Blueprint
UPPER INTERMEDIATE

Teacher's Book

Brian Abbs
Ingrid Freebairn

Longman

Longman Group UK Limited
Longman House, Burnt Mill, Harlow,
Essex, CM20 2JE, England
and Associated Companies throughout the world.

First published 1993
Reprinted 1994

Set in 10/10.5 pt Times

Printed in Spain by Mateu Cromo, S.A. Pinto (Madrid)

ISBN 0 582 09911 0

Contents

Introduction

The course

Blueprint Upper Intermediate is for students who have completed an intermediate course such as Blueprint Intermediate, Intermediate Matters or Sourcebook Intermediate. It provides approximately 100-120 hours of classroom study. The course consists of a Students' Book, a Workbook, this Teacher's Book, a set of two Class Cassettes and a separate Student Cassette, linked to the Workbook.

The needs of the upper intermediate student

Although they may have come from a variety of learning backgrounds, students at the upper intermediate level have certain needs in common.

1 Revision

By the time students reach the upper intermediate level, they will be familiar with the main structures of English. However, despite a certain level of fluency, they still make basic errors in important areas, such as the use of verb forms, tenses and prepositions. What they now need is to revise and refine their existing knowledge of grammar without feeling that they are simply repeating work that they have already covered.

2 Increased range and depth

If they are to progress, students at upper intermediate level need to develop a more profound understanding of language and a greater awareness of possible structural and stylistic variations. They need to broaden their range of vocabulary and expression so that they can use the language with more precision and subtlety. Plenty of practice in word formation and collocation, as well as consistent exposure to new words and expressions are both essential at this level.

Skills development is also vital. Students need practice in processing information from longer, more demanding listening and reading material which is taken from a variety of different sources. Moreover, when speaking and writing, they need to be able to express themselves more intelligibly, more accurately and with a greater range of expression.

3 Challenge and involvement

To sustain motivation and a positive attitude to learning, students at all levels need to be challenged, both intellectually and linguistically. Students easily become bored and lose concentration if they are not involved in what they are doing, or if the texts or activities are too easy. The subject matter and language work must engage the students' minds and challenge them to think.

4 Learner independence

Although students have now reached a relatively high level of competence in English, they still need clear goals and objectives so that they can themselves measure their progress at regular intervals and assess how well they are doing. They need to reestablish those learning strategies which will help them study and make progress independently. In particular, they need advice on how to tackle authentic listening texts, how to learn vocabulary and use monolingual dictionaries and how to approach writing assignments in an organised way.

5 Examinations

Students who have the First Certificate Examination as a potential goal need not only to gain familiarity with specific examination-type tasks, but also to concentrate on grammatical accuracy and on developing their writing skills more comprehensively.

In short, what students need at the upper intermediate level (whether for general study or for examination purposes) is material which will enable them to perfect their grammar, broaden their vocabulary and refine their language skills so that they can produce language accurately, fluently and with a greater degree of subtlety.

How Blueprint meets these needs

1 Grammar

Grammar extension and revision has a central role in Blueprint Upper Intermediate. Every teaching unit includes explicit structural work on a major or minor grammatical point. New grammar is presented in Grammar Focus boxes. Grammar revision is presented in Grammar Review boxes by means of inductive questions and language awareness tasks which encourage students to reflect on how the language works.

All the grammar points are backed up by Practice exercises and separate Workbook exercises.

To aid revision, there is a comprehensive Grammar Reference section at the back of the Students' Book. This is cross-referenced to the Grammar Review boxes. A note at the end of each Grammar Review box indicates the page of the Grammar Reference where students can find more detailed information about the particular grammatical point. The Grammar Reference section has the added advantage of giving students free access to the rules of the language when they need them.

Regular Study Point sections highlight language points which are more relevant to writing, such as 'Adverbial linking phrases' and 'Expressions of cause and effect'.

2 Vocabulary

Blueprint Upper Intermediate contains many varied types of activity to aid vocabulary building. *Guess the meaning* and *Study the words* exercises in the Students' Book isolate important new vocabulary from the reading texts. Separate Vocabulary sections expand topic-related vocabulary into word fields and pay special attention to word-building using prefixes and suffixes. In addition, regular Phrasal Verbs and Idioms sections help to extend the students' knowledge of colloquial expression.

Vocabulary is also practised in the Workbook, and key vocabulary areas are tested in the Check sections in the Students' Book and the Progress Tests in the Workbook.

The teacher's notes make a specific point of encouraging the students to explore the meaning of new words and expressions and to use them in sentences of their own.

3 Skills development

Reading

The reading texts are designed to develop the students' reading skill more comprehensively. Students are exposed to a wide range of texts including extracts from newspapers, magazine articles, popular scientific journals, novels, poems and short stories. An additional reading dimension is provided by charts, diagrams and graphs.

All the reading texts have a 'warm-up' activity labelled *Talk about it* or *Before you read.* These sections contain questions or tasks to stimulate discussion and ideas in preparation for the text and to raise key vocabulary. Different types of comprehension tasks include *Read and answer* to check general comprehension and *Read and think* to encourage students to read for inference. Style questions after the literature texts guide students towards the use of a particular stylistic device of the written language.

Listening

Listening practice in Blueprint Upper Intermediate is provided by a balance of scripted and authentic recordings. Dialogues give intensive listening practice while authentic interviews and conversations provide practice in listening for gist, for information and for attitude. Most listening texts are preceded by a *Before you listen* activity which prepares the students for the text. The listening tasks include note-taking and chart completion tasks as well as multiple choice and straight comprehension questions.

Writing

The writing skill so essential at this level (particularly for examination purposes) is developed consistently and thoroughly in Blueprint Upper Intermediate. Students are given the help they need to produce more accurate, more fluent and more coherent pieces of writing. They are shown that the planning and organisation of their thoughts and ideas is as important as the actual writing of the composition or letter.

In some units writing practice is linked to the consolidation of a particular structure; in others it is linked to a communicative function. Detailed guidance is given in the writing of certain types of texts, such as formal and informal letters, narrative and argument.

The writing tasks are generally preceded by a *Before you write* section which encourages students to discuss the task in hand and organise their writing. Study Point sections highlight special features of written English, such as 'Narrative linking devices' and 'Topic sentences' as well as offering help on 'Commonly confused words and phrases'.

Speaking

To help improve students' oral fluency, Blueprint Upper Intermediate contains a variety of activities aimed at encouraging free expression. The pictorial page which opens each block of five units, the *Talk about it* and the *About you* sections all offer students opportunities for discussion and allow teachers to move away from the texts or themes and to involve the students personally. Roleplays also provide the students with the chance to practise communicative exchanges in situations with which they can easily identify.

A selection of Fluency Projects appears at the back of the Students' Book for extra fluency practice. As these are not closely linked to specific language points, they may be used at any stage of the course.

Speechwork is given detailed attention throughout the course. The stress and intonation of functional language and conversational strategies is practised in those units which have a special communication focus.

Speechwork exercises in the Students' Book focus on the elision of spoken English as well as on the problems of 'sound-to-spelling' (e.g. the various spellings of the sound /ɜː/) or of 'spelling-to-sound' (e.g. the various sounds attached to the spelling 'ough').

A special section in the Workbook deals with common problem areas which students experience in pronunciation and word stress.

4 Challenge and relevance

In Blueprint Upper Intermediate the students' minds are challenged both on an intellectual and a linguistic level. They are engaged intellectually through the topical and sometimes controversial subject matter of the reading and listening texts, while the inductive approach to grammar and the use of authentic literature texts challenges them linguistically.

To make learning more relevant, students are encouraged to relate material to their own lives and experiences. Revision of verb tenses, practice of new vocabulary and topics and the issues covered in each unit are bought into the students' realm of experience by means of *About you* or *Talk about it* sections.

5 Learner independence

The Students' Book opens with a two-page Study Skills Review to help students make the most of their time in and outside the classroom. It identifies typical problems many students have in learning English, and suggests ways of overcoming them.

The material is organised into short, manageable units with clearly-defined learning objectives. The unit title indicates the theme of the material and there is clear signposting within the unit of the grammar, function or vocabulary in focus. All activities are clearly labelled so that students know what they are doing at every stage of the lesson.

The learning goals in each lesson of the Students' Book are highlighted graphically in coloured boxes which carefully distinguish between Grammar Review, Grammar Focus, Communication Focus and Study Point.

A Check section after every five units of the Students' Book helps students to measure their progress as they go along. This gives them the chance to spot special areas of difficulty which need extra practice. A separate Progress Test after every five units of the Workbook offers an alternative way of testing the same material, based on question-types used in the Cambridge First Certificate Examination.

The Grammar Reference section at the back of the Students' Book provides clear, concise grammar explanations and allows students access to the rules of the language at any point that suits them.

6 Examination skills

Specific exam-type exercises and tasks are introduced at frequent intervals. In particular, the test pages of the Workbook give special practice in multiple choice, transformation and word formation techniques often found in the First Certificate Examination. Oral ability is developed through a variety of techniques, including the use of the pictorial pages at the start of each block of five units. These stimulate the students to express their opinions on a range of topics. Many of the writing tasks resemble those found in the First Certificate Examination.

Description of the course

1 Students' Book

The main body of the Students' Book consists of forty teaching units. These are divided into blocks of five units followed by a Check section. A key to each Check is included at the relevant point in the Teacher's Book.

Each block of five units opens with a pictorial page to stimulate discussion around the theme of the first unit in the block. Each unit has a balance of skills work and grammar practice.

At the back of the Students' Book, after the forty teaching units, there are four Fluency Projects to be used either at ten-unit intervals or at the end of the course. There are also two pages of rolecards printed back-to-back for use in the roleplay sections of those units which have a special communication focus.

A ten-page Grammar Reference section, which gives fuller explanations of the grammar points highlighted in the units, and a unit-by-unit list of key vocabulary with phonetic spelling are also included at the end of the Students' Book.

2 Class Cassettes

The set of two Class Cassettes contains all the dialogues, speechwork exercises and listening texts from the Students' Book, as well as dramatic readings of the literary texts. The cassettes are an important accompaniment to the course in that they provide exposure to a wide range of speakers from different parts of the English-speaking world and give practice in a variety of listening tasks.

3 Workbook

Extra practice of grammar, functions and vocabulary as well as further listening and reading comprehension activities are provided in a separate illustrated Workbook.

Speechwork is given special attention through oral exercises and through a special revision section at the back of the book which concentrates on word stress and problem areas in pronunciation. All the listening texts, oral exercises and speechwork exercises are recorded on the Student Cassette. A key to the Workbook exercises is provided at the end of this Teacher's Book.

4 Student Cassette

The Student Cassette contains all the listening material from the Workbook. Simplified listening comprehension material, oral exercises and speechwork exercises enable students to practise comprehension, word stress and problem areas in the pronunciation of spoken English, such as elision and consonant reduction. The cassette allows students to work independently at their own pace, and helps to develop greater confidence in listening.

5 Teacher's Book

This Teacher's Book has an introduction which describes the contents, rationale and methodological principles of Blueprint Upper Intermediate. This introduction is followed by unit-by-unit Lesson Notes for the Students' Book. These include answer keys to the Practice exercises, tapescripts of the listening materials and suggestions for Extra Activities. Keys to the Check exercises are included after every five units; keys and tapescripts for the Workbook are printed at the end of the Teacher's Book.

Abbreviations used in the Teacher's Book

T	Teacher
S	Student
T-S	Teacher speaks to student
S-S	Student speaks to student
S1-S2	First student speaks to second student and so on
L1	Native language
OHP	Overhead projector
OHT	Overhead transparency
Ex.	Exercise
e.g.	for example
etc.	etcetera
i.e.	that is
c.f.	compare with

Lesson notes

UNIT 1 Taking risks

Suggested lesson break: after Exercise 6

BACKGROUND NOTES
blind date: a social meeting between a boy and a girl who have not met before
Bordeaux: a port and city in the south west of France

Exercise 1 Talk about it

Ask students to identify the activity in the picture. Ask if any of them have done any rock climbing before. Those who have, or who know something about it, may like to describe what it involves, what equipment you need and what precautions you have to take to avoid accidents. Ask the next two questions to the class as a whole. Then ask the last question as a lead-in to the following activity:

Ask students in pairs to write down five sporting activities which they consider to be very risky. Collect a list of all the risky activities on the board and ask students to choose five and rank them in order of riskiness.

Exercise 2

As a warm-up to the questionnaire, ask students if they can think of any other non-sporting or non-physical activities which require courage e.g. making a speech in public, telling someone bad news, complaining about food in a restaurant. Ask if they think some people are naturally daring and others naturally cowardly. Which do they think they are? In this way, lead in to the questionnaire and ask students to work in pairs and find out what sort of person they are. Tell them to use a dictionary for any words they do not know, e.g. *frustrated, caution/ious, realistic, mature*.

Check how individual students scored on the questionnaire. Ask if they can think of other similar questions to ask in a questionnaire of this type. Check comprehension of any new words by getting students to use them in a sentence of their own.

GRAMMAR REVIEW

Ask a student to read the first question of the questionnaire again and to say what tense is being used. Ask what part of the verb phrase is a clue to the tense (e.g. the auxiliary *have* and the adverb *ever*). Ask another student to read Question 9 and ask similar questions. Ask if any student can say when each tense is used. Do not expect perfect answers. Ask them to do the first exercise in the Review box individually or in pairs, and check the answers immediately.

KEY

Name of tense	Clue words
1 Present perfect	*already*
2 Past simple	*at eleven thirty last night*
3 Present perfect	*so far today*
4 Present perfect	*yet*
5 Past simple	*three weeks ago*
6 Present perfect	*just*

Once the 'clue' words have been checked, the next exercise can be done with the class as a whole. Explain the statements in your own words if you think it will help your students.

Matched sentences: 1+4b 2+5a 3c 6d

Select a weaker student to answer the final question.
Correct answer = b

Exercise 3 PRACTICE

Students work individually or in pairs. Remind them to use short forms where appropriate. Check answers with the whole class.

KEY

1 've just finished 2 went 3 Have you ever eaten 4 has written 5 moved 6 've torn

Exercise 4

Work T-S with the example conversation omitting the questions in italics. Then choose another student for the second prompt, like this:

T: Have you ever broken an arm or a leg?
S: Yes, I have.
T: How did you break it? etc.

In this way, you can show that the follow-up question can start with any appropriate question word, provided the question is expressed in the past simple tense.

Students can either work in pairs, or move round the class trying to interview as many others as possible. After a few minutes, ask different students to report back their findings.

Now ask which students gave positive answers to questions 1, 5 and 6 of the questionnaire. The other students can ask them questions about their experiences, using *When/Where/How did you ...* questions. However, save any parachuting experiences until Exercise 6 Listening.

GRAMMAR FOCUS

Ask students to read the Grammar Focus box silently and to do the task. If appropriate, draw comparisons with the students' own language to show the difference in usage.

Exercise 5 PRACTICE

Work T-S with the example exchange, then ask students to work in pairs. Check round the class afterwards.

KEY

2 I don't know. It's the first time I've eaten it.
3 No. It's the first time I've been to an opera.
4 Actually, it's the first time he's spoken in public.
5 Thank you. It's the first time I've made one.

Exercise 6 LISTENING

Ask if any students have done any parachuting or know anything about it. Try and elicit what the preparation might be, what the risks are, and what the sensations might be. Elicit the word *ripcord* as in *to pull the ripcord to open the parachute*. Ask students to look at the questions and see if anyone can explain *back out*. Play the tape twice and then check the answers. Some students might like to go through the tape again for a more detailed study of the content.

TAPESCRIPT

CELIA: This particular course was held in Hampshire in the south east of England. The course was just for one weekend - you learnt how to do it one day and you did it the next day. So we spent Saturday learning how to fall properly by falling off benches.

The benches were really quite low - they were probably about three or four feet off the ground and we just had to learn to fall sideways off them because when you land on the ground from parachuting, you do land with a tremendous thump and you've got to learn to be able to roll into the ground to absorb some of the shock of landing. And that's … that was what we had to learn to do. And then we were also taught about, um, we were given training in obviously exactly what to do when you leave the plane. For example, we were told what to do if our parachute didn't open automatically. We had spare … a spare parachute and you have to pull the ripcord for it to open.

INTERVIEWER: OK. So that's how you spent the first night - the first day. The next day - how were you feeling the next day?

CELIA: Oh well, I think we were all very frightened and we also knew that it wasn't absolutely certain that we'd jump because it depends very much on the extent of the wind. If there's too much wind, you can't jump and England on the whole is a very windy place. And they said, 'Right. We're going to take the three lightest people first.' And they looked at all of us and I was one of the three and they said 'And of the three of you that are going, the heaviest of the three lightest will jump.' And I was the heaviest of the three lightest. So I was the very first one to jump. So of course, as it was the first time I'd ever experienced anything like this, I was very frightened indeed. But of course, you can't really show it. You've chosen to do this thing, you know. And I really felt by that stage, I didn't have an option. You know, the pressure on you to do it was so great, you couldn't stick up your hand and say 'After all, I don't think I will'.

So we went up to about 2,000 feet, which isn't very high, but you always have a low jump when you first start and it was tremendously cold because the side - the door - of the little plane was open and you'd have this freezing cold air coming in. Then they said 'Right! You!' and I had to get up. And then you stood there - it was probably half a second, but it felt like forever. And then they say 'Go!' with this tremendous imperative. And you just jump backwards into space. And what was interesting was the fantastic difference between rushing through the air at this great speed and then suddenly being pulled up short because the parachute opened, and then there was a beautiful few moments of absolute quiet and tranquility when you float slowly through the air.

INTERVIEWER: And during those moments when you were floating through - were you able to realise anything?

CELIA: I think there were three stages really. There was the stage of just jumping backwards out and that was the moment … a moment of just total feeling. I don't know what … how to describe the feeling. It's an enormous mixture of absolute fear and absolute exhilaration at the same time. For just … for one second you're absolutely out of control of everything and you have nothing but a complete physical experience of cold wind and just falling through the air. So that's sort of one moment in it, and then the next phase is this beautiful, er … moments of tranquility when you feel you can look around you - you can look down. And the sky was blue and there were these little tiny cars and cows down below. And then there's this next moment of panic when you think, 'I'm going to land and am I going to be able to land alright?' and this great physical experience of sort of dashing your body onto the ground. So three really quite different senses. I mean I think I had three feelings, three different sorts of feelings.

SUGGESTED LESSON BREAK

READING

Introduce the topic of the text, i.e. the experiment to treat problem teenagers by teaching them to do a parachute jump. Ask students to look up the word *grace* in the dictionary and to find the meaning which best fits the context. The expression *falling to grace* does not actually exist in English. It is the opposite of the expression *to fall from grace* (to fall from a position of favour, or to fall into bad ways of behaving). In other words, the teenagers were hopefully falling into good ways of behaving.

Ask students to read the text and make a note of any words or expressions which are new. Tell them not to look them up in a dictionary yet. Ask them also to note any detail about the parachuting experience which strikes them as different from what they heard in the listening text. (In the listening text, for example, the weather seemed to be quite chilly and the aeroplane cabin was very cold, whereas in the reading text, it was high summer and the aeroplane was very hot.)

Exercise 7

Students work in pairs. They can take it in turns to read out each statement and together decide if it is True or False. Check the answers and get them to justify their answers with extracts from the text.

KEY

1 False 2 False 3 True 4 False 5 False

Some students may differ on the answer to Question 3. If so, ask what evidence they can find in the text to suggest the opposite.

Exercise 8 Study the words.

Check the words and expressions by asking individual students. Check the pronunciation of the words from the text and spend some time talking about each word, giving other contexts for its use, e.g. with *breeze* you can say 'a gentle breeze', 'a stiff breeze', 'the flags flapped gently in the breeze', etc . You can also say 'he breezed into the room' meaning 'he came in carelessly and confidently'.

KEY

1 breeze 2 makes your head swim 3 palpable
4 firmly 5 surge 6 charge

Ask students to try and explain in their own words what the expressions (1–4) mean.

KEY

1 commonly called so but often inaccurately or improperly
2 indicating a knot of anxiety or fear, i.e. very frightened
3 were too afraid to jump
4 from a different point of view

Ask if students have any words still left unexplained from their initial reading.

Exercise 9 Talk about it.

Discuss the questions with the whole class. Bring up the question of risk, and if it is fair to ask teenagers to do something if they are very frightened. Mention other forms of rehabilitation programmes, e.g. community work. Ask what they see as the main difference in the two approaches (community work versus parachuting).

Exercise 10 VOCABULARY

Students can do the exercise individually using a dictionary if necessary.

KEY

Fear: frightened, anxious, nervous, petrified, apprehensive, uneasy, scared, terrified
Courage: courageous, daring, fearless, reckless, bold, brave

After checking the answers, go through each word in turn, making sure that students understand the nuances of meaning. Give examples of sentences in which they are used.

As a check, read out the following situations in turn to the whole class and ask the students to select appropriate words to match the emotions and feelings involed in them, e.g:

T: Someone is about to go into an interview. How do you think they feel? (or: How would you describe that person?)
S1: Nervous/apprehensive.

SITUATIONS

1 It's late at night. Some parents are waiting up for their teenage daughter or son to return home after a party or a visit to a disco. (anxious/apprehensive/uneasy)
2 A professional downhill skier is about to race down a steep mountain (daring/fearless/reckless)
3 A person thinks he or she has seen a ghost. (petrified/terrified)
4 Someone is fighting a life-threatening disease like cancer but trying not to show pain or distress to relatives and friends. (courageous/brave)
5 Two circus trapeze artists are about to change swings in mid-air high above the circus ring without a safety net. (daring/bold/nervous/fearless)
6 A beginner on skis faces a steep mountain slope in order to get home. (frightened/scared/terrified)

For homework, allot six words to different students (so that all the words in the box are covered) and ask them to write a sentence for each word which shows its meaning.

Exercise 11 WRITING

Ask students to name a few sports or activities which require skill and write them on the blackboard (e.g. *windsurfing, skiing, snorkelling, scubadiving, sailing*). Ask students to choose a sport and note down:
-when they first tried it
-how they felt about trying it (keen? excited? apprehensive?)
-what training or preparation they had to do first
-how they felt about it after this stage
-how they felt the first time they actually did it

Ask one student to read out his/her first few sentences using the model as a guide.

EXTRA ACTIVITIES

1 Tell a story

Students form groups to think up a frightening story that incorporates as many of the words from Unit 1 as possible. One or several students can be chosen from each group to tell the story to the rest of the class. Alternatively, students may like to write the 'blurb' or trailer for the cover of a horror video.

2 Question the expert!

A student who has knowledge and experience of an unusual activity or sport takes the 'hot seat' in front of the class to answer quick fire questions. The other students prepare as many questions as they can to ask the 'expert' in order to find out information, such as the physical and mental qualities which are needed, the special equipment which may be required, the amount of training necessary, what it feels like the first time you do the activity, and how to get started.

Students note the answers to the questions to form the basis of a project on 'Dangerous sports and activities'.

UNIT 2 Social occasions

Suggested lesson break: after Grammar Review

Give back or correct homework from the previous lesson. Revise new vocabulary from Unit 1.

(Note that in future all new lessons should start with, or include at some point, correction of homework and revision of vocabulary from the previous lesson.)

Exercise 1 Talk about it.

Do the exercise with the class as a whole. Dramatise the five opening lines using students in the class. Students can then give their opinion on what is or is not appropriate. With a multilingual group, you may be able to stimulate some interesting discussion if social conventions are different. If students are not sure, tell them that sentences 2, 4 and 5 are all acceptable openings whereas 1 and 3 are considered too direct and intrusive. Point out that the British consider any direct question from a stranger about how much they earn or how much they get paid for something to be impolite.

Some teachers may wish to direct students at this point to the note which starts *When British people* ... on the next page of the unit. Exercise 9 can follow directly on from this note or can be left until the end of the lesson.

Exercise 2 LISTENING DIALOGUE

Ask students to work in pairs to see if they can think of suitable words to complete the gaps in the dialogue. Stress that there are often several possibilities. When they have finished this, check with the whole class to see what they have suggested for each gap. Eliminate the ones that don't make sense or are grammatically inaccurate. Then play the tape and ask students to make any corrections to their versions.

TAPESCRIPT AND KEY

SAM: *It's* great music, *isn't it*?
TARA: Yes, it's good.
SAM: *Haven't I seen* you somewhere before. In Garbo's, for instance?
TARA: No, I've never been there. *Is it* any good?
SAM: Yes, it's OK. It's a bit expensive. So *how do you know* Jenny?
TARA: I'm her cousin.
SAM: Oh, I thought you were one of her friends from college. *My name's* Sam, by the way.
TARA: And I'm Tara. Hi! *Do you want* one of these cheese biscuits? They're really tasty.
SAM: Thanks. Mmm! *They're* good, *aren't they? Can I get you* something to drink?
TARA: No, thanks. I'd rather dance.

Play the tape again, pausing after each line for students to listen and repeat.

Exercise 3

Play the second version of the tape with 'bleeps' instead of Sam's lines and ask individual students to say Sam's lines after the bleeps. Correct any serious stress or intonation errors.

COMMUNICATION FOCUS

Say each sentence, asking students to repeat them after you. Point out that the first three introductions can be used in informal or semi-formal situations whereas the last is much more formal. With monolingual groups, see if they can think of equivalent introductory phrases in their own language. Go through the rest of the sentences in the box in the same way, making sure that students have a chance of practising the intonation of each one. Do not draw attention to the grammar of the question tags or negative questions yet, unless you get a specific request from a student.

Exercise 4 PRACTICE

Work T-S with one or two remarks or questions from each section of the box, encouraging students to make a suitable response each time. Students then work in pairs, working alternately to practise the exchanges.

GRAMMAR REVIEW

Go through the questions, working as a class or asking students to work individually.

KEY

Sentences 1 and 3 imply that the speaker is fairly sure of the answer *'Yes'*.

Sentence 3 is a negative question. Sentence 1 is a question tag.

Which tags follow these statements?
1 aren't you 2 haven't you 3 did you 4 could you

If students are confused about the tag endings, refer them to p.135 of the Grammar Reference section and give them more incomplete sentences to practise on.

SUGGESTED LESSON BREAK

SPEECHWORK

Play the tape to accompany the note about intonation, pausing before each question. You may like to build a situation for each question to make it more real for the students. e.g. (first example):

T: You're in the street and you bump into someone whom you met last week at a party. You think he may be called John but you're not sure because you were introduced to so many other new people at that party. You're uncertain and so you say: *You're John, aren't you?* (with a rising intonation)

Get students to repeat each question as they hear it on the tape each time.

Point out that when negative questions are comments (i.e. with a falling intonation) the question mark is often replaced by an exclamation mark. The grammatical description is, however, still a 'negative question'.

Exercise 5

Play the tape with the three example question tags and show that the intonation indicates the attitude described in brackets. Then ask students to listen to the rest of the question tags and to suggest the attitude. Repeat with the negative questions. Play the examples and discuss them first before playing the rest of the tape.

When students are clear about the intonation, play the tape again so they can listen and repeat all the questions.

TAPESCRIPT AND KEY

Examples:
You're Spanish, aren't you? (certain)
You're British, aren't you? (uncertain)
You aren't British, are you? (surprised)

1 You aren't serious, are you? (surprised)
2 You're an artist, aren't you? (uncertain)
3 You haven't met Jane, have you? (certain)
4 She's a friend of yours, isn't she? (uncertain)

Examples:
Isn't it hot! (comment)
Don't you like tea? (surprise)

1 Don't you like Tom Cruise? (surprise)
2 Isn't it beautiful! (comment)
3 Haven't you met Mike before? (surprise)
4 Aren't they delicious! (comment)

Exercise 6 PRACTICE

Ask students to work in pairs to complete the dialogue. Check that they are sure they know how to convert the cues. It may be useful to go through each one and get students to say first of all if they are going to use a tag or a negative question. Elicit an example from a student before putting the pairs to work. Check afterwards by getting different students to write the missing sentences on the board.

KEY

JOHN: *Your name's Sue, isn't it?*
CHRIS: No, it isn't actually. It's Chris.
JOHN: Oh, *you played in the tennis tournament last week, didn't you?* or (*Didn't you play in the tennis tournament last week?*)
CHRIS: What tennis tournament?
JOHN: *Don't you know about it?* They have one every year. Do you want a Coke, by the way?
CHRIS: No thanks.
JOHN: *Don't you like Coke?*
CHRIS: Not much, no. I've got to go.
JOHN: *You're not leaving already, are you?*
CHRIS: Yes, I came here to meet someone and he's not here.
JOHN: Oh, *you wouldn't like to join me in a game of badminton, would you?*
CHRIS: No, thanks. To tell you the truth, I can't play any sports at all!

Exercise 7

Students read the finished dialogue in pairs, changing parts afterwards.

Exercise 8 ROLEPLAY

Divide the class into 'A' students and 'B' students and ask them to read their respective rolecards. Go round and help any students who are not clear how to interpret their rolecards. Pair the students in As and Bs and ask them to perform the roleplay. Encourage them to carry on the conversation as long as they can. Go round and monitor performance, making notes of recurring problems. Ask one of the pairs to perform in front of the rest of the class. Spend a few minutes giving feedback to the pairs and dealing with common errors.

Note

Ask students to read the note on British social conventions and check by asking a few comprehension questions.

Exercise 9 About you

Spend a few minutes discussing the questions with the class as a whole. Highlight any differences in social conventions between the students' own culture and that of the British. This discussion will be more productive in a multilingual class.

The cartoon

Ask if any of the students can explain the joke in the cartoon (that all penguins look alike).

EXTRA ACTIVITIES

1 Question tag bingo

Write on the board the following twenty question tags: *can't you, isn't it, have you, were they, could you, did he, doesn't she, won't you, haven't you, isn't he, aren't you, aren't I, wasn't it, do we, has it, wouldn't you, shall I, couldn't he, didn't you, will she.*

Ask students to draw a bingo box containing twelve squares (4 by 3) to select any twelve of the tags, on the board and to write one each in any square they like. Tell students that you are going to read out some sentences which can precede a question tag. If they have the appropriate tag in their box, they should cross it out and put the number of the statement in the box (so you can check afterwards that they have matched the right tag to the right statement). The first student or students to cross out all their twelve squares shouts 'Bingo!'.

BINGO SENTENCES:

1 She lives quite near here, ...
2 I'm stupid, ...
3 You met Sally the last time you were here, ...
4 You can understand me, ...
5 She won't mind about it, ...
6 You've met John before, ...
7 They weren't angry with us, ...
8 It's an awful story, ...
9 You couldn't lend me ten pounds, ...
10 He's going to phone me tonight, ...
11 I'll come along at seven o'clock, ...
12 You're leaving soon, ...
13 This hasn't caused any problem, ...
14 He didn't say where he was going, ...
15 You haven't seen my glasses anywhere, ...
16 We don't have to be there until nine, ...
17 You'll be very quiet about this, ...
18 He could borrow your car, ...
19 It was lucky you were here, ...
20 You'd help me if I had a problem, ...

2 Party time: the rich and famous

Give each student a name tag with the name of somebody famous and still alive. Choose from the areas of film, TV, pop stars, actors, musicians, writers, politicians, sports personalities, etc. Students then go round a 'cocktail party' making conversation with the other characters. Tell them that they must start with a special opening phrase taken from the Communication box but from then on their conversation may take any direction they wish. The only restriction is that they must talk to at least four people in the party.

UNIT 3 Different tastes

Suggested lesson break: after Exercise 6

BACKGROUND NOTES

(Note that while this book was being written John McEnroe and his wife, Tatum O'Neal legally separated.)

John McEnroe: an American tennis player who won the Men's Singles Final Wimbledon in the 1980s. As well as his skill at tennis, he is well-known for losing his temper during tennis matches and for loudly and aggressively questioning umpires' decisions. He is particularly remembered at Wimbledon for his remark to an umpire, 'You cannot be serious!' when he disagreed with a decision.

Tatum O'Neal: an American actress, daughter of Ryan O'Neal. Tatum established herself as a child star in the film *Paper Moon* in which she co-starred with her father.

Exercise 1 Talk about it.

Divide students into small groups of three or four and ask them to talk about the different aspects of friendship. Ask them to put them in order of importance. After five minutes, call the class together and compare the results of the different groups. As they discuss, you may like to remind them on the blackboard of these structures:

We have	*similar* *different*	*tastes.*
but		
My tastes are	*similar to* *different from* *the same as*	*his/hers.*

Exercise 2 READING

Ask students what they know about the two characters in the photograph and if they can name a film that Tatum O'Neal has been in. (See Background Notes)

Exercise 3

Ask students to read the text silently while completing the chart. Ask them to note or underline any words or expressions they do not know but discourage them from using a dictionary at this stage. Expect difficulties with: *teamed up, lobster, hermit, invasion of his privacy, self-sufficient* and *tantrums.*

KEY

	SHE	HE
New York in winter	×	✓
modern furniture		✓
steak and lobster		✓
going out at night	✓	
the attention of the press	✓	×

Exercise 4 Study the words.

Students may work individually or in pairs.

KEY

1 teamed up 2 reaction 3 antiques 4 hermit
5 self-sufficient 6 tantrum

Explain any other words or expressions from the text that students still have problems with.

Exercise 5 Talk about it.

Discuss the questions with the class as a whole. Prompt the discussion by mentioning any other well-known 'unusual' couple who may be currently in the news because of difficulties with their relationship.

GRAMMAR REVIEW

Students work individually or in pairs. When they have completed the lists, ask them to make a true statement about their own likes and dislikes with one verb or expression from each list, provided it is not *like* or *dislike*. Explain that *be mad about* is quite colloquial, and that *have a horror of* is unusual in spoken English.

KEY

Like	Dislike
like (mild/neutral)	hate (strong)
adore (strong)	can't stand (strong)
be keen on (mild/neutral)	have a horror of (strong)
prefer (mild/neutral)	
enjoy (mild/neutral)	dislike (mild/neutral)
be fond of (mild/neutral)	detest (strong)
be mad about (strong)	
not mind (mild/neutral)	

The gerund is used after verbs or phrases expressing likes and dislikes.
You make a negative gerund by putting *not* before the gerund.

After answering the last question, get students to make some sentences with negative gerunds in the context of their own lives. According to your knowledge of your students' background, write one or two 'cue' sentences on the board to help them, e.g. (if the students are still at school):

I hate | *X earn any money*
X have my own transport

(if the students have left school):

I enjoy | *X go to school any more*
X have to get up early/do lots of homework

(if the students are living away from home):

I don't like | *X have a telephone*
X see my friends every day
X have any (name of special food they can only get at home)

Exercise 6 PRACTICE

KEY

1 doing/cooking 2 lying 3 not being able to
4 walking 5 not having to get up

SUGGESTED LESSON BREAK

GRAMMAR FOCUS

Read the Grammar Focus aloud in short sections. After each example, ask different students to think of a similar sentence using the same structure. When it comes to the section on *would rather*, prompt students with:

He likes a big breakfast in the morning but she ...
She wants to use the money to decorate the house but he ...
I'd rather spend Saturday night alone ...

Exercise 7 PRACTICE

Rewrite the two lists of preferences on the blackboard so that they are side by side. This will help students to make parallel sentences. Read out the three different ways of expressing the contrast and remind students of the use of *whereas*. Elicit three different types of sentence for the second pair of prompts (*spend the day at home/visit friends*), to make sure students understand the variety of ways of expressing the same contrast. Divide the class into two teams. One member of each team calls out a suitable beginning and the equivalent member of the opposite team finishes the sentence in a suitable way, e.g:

A: Mark likes eating at home / Mark prefers eating at home ...
B: ... whereas Sarah prefers to go out to eat. / whereas Sarah would rather go out to eat.

Exercise 8 About you

Students now work in pairs and talk about how they like spending their weekend. Go round and monitor, collecting any errors that you would like to raise with the class as a whole. Ask students to tell the rest of the class any interesting differences in their lifestyles.

Exercise 9 WRITING

Ask students to think quietly for a moment or two and then talk to a partner about the person they intend to write about. Tell them that they can also refer to people's habits and personality as well.

Remind students of the different ways of expressing contrast:

X ... but I ...
Although X ..., I ...
X ... . However, I ...
X ... whereas I ...

Suggest ways of starting the paragraph:

I would like to describe my relationship with ...
I have known ... for ... years and although ...
Although ... is my sister/brother, I must say that we don't always get on very well. The problem is that we are very different.

EXTRA ACTIVITIES

1 Personal statements

Each student writes on a piece of paper between 6-8 personal statements about themselves. Students should not identify themselves by name. The sentences must use the following verbs: *love, dislike, hate, can't stand, be fond of, be keen on, enjoy, not mind, prefer, would rather.* The personal statements are then collected and distributed evenly among groups of students. One person elects to read the statements and the rest must try to identify whose statement it is. Obviously, the handwriting must be concealed by the person reading the statement aloud.

2 Opposites

One student starts by calling out a 'like or dislike' sentence and naming another student who has to give an 'opposite' sentence, e.g:

S1: I like getting up early. Carla.
S2 (Carla): I like sleeping late.

S2 now calls out another sentence, names another student and so continues the chain. If a statement doesn't have an obvious opposite, the student must try to think of a reasonable contrast, e.g:

S1: I like tea.
S2: I like cold milk.

UNIT 4 Good days, bad days

Suggested lesson break: after Exercise 5

The cartoon

Ask a student to describe what is going wrong in the kitchen. Ask students what *those* means in the expression *one of those days* (the sort of day when everything goes wrong).

Exercise 1 Talk about it.

Ask the questions of the class as a whole and find out if any of the students have heard of 'biorhythms'. If so, encourage those students to try and explain what biorhythms are. Ask students if they have any further questions about biorhythms and write these on the board.

Exercise 2 READING

Ask students to read the text once through and find the answers to the questions on the board (if they are given) as well as the questions in Exercise 2. While they read, ask students to note or underline any words or expressions they are uncertain of. They should not use a dictionary but try and guess the meaning of the words from the context. Check the answers.

It may be useful to point out that several people disagree entirely with the 'biorhythm' theory. Contrary to what certain scientists say, it is not a scientifically proven fact.

Exercise 3 Read and think.

Discuss the questions with the class as a whole.

SUGGESTED ANSWERS

1 An artist is unable to paint and a writer is unable to write. (not in an absolute sense but in a creative sense)
2 a) start learning how to drive b) make an important decision at work c) take an exam
3 You might end up organising your life around your body clock, which may make you miss out on life, e.g. If someone invited you to a party and it was a long drive away, you might say no if you were at a weak part of your emotional or physical biorhythm.

Exercise 4 Study the words.

Students will already have noted some of these words and expressions on first reading the text and will have attempted to guess their meaning. Use this exercise to check that everybody is clear about the words, and explain any other words or expressions that students may have noted.

KEY

1 clumsy 2 you cause a lot of accidents to happen 3 you lose your temper easily 4 the other way round

Match the word from the text with a word with a similar meaning:
1c 2c 3b 4a 5d 6a

Exercise 5 Talk about it.

Students work in pairs to interpret the diagram.

KEY

The heads represent the intellectual, the body the emotional and the legs the physical biorhythms.

Intellectual:
Glowing yellow head = strong
Dark-grey head cracked open = critical

Normal light-grey head = weak

Emotional:
Yellow body with glowing heart = strong
Dark-grey body with broken heart = critical
Normal light-grey body = weak

Physical:
Yellow running legs = strong
Dark-grey shaking legs = critical
Light-grey straight legs = weak

Physically 'critical' days in the coming week = Friday and Saturday
Emotionally 'critical' day = Tuesday
Intellectually 'critical' day = Thursday

Note that this would not be a typical week. It is unlikely for so many critical days to coincide in one week.

SUGGESTED LESSON BREAK

Exercise 6 SPEECHWORK

Tell students to listen while you pronounce *girl* and *heard*. Ask: *Is the vowel sound the same or different? What about the spelling?* Play the tape and tell students to write the words they hear.

Check answers and then play the tape again, asking students to listen and repeat the list of words. Point out that in most parts of Britain the 'r' in these words is not pronounced.

TAPESCRIPT AND KEY
earth first work turn were alert internal thirty word learn

GRAMMAR REVIEW

Put students into groups to discuss these sentences. If students are not sure of the rules, refer them to the relevant section of the Grammar Reference on page 127.

KEY

Sentences 1-8:

1 No article when referring to plural countable nouns when making general statements
2 Definite article to refer to specific things
3 No article with abstract nouns, especially school/academic subjects
4 Definite article to refer to something specific, e.g. the architecture of a certain historical period
5 The indefinite article in front of a singular countable noun mentioned for the first time; the definite article is used when it is mentioned again.
6 *The glass* = specific item already mentioned; *the floor* = the definite article to refer to something unique - there is only one floor in a room (c.f. *the ceiling, the roof*)
7 No article with uncountable nouns when they are unspecific
8 No article with abstract nouns when they are unspecific

Exercise 7 PRACTICE

Do this exercise with the whole class or set for homework.

KEY
1 Life 2 The oranges 3 a restaurant/the food
4 loud music 5 the music 6 blood 7 divorce
8 The truth

LISTENING

Exercise 8 Before you listen

Ask students to use dictionaries and discuss the words with each other. Explain that *secretion* comes from the verb *to secrete* and has nothing to do with *secret*. Ask what the adjectives from the various abstract nouns are (*anxious, nauseous, unstable* not ~~*instable*~~, *irritable*).

Ask students if, on the basis of these words and expressions and the title of the unit, they can make any guess as to what the experiment was about.

Exercise 9

Play the tape once through for students to answer the gist questions. Then play the tape again, pausing at intervals for them to note the activities under the relevant times. Finally, ask students how they think the old timetable differed from the new one.

TAPESCRIPT

Well, the Council of Europe have been funding a very interesting experiment just recently, to see if children learn better in a school situation if they're allowed to follow their natural biorhythms of waking and sleeping, and so a school in south west France – in Pau, actually – a primary school was selected for this purpose and one particular class of seven and eight year olds were put into this natural kind of timetable while the rest of the school carried on in a more controlled conventional system.

The whole programme was based on the theory that they need a lot of sleep at that age and while they're sleeping the growth hormone is secreted, so if the sleep pattern is disturbed then that child is likely to wake up irritable, suffering anxiety, maybe nausea in some cases. Emotional instability and irritability are … are quite often notable in … in children of that age. So, the first thing was that the children started school at nine o'clock instead of eight thirty. As children are at their most intelligent and alert in the morning, it was between ten and eleven, these … this most energetic period that the most serious study was done. Then by the time it got to lunch time, a break would be taken at one o'clock, and this experimental group could go home until three fifteen or they could read quietly, or they could take part in a drama activity, or a gentle sport like table tennis, or even, in some cases, they could take a little siesta in a … a darkened room in the school.

After lunch, from three fifteen onwards, it was found that the physical alertness is greater at that time of day, and so they were encouraged to play sport, quite energetic sport. Their … the memory is at its most active during that time, so after an hour's sport, the last two hours of the day, four fifteen till six fifteen, was spent studying mathematics because that's a good time for memory retention.

Well, the result of all this was very exciting – enormous enthusiasm from the children, and also the parents and teachers. The children … the children's results in various tests were noticeably better, I mean they were equal if not better to those from tests in the controlled classes in the conventional system, and they … the children themselves gained enormously in confidence. In fact, the report has recommended that they go on for another year. So all in all it's been a very successful, very interesting experiment on the part of the Council of Europe.

Exercise 10 Talk about it.

Discuss the questions with the class as a whole. If appropriate, ask students if they can remember what their timetable was like during primary school. Ask them what problems might arise in their own country if it adopted a timetable like the one suggested in the experiment.

EXTRA ACTIVITIES

1 Gapped text

Write part of the reading text on biorhythms on the board with gaps for students to fill in from memory. The gaps may replace articles, abstract nouns or prepositions or even longer phrases, according to what type of practice your students need most.

2 Countable or uncountable?

Make up a list of nouns from this unit, making sure that there is a mix of countable and uncountable nouns. Call the words out one by one and ask students to write a C or a U according to whether they are countable or uncountable. e.g:

1 car 2 life 3 blood 4 cycle 5 water 6 energy
7 period 8 insurance 9 temper
10 coordination

They need not write the word, only the number and the correct letter.

UNIT 5 A letter of application

Suggested lesson breaks: after Exercise 5 and Exercise 8

BACKGROUND NOTES

health club: a place with special equipment where people can go to take exercise and join in social activities. Entry is usually restricted by membership. A health club is not the same as a health centre, which is a medical clinic where doctors see patients.

Windsor: a town in the south of England on the River Thames famous for the castle which is one of the homes of the British Royal family.

Before asking students to open their books, give them each a piece of paper and ask them to imagine they are writing a formal letter to a secretarial agency in England (think of a name and address) in answer to an advertisement for a translator. Tell them that all you want them to do is to start writing the letter, (just the first line of the letter will do), and to show also how they would end the letter. (If students have already looked ahead and checked how to do this, all the better.)

This will give you an idea of what problems students still have in the formal aspects of letter writing, i.e. the position of their address, the addressee's name and address, the date, the salutation, the ending and so on.

Now tell students to open their books and check if their letter looks similar to the one in the book. Tell them to note any errors in content and style and then to read the letter.

Exercise 1 READING

Ask students to look at the picture of Paulo and to guess which nationality he is (Portuguese). Ask them to look at the advertisement and ask: *What job is he applying for? Where is it situated?* Now ask them to read the letter while you write these questions on the board: *How old is Paulo? Where does he live? What are his qualifications? What hours does he prefer? When can he start work?*

Students now work in pairs to do the matching exercise.

KEY

keen on sport: I am interested in sport and fitness and at home I go to a sports centre three times a week. I am also a member of the college swimming team.

outgoing: I get on very well with people and I like making new friends.

part-time work (including late hours): I am prepared to work any hours but ideally I would like to work in the afternoons and evenings only so that I can attend English classes in the mornings.

June to September: My term ends on 28th May, so I would be able to start on 1st June.

good command of English: I have studied English for six years but I want to spend some time in England in order to improve my spoken English.

must be adaptable: I don't mind doing any sort of work including cleaning, washing up and helping in the gym.

Point out how important it is when writing a letter of application for a job that you try to 'answer' the advertisement like Paulo has done.

Exercise 2

Ask students to notice how Paulo has laid out his letter and to name four features which show that it is formal rather than informal. You may like to remind them here how to start and end an informal letter. Any of the following features may be mentioned:

KEY

1 Name and address included of person receiving the letter, usually placed above the salutation
2 Use of titles: *Dear Sir/Madam*
3 Formal introduction, e.g: *I am writing in reply to your advertisement*
4 Use of full forms, e.g: *I am writing* not *I'm writing.*
5 Formal closing formula, e.g: *I look forward to hearing from you.*
6 Closing salutation: *Yours faithfully* not *Yours sincerely* or *Yours*

Students can now correct their own letters bearing in mind these points.

GRAMMAR REVIEW

Students can work in pairs.

KEY

Present simple

- to talk about routine or frequency: *I go to a sports centre three times a week.*
- to talk about general facts: *I come from Coimbra in the north of Portugal.*
- to talk about fixed times in the future: *My term ends on 28th May*

Present continuous

- to talk about events which are happening now or around the time of speaking: *I am still studying at college*
- to talk about definite future arrangements: *I am taking my final exams in May.*

Exercise 3 PRACTICE

Read out the phrases and let students call out 'present simple' or 'present continuous'. If they make a mistake, ask them to make a sentence with the phrase, without telling them that they are wrong. Often when students hear the phrase used with the wrong verb tense in a complete sentence, they will realise their mistake.

KEY

The present simple tense: generally, about this time of the year, every day
The present continuous tense: at the moment, at present, tomorrow, for the time being, currently, right now, next week

Exercise 4

Ask different students to make up a true statement about themselves using one or two of the phrases, then ask them to make sentences with the remaining phrases as part of their homework. Point out that the phrases may come in different places in the sentence, e.g. at the beginning, at the end, before the main verb, etc.

Exercise 5

Read the example paragraph, then give another model of your own, referring to a member of your family. Students then write a similar paragraph of their own while you go round, helping with vocabulary and checking tense usage.

SUGGESTED LESSON BREAK

GRAMMAR FOCUS

Ask students to find two examples of clauses of purpose in the letter. Refer to the first example at the end of the second paragraph of Paulo's letter: *in order to improve my spoken English.* Point out that Paulo could also have expressed purpose by saying *to improve my spoken English* or *so I can improve my spoken English.*

Ask students to read the Grammar Focus silently. Note that it is possible to make a negative with *in order to (in order not to)* but it is fairly formal. It is useful for students to know that they may meet this negative form but point out that it is not as common as *so that...not.*

Exercise 6 PRACTICE

Go through the exercise with the whole class. Sometimes more than one version is possible.

KEY

1 I'll give you my telephone number so (that) you can phone me at work.
2 Take some suntan cream so (that) you won't get sunburnt.
3 I'm going to the post office to post a parcel.
4 We are organising a 'Fun Run' (in order) to raise money for the local hospital.
5 They took the phone off the hook so (that) nobody could phone them.
6 Speak louder so (that) Granny can hear you.
7 Turn the sound down so (that) you don't disturb the neighbours.
8 We are installing solar heating (in order) to save energy.

Exercise 7

Go round the class eliciting reasons, e.g. *in order to pass my exams, so I can get into ... College, so I can get a good job, in order to understand English people when I go abroad,* etc.

Exercise 8 PHRASAL VERB: *get*

Refer back to the phrase in Paulo's letter which reads *I get on very well with people.* Ask: *What sort of verb is this? Why is it different from other verbs? Can you think of a phrasal verb with 'give'? 'look'? 'take'? Can you think of any more with 'get'?* Elicit *get up* and *get down.*

Set students to work on the exercise. Check the answers briefly. Then ask different students to use the phrasal verbs in sentences of their own.

KEY
1f 2d 3g 4c 5b 6a 7h 8e

STUDY POINT

Ask students to try and work out the three types of phrasal verbs before looking at the Grammar Reference section.

KEY
Type 1 e.g. *get on* (sentence 6): intransitive phrasal verb which cannot take an object
Type 2 e.g. *get over it* (sentence 5): transitive phrasal verb where the object can only come after the preposition, i.e. after the complete phrasal verb
Type 3 e.g. *get his ideas across* (sentence 3): transitive phrasal verb where the object can come after the preposition or between the verb and the preposition

Ask students to categorise the other phrasal verbs in Exercise 8 and see if they can say which type they belong to.

KEY
Type 1: get away, get up, get on
Type 2: get up to, get over, get round to
Type 3: get across, get down

Now ask students to turn to the Grammar Reference section (page 134) and read the note about phrasal verbs and how they are signalled in the dictionary. Distribute a number of good-sized monolingual dictionaries like the *Longman Dictionary of Contemporary English.* Ask students to find the following phrasal verbs and note the type according to the entries: *take up* (a sport), *break down* (of a car), *give up* (after many attempts), *put up* (give a bed for the night), *put up with* (suffer).

SUGGESTED LESSON BREAK

Exercise 9 Talk about it.

Ask students to look at the photos and say what each person is doing in each. Then ask them to look at the list of jobs and say what job each person in the photos has.

KEY
Selling icecream in the street/Being a waiter in a café/Picking fruit on a farm/Being a tour guide

Check that students know that *a sun lounger* is a long beach chair used for sunbathing which often folds out into different positions.

Ask the questions to the class as a whole, drawing out any relevant experiences. Those who have never had any of these jobs can be asked to name one which they would like to do.

Now put students into groups of three or four and tell them they must try and agree on an order of preference. If the members of any group are very divided in opinion, they can each do an individual order of preference. Each group gives feedback on their discussion and compares their order of preference with the others. See if any agreement emerges over the most and the least desirable jobs.

WRITING

Exercise 10 Before you write

Ask students to skim-read the advertisement and ask a few comprehension questions. Check that students understand *casual, lifeguard* and *first aid.* Ask if any of them have taken any life-saving certificate. (This could lead to a discussion of what is involved in lifesaving a person.)

Ask students to work quietly making brief notes under the headings. Tell them that they may invent suitable qualifications if they wish. Have a quick general discussion as to what questions one might want to ask in a letter.

Exercise 11

Ask one student to come to the front of the class and write on the board how she or he might start the letter. The other students may comment as the student writes. Then ask students to complete the letter for homework.

EXTRA ACTIVITIES

1 Mime a job

Students work in groups. Each student takes it in turns to mime one of the jobs in the list in Exercise 9. The rest of the group have to ask *Yes/No* questions in order to guess the job.

2 Jigsaw letter

Write a letter of application for a job. Photocopy it so that you have one copy of the letter for each group of 4-5 in the class. Cut each letter up into several sentences, mix them up and put them in an envelope. Give the envelope to each group and tell them that the first group to manage to reorder the letter correctly wins. (Don't make it too easy.

Remember that it is also possible to cut off a sentence in the middle of a phrase.)

Ex. 9 1 get on 2 get round to 3 get over 4 gets up 5 get it across

CHECK 1 Units 1-5

Before the lesson, photocopy the key or copy it onto an OHT. When students have completed the Check exercises (either at home or in class), they can either correct each other's answers or correct their own. At this stage the students should note down their grammatical difficulties under headings, e.g: use of article, present simple/ continuous. Refer them to the relevant parts of the Grammar Reference section at the back of the Students' Book and give them some more remedial exercises.

The results of these Check units can help identify those areas of grammar and usage which will need more attention in the future.

KEY

Ex. 1 1b 2c 3a 4b 5c 6c 7a

Ex. 2 1 Have you ever written 2 've made 3 was, saw 4 is business going, are not doing, made 5 was, had seen 6 have you had 7 aren't working/ haven't been working

Ex. 3 1b 2c 3a 4c 5b 6a

Ex. 4 1 aren't they? 2 will you? 3 doesn't it? 4 didn't it? 5 were you? 6 isn't it? 7 have you? 8 didn't they? 9 didn't she? 10 wouldn't you?

Ex. 5
1 Don't you work in the accounts department?
2 Haven't we seen this film before?
3 Don't you want an icecream/Don't you like icecream?
4 Aren't you/Isn't Alison going away on holiday soon?
5 Doesn't she work in the library?
6 Didn't you/they hear the fire alarm go off?
7 Don't you want to do something/anything more interesting this evening?
8 Shouldn't we tell the police?

Ex. 6 1 getting 2 fishing 3 watch 4 being 5 lying 6 having 7 washing up 8 gardening 9 not having 10 going

Ex. 7 1 the 2 - , - 3 the 4 The 5 - 6 -, - 7 the 8 - 9 the 10 -, -

Ex. 8
1 I'll give you my address so (that) you will be able to/you can write to me.
2 They called a meeting in order to discuss a problem.
3 Let's go next door so (that) nobody can hear us.
4 He gave a false name in order to confuse the police.
5 He studied hard every night in order to catch up with the others.
6 She always sits at the back of the class so (that) she doesn't have to answer any questions.

UNIT 6 Physical description

Suggested lesson break: after Exercise 6.

BACKGROUND NOTES

Cézanne, Paul: (1839-1906) a French painter who influenced the development of cubism and abstract art.
Toulouse-Lautrec, Henri de: a French painter (1864-1901), well-known for his brightly-coloured posters.
Modigliani, Amadeo: (1884-1920) an Italian painter influenced by Toulouse-Lautrec, Picasso and Cézanne. He is especially known for his pictures of people, in which their faces and bodies are much longer than in real life.
P.D.James: (b. 1920) A British writer of detective stories.
Anita Brookner: (b. 1938) a British novelist whose books are notable for their wistful portraits of women. She won the Booker Prize in 1984 for her novel *Hotel du Lac.*
William Boyd: (b. 1952) a novelist and screen writer. He won critical acclaim for his first novel *A Good Man in Africa.* His novels are known for their dry humour and comic detail.

Exercise 1 Talk about it.

Ask the first two questions. Possible answers for the second question: the hat and scarf of the man on the right; the shape of the face of the girl on the right; the hat and pipe of the man on the left. Ask if students can identify the portraits and if they have any favourite painters. Extend the discussion, if students are interested, into other areas such as: other styles of portrait painting (Picasso, pencil sketches), other famous impressionists, if there is a difficulty in capturing likeness in portraits, the difference between a photograph and a portrait, etc.

KEY

The portraits are:
Top left: Modigliani's *Femme à l'écharpe bleue*
Top right: Toulouse Lautrec's *Ambassadeurs: Aristide Bruant*
Bottom left: Cézanne's *L'homme à la pipe*
Bottom right: Modigliani's *Fillete vers 1918*

Exercise 2

Students may use a dictionary if they wish. Use your face and body to show the difference between the neck (the whole area), the throat (just by the Adam's apple), the chin and the jaw. Give the two pronunciations of *forehead* (/ˈfɔːhed/ and /ˈfɒrəd/). Finally, ask different students to point to the parts of their own faces and say what they are.

KEY
1 throat 2 mouth 3 nose 4 fringe 5 cheek
6 jaw 7 chin 8 beard 9 moustache 10 eyebrow
11 forehead 12 parting 13 eyelash 14 ear
15 neck

Exercise 3 LITERATURE

Note that recorded versions of all the Literature texts from the Students' Book can also be found on the Class Cassettes at the appropriate places within each unit. Teachers may like to use these taped readings instead of or alongside the printed versions.

Ask students to look at and describe the woman on the bottom left hand side of the page (under the P.D. James text). Now ask them to read or listen to the text and note any differences. Direct them to the glossary but tell them to note any other new words as they read. Check the differences afterwards and continue in the same way with the other two texts.

KEY

1 The woman in the text has straight brows and has her hair in a chignon, whereas the woman in the picture has curved brows and loose hair.
2 The woman in the text has blonde/brown hair and a black hairband, whereas the woman in the picture has black hair and a white hairband. The woman in the text has large eyes, but the woman in the picture has small eyes.
3 The man in the text has a parting in the middle and a moustache, whereas the man in the picture has a side parting and no moustache. In the text the man has a small, almost snub nose, whereas the man in the picture has a large nose.

This might be a good time, if students have an interest in literature, to tell them some more about the authors (see Background Notes above).

Exercise 4 VOCABULARY

Students work in pairs to categorise the vocabulary. If they like, they can add other categories, e.g. colour, eyes, facial features. Show that, under *hair*, they can write phrases like *swept upwards*.

KEY
CLOTHES (articles): sweater, scarf, trousers, skirt, band (materials): cashmere, silk, flannel, velvet
BUILD: tall, stocky
HAIR: strong, greying, swept upwards, curled into a chignon, thick, blonde, brown, pepper and salt, cut short with a parting in the middle
SKIN: fine
GENERAL APPEARANCE: handsome, distinguished, younger than her age

Exercise 5

Students may use a dictionary for this exercise. Alternatively, do the exercise with the whole class. Check and practise the pronunciation of *broad-shouldered, balding, plait, freckles* and *wrinkles.*

KEY
BUILD: overweight (adj), skinny (adj), well-built (adj), broad-shouldered (adj)
HAIR: wavy (adj), ponytail (n), straight (adj), plait (n), curly (adj), balding (adj), shoulder-length (adj), bun (n)
SKIN: pale (adj), wrinkles (n), sun-tanned (adj), spots (n), freckles (n)
GENERAL APPEARANCE: pretty (adj), plain (adj), beautiful (adj), ugly (adj)

Exercise 6

Students should first note which words and phrases are nouns and which are adjectives, as in the key above, before they complete the sentences.

KEY

1 She wears her hair in a ponytail/plait/bun.
2 His/her hair is curly/wavy/straight/shoulder-length.
3 She doesn't like her skin because she's got freckles/wrinkles/spots.
4 She's on a special diet because she is skinny/overweight.
5 Unlike his brother, who's rather thin, he's tall and well-built/broad-shouldered/(overweight).
6 The best models always seem to be beautiful/skinny/suntanned/(pale).

SUGGESTED LESSON BREAK

STUDY POINT

Read the note aloud to the students. Ask them to give other examples for each of the categories.

Exercise 7 PRACTICE

KEY

1 She wore a tight-fitting red velvet dress.
2 He's got large brown deep-set eyes.
3 The girl had long wavy auburn hair.
4 I'm looking for a large white cotton sweater.
5 The boy had long dark hair.

Exercise 8

In this exercise students must try to describe each other's appearance from memory. Choose a student in the class and sit back to back with him/her. Give an example of what you expect students to say. e.g: *You've got short wavy blonde hair with a fringe and a side parting. You're wearing a red and white striped shirt and blue jeans and boots with a silver buckle.* Point out that they should try and include as much detail and new vocabulary as possible. Students judge each other's description on a scale of one to ten.

STUDY POINT

Students work individually to complete the phrases and to find the examples.

KEY

a stocky man *in* his early/mid/late forties
a girl *with* dark hair
a woman *in* a biege raincoat
The girl *with* a ponytail

The preposition *in* is used with age and clothes; *with* is used with hair.

Find two examples of an adjectival phrase:
dressed with careful and expensive informality
swept upwards and curled into a chignon

Ask students to search the second text to find one more adjectival phrase *(held back by a black velvet band.)*

Exercise 9

The exercise can be done orally with the whole class.

KEY

1 She was a slim woman in her thirties.
2 He wore a jacket with gold buttons.
3 He had greasy black hair pulled back into a rubber band.
4 She wore a scarf tied loosely round her neck.
5 He was an unusual-looking man with a short ponytail.

Exercise 10 LISTENING

Students copy the headings from the chart into their notebooks, leaving plenty of space in which to write the details.

Pre-teach the following words:
foot (measurement), *hazel* (adj), *sparkling* (eyes), *highlights* (in hair), *cool* (*coll.* = fashionable and aloof) and *skinny*.

Tell students not to write anything until they have heard the tape through once. Play the tape a second time, pausing for them to write. To help students you might like to put the following headings on the board under each speaker:

FRIEND 1	FRIEND 2
Hair	*Hair*
Eyes	*Clothes*
Build	*General appearance*
Clothes	

TAPESCRIPT

1 I was quite shocked to see how much a friend of mine had … had changed when I saw her recently. I first knew her, oh, about twenty years ago when we were both about twenty two or so, and she was a bright, fun-loving person with long brown hair and hazel coloured eyes which … which were smiling eyes. They were eyes which lit up when you met her and they always attracted people to her. And she was a heavyish sort of person - not tall - she was about 5 foot 3, 5 foot 4 and she used to wear dresses - long, long skirts with flower designs, but I was quite amazed when I saw her recently to see that she was physically different and she was wearing very, very different clothes. She was much slimmer, much fitter looking. Her eyes of course were still those wonderful sparkling eyes but their focus was a little bit more serious now. And her … her hair was now short. It was … it had changed colour. It had highlights in it ... little streaks of colour but it was short. And whereas she'd had a sort of rather round, sort of almost baby face, now it was … it was … it was a much tighter, sharper look. And her clothing … she was wearing jeans and a T-shirt and trainers, and she said that she most often wore that kind of clothing now. So I was … I was quite surprised how much she'd changed.

2 It's strange how much people change. I once had a friend whom I knew from my childhood and when I knew him, he was this sort of young, hard teenager, concerned with his ... his cool image and he was terribly skinny. He wore tight trousers. He had really short hair that was shaved at the back. He had these big, heavy black boots that he used to wear and a ... dark leather jacket. And he always wore the same clothes – he never, ever changed. He never wore a suit for any special occasion or smart trousers. I think the big change in my friend happened when he went to college. I think his dad persuaded him to go and study there and he got accepted onto a business course and from that moment on he really changed drastically. He became interested in … in the business world. He read the newspapers. He watched TV and he even studied quite hard. He dropped his cool image and changed physically quite a lot as well. He let his hair grow much longer and he put a bit of weight on and he actually started wearing normal clothes - jeans and smart trousers. He even wore office suits sometimes when he had to go to interviews or meet with people in companies. I think he realised that there was really more to life than just looking cool.

Exercise 11 WRITING

Make sure that students have someone in mind to write about. It should preferably be someone famous. Students write a paragraph for homework. Point out that the description will be mostly about physical appearance but they can write in general about the person's clothes, e.g: *X usually wears … and …*

At the beginning of the next lesson, students find a different partner in the class to read their paragraph to without revealing the person's identity. The partner has to try and guess who it is.

EXTRA ACTIVITIES

1 The adjective game

Students work in groups of four or five. One

student starts by giving a sentence describing either a person's hair or clothing, e.g: *He had dark hair* or *She wore a sweater*. In turn, a student must add an adjective or an adjectival phrase to the preceding sentence so that it makes sense and the words are in the right order. e.g:

S1: She wore a jacket.
S2: She wore a red jacket.
S3: She wore a red woollen jacket.
S4: She wore a red woollen jacket with gold buttons.

A player must drop out if he/she cannot think of a word or phrase, puts the adjective or phrase in an unacceptable position or says something nonsensical or contradictory (e.g: ~~*He had red black hair*~~).

Students report back to the other groups their final sentence.

2 Guess who?

Ask students to bring in a photograph of themselves (preferably portrait-size), taken before the age of ten. These are then displayed on a notice board and numbered. Students walk round and identify each of the portraits. The answers are then discussed with questions like: *Who is number 6?* (Antonia) *How do you know it's Antonia?* (You can tell by the eyes which are quite deep-set and the nose.)

UNIT 7 First Impressions

Suggested lesson break: after Exercise 5

BACKGROUND NOTES
reggae: a kind of popular music from the West Indies with a strong regular beat which developed in Jamaica in the 1960s.
East End of London: the eastern part of central London, north of the river Thames, containing much of the Docklands.
Taiwan: an island off the south-east coast of China, whose capital is Taipei.
West End: the western part of central London, considered a fashionable place, where there are large or important shops, theatres, hotels, etc.

Exercise 1 Before you read

In the general discussion arising from these questions, try to encourage students to use some of the vocabulary from the previous unit.

Exercise 2 READING

Either ask students to make suggestions about the jobs the people in the photographs might do or write the following three jobs on the blackboard: *veterinary surgeon (a vet), hairdresser, secretary* and ask students to say which of these jobs they think the people do for a living. Do not give the answer yet but ask the reasons for their choice. Now ask students to skim-read the text and correct their guesses if necessary.

Exercise 3 Read and answer.

Students read the text again, underlining or noting down any new words and expressions. They should not use a dictionary yet.

Ask the questions of the class as a whole.

Exercise 4 Read and think.

Ask the questions to the class as a whole.

(Some possible answers)
1 Taiwan is a long way away from the UK ('in the Far East') and it is comparatively rare to meet Taiwanese people in Britain, apart from tourists. Also, British immigration and employment regulations would make it very difficult for someone from Taiwan to get a long-term work permit to work as a salon hairdresser. Western hairstyles and hair fashions for women are very different from those in Taiwan and most qualified salon hairdressers would return home to use their skills in Taiwan's rapidly developing economy. Finally, hairdressing involves close contact with clients, so language might be a problem.
2 Because although she has an established professional job, she lives in a shared flat with friends. Her appearance is unconventional (people expect professionals to dress conservatively). Also, people might expect an attractive young woman to have a boyfriend but she hasn't.

Exercise 5 Study the words

Check the words and expressions with the students and ask if there are still any words or phrases underlined in the texts which they are uncertain of. Use the Background Notes if necessary.

KEY
1 to form a judgement too quickly 2 instant opinions 3 a multi-storeyed tower block of flats 4 having enough money to live comfortably 5 neat and clean in appearance 6 extremely tiring

Ask if students can make sentences of their own using these words and phrases.

SUGGESTED LESSON BREAK

Exercise 6 VOCABULARY

Ask different students to describe what is happening in each picture, using the appropriate verb, e.g: *In Picture 1 a detective is examining something with a magnifying glass.*

KEY
1 examine 2 search 3 watch 4 glance 5 stare 6 look at

Spend some time talking about the verbs and getting students to suggest new sentences and contexts in which to use them.

Exercise 7 PHRASAL VERB: *look*

Students work individually or in pairs.

KEY
1 looks like 2 looking for 3 look up 4 Look out 5 look into 6 looks after

Look up can be separated by an object.

Ask a student to rephrase sentence 3 to show its alternative form with the object in between *look* and the preposition. Check that students can use the phrasal verbs by asking a series of questions, e.g: *What does an au pair job involve? What would you do if you wanted to know what Einstein was famous for? Who do you most look like in your family?* etc.

Exercise 8 Talk about it.

Do this exercise with the whole class. To stimulate discussion, write a selection of jobs on the board to focus students' ideas. e.g: a teacher, a managing director of a company, an advertising copywriter, a sales assistant, a gardener, a beautician, etc.

GRAMMAR REVIEW

Students work individually.

KEY
1a 2b 3a

1 The simple tense is correct because the activity is complete.
2 The continuous tense is correct because it emphasises that the activity of eating blueberries began at a point in the past and continued over a period of time. The activity may or may not be over at the time of speaking.
3 The simple tense is correct because certain verbs like *know, like*, etc, are normally only used in the simple form.

Exercise 9 PRACTICE

Students work individually or in pairs. Ask them to use contracted forms in their answers.

KEY
1 you haven't been waiting, I've only been 2 's been sitting 3 's been 4 has he phoned 5 have been going out 6 've been having 7 've known

Exercise 10 WRITING

Build up the first four lines of the conversation on the board with the help of the students, then ask them to continue. Explain that there is no 'correct' conversation and that there are various ways of expressing the information. They should use the basic facts in Mei-Yu's text but they can add other details if they like. The conversation should include about seven or eight exchanges.

SUGGESTED CONVERSATION

CUSTOMER: How long have you been a hairdresser?
MEI-YU: Over fifteen years.
CUSTOMER: That's a long time. Have you always worked in this country?
MEI-YU: No, I was a hairdresser in Taiwan first.
CUSTOMER: I see. How long have you been here in London?
MEI-YU: Since 1983.
CUSTOMER: And you've always worked in this salon, have you?
MEI-YU: Yes, I like it here. It's a nice place to work.
CUSTOMER: Do you have any family here?
MEI-YU: Yes, I'm married. We've got one son.
CUSTOMER: How long have you been married?
MEI-YU: We've been married for over ten years now.
CUSTOMER: Really? What does your husband do?
MEI-YU: He works for a computer company.
CUSTOMER: Do you ever think of going back to Taiwan?
MEI-YU: Not any more. We've been here too long. We've got lots of friends here now.

Exercise 11 ROLEPLAY

Set the scene for the roleplay and ask students to read their respective rolecards at the back of the book. Explain that you want them to use all the information on their rolecards. This means that when they talk to their friend they must mention how they have spent their morning so far. They may add extra details if they wish. Write a suitable opening exchange on the board to start them off, e.g:

A: *Oh, hello, Carmen. Fancy seeing you here!*
B: *Hi, Alma.*
A: *Have you been shopping here all morning?*
B: *No, I've been swimming. I only arrived about twenty minutes ago. In fact I've just bought ...*

EXTRA ACTIVITIES

1 What turns you off?

In groups, students discuss what it is about people that gives a bad impression or 'turns them off' at a first meeting, e.g. their voice, their laugh, if they smoke, if they are obviously drunk, if they haven't bothered at all about their clothes and appearance. The class then convene and decide on the 'Top Five Turn-offs'.

2 Interview questions

Students imagine they are staying in Britain and have been asked to do a project about old people in the community. Ask them to make a list of questions to ask. Give a couple of examples, e.g: *How old are you? How long have you been living here?* Other questions which the students might think of are: *Have you always lived in the same place? Where did you work? How long have you been retired? How do you spend your time?* (If the old people are ill): *What help have you been getting? Who cooks and cleans for you?* If students are studying in an English-speaking country, they can use these questions to conduct a survey in their local community.

UNIT 8 Polite requests

Suggested lesson break: after Exercise 4

BACKGROUND NOTES
Paddington: one of London's mainline stations serving the west of England
'Bambi': a classic animated film by Walt Disney about a small deer
Kings Cross: one of London's mainline stations serving Scotland and the north of England
Edinburgh: the capital of Scotland

Exercise 1 Think about it.

Ask students to describe the scene in the photograph and to discuss the questions.

Exercise 2 LISTENING DIALOGUE

Students read the dialogue in pairs and note what they think are the missing words. Explain that several answers may be possible and that the dotted line means one or more words are missing.

Ask students to guess the meaning of *stuffy*. Check what students have written and eliminate any suggestions which are not grammatical or appropriate. Then play the tape and ask them to adjust their versions. Students can then read the completed dialogue in pairs.

TAPESCRIPT AND KEY

LIZ: Excuse me, *is anybody sitting* there?
WOMAN: No, no. It's free.
LIZ: Oh, good. Goodness, it's stuffy in here, isn't it! *Do you mind very much* if I open the window a little?
WOMAN: No, *not at all*. It is rather hot.
MAN: Tickets, please.
LIZ: *Excuse me*, but do you know what time this train gets to Paddington?
MAN: 10.35, madam.
LIZ: Thank you. Er, *could I possibly* borrow your newspaper for a moment?
WOMAN: Yes, certainly. *By all means.* I've finished with it.
LIZ: Thanks. I just wanted to check the times of a film I'm going to see this afternoon.
WOMAN: *Are you going to see* anything interesting?
LIZ: Well, actually, I'm taking my four-year-old niece to see *Bambi*!
/some time later/
MAN: Any more tickets?
LIZ: Oh, excuse me, but *do you think you could* help me with my case?
MAN: *Certainly,* madam. There you are!
LIZ: Thanks very much.

Exercise 3 Answer the questions.

1 1 Excuse me, is anybody sitting there?
  2 Do you mind very much if I open the window a little?
  3 Excuse me, but do you know what time this train gets to Paddington?
  4 Could I possibly borrow your newspaper for a moment?
  5 Excuse me, but do you think you could help me with my case?

2 Do you mind very much if I ...
Do you know what time ...
Could I possibly borrow ...
Excuse me, but do you think you could help me ...

3 The dialogue expressions have extra politeness markers (e.g: *very much, possibly*) and the use of indirect questions. These make the speaker sound more polite, especially when speaking to strangers.

COMMUNICATION FOCUS

Go round the class asking different students to read different polite requests and responses. Point out that the words in brackets are optional but that they do add an extra measure of politeness. Make sure that students are producing the correct intonation for the polite openers, e.g:

Excuse me but ..., I'm sorry to disturb you but ...

(This will be practised further in the Speechwork section that follows.) In order to provide some brief practice of the requests, write the following cues on the board:

Factual information
Where's the information desk?
How much are the tickets?

Ask people to do things
-check my spelling
-sign this form

Ask permission
-put the heating on
-turn the sound down

Exercise 4 SPEECHWORK

Play the tape for students to practise the intonation of polite requests.

TAPESCRIPT
(Opening remarks):
Excuse me but ... I'm awfully sorry but ...
I'm sorry to trouble you but ... Sorry to disturb you but ...

(Complete requests):
1 ... a buffet car on this train?
... do you know if there's a buffet car on this train?
Excuse me, but do you know if there's a buffet car on this train?

2 ... close the window a little?
... you could close the window a little?
Excuse me, but do you think you could close the window a little?

3 ... help me with my suitcase?
... could you possibly help me with my suitcase?
Sorry to bother you but could you possibly help me with my suitcase?

4 ... looking after my bag for a moment?
... would you mind looking after my bag for a moment?
I'm sorry to disturb you but would you mind looking after my bag for a moment?

SUGGESTED LESSON BREAK

GRAMMAR REVIEW

Go through the questions working with the whole class.

KEY
Sentence 2 sounds more polite.
Sentence 2 is an indirect question.
The verb follows the subject in the second part of an indirect question.
Other phrases which can introduce an indirect question are:
Do you know..., Have you any idea...,
Could you tell me/let me know..., I wonder...,
I don't know...

Exercise 5 PRACTICE

Divide the class into small groups. Give each group a situation in each section, e.g: Group 1 gets Situations 1, 4 and 8. Group 2 gets Situations 2, 5 and 9, etc. Some groups may have to work on the same situations if you have a large class. Ask them to prepare what they are going to say in each situation, using the expressions in the Communication Focus box. Tell them that you want them to sound as polite as possible each time and that they should give an appropriate response to the request in each case. When the groups have worked out their three situations (set a time limit of 4-5 minutes) ask each group to perform their situations for the others. For homework, students can write requests and responses for the whole exercise.

Exercise 6 VOCABULARY

See if students can do this on their own. After checking the exercise, ask students to work in pairs making two-line exchanges for each expression.

KEY
1 Do you mind 2 mind your own business
3 changed my mind 4 make up your mind
5 Never mind 6 Mind out! 7 Mind you

Exercise 7 ROLEPLAY

This roleplay needs plenty of time for students to prepare and perform. Ask a student to read aloud the train information notice. Divide students into 'A's and 'B's and refer them to their respective rolecards. They should have a few minutes to read and make notes about what they are going to say. The conversation falls into two parts. In the first part, students have to establish the conversation and talk about what they are doing or where they are going. In the second part (after a small pause), both A and B have to make requests.

Help students by writing the opening lines of the conversation on the board:

B: *Excuse me but is anybody sitting here?*
A: *No, it's free.*
B: *Do you mind if I sit here, then?*
A: *By all means.*
B: *I'm meeting a friend but the train's late. Typical, isn't it?*
A: *My train's been delayed as well. ...*

Go round and listen while students perform, making notes of any recurring errors. Call the class together and choose two pairs to act out their conversation in front of the class. Go through the errors and ask students to write the conversation for homework.

EXTRA ACTIVITIES

1 Request chains

Students form groups of four or five. In turn, each student gives a basic order, e.g:

S1: Open the window.

The next person must add or change an element to make it more polite, e.g:

S2: Open the window, please.
S3: Could you open the window, please?
S4: Could you possibly open the window, please?
S5: Excuse me, but could you possibly open the window, please?
S6: Excuse me, but would you mind very much opening the window for me, please?
S7: Excuse me, sorry to disturb you, but would you mind very much opening the window for me, please?

2 Indirect questions

Everyone has to write five direct questions for factual information in their books starting either with a *Wh-* or a *Yes/No* question, e.g: *1 What's the time? 2 Has the train to Paddington arrived yet?* etc. Choose one student to start. This student reads out the first question and calls out the name of another student who then has to make it indirect by starting with *Can you tell me...?* e.g:

S1: What's the time? Jessica!
S2 (Jessica): Can you tell me what the time is? Where's the post office? Bruno!
S3 (Bruno): Can you tell me where the post office is? etc.

UNIT 9 Personality of the year

Suggested lesson break: after Exercise 4

BACKGROUND NOTES

Gary Lineker: Gary Lineker was born in 1960 in Leicester, a city in the Midlands of England. He made his debut for England in 1984. In 1986 he was voted Footballer of the Year and in June of that year he was sold to the Spanish team of Barcelona for £2,750,000. He was appointed captain of the England team in 1990 and was voted Footballer of the Year again in 1992. In 1993 he left England to play for the Japanese Club, Grampus Eight. During his career, Gary Lineker scored forty-eight goals for England, one goal short of the record held by Bobby Charlton.

Exercise 1 Before you read

Ask students if they have heard of Gary Lineker (a professional footballer). Then ask them to look at the pictures and the newspaper headlines and to say what it tells you about Lineker and his personality.

To set the context of the text as a competition entry, read the advertisement for the 'Sports Personality of the Year' competition. Ask students what qualities they think are important in a sports personality.

READING

Exercise 2 Read and answer.

Ask students to read the text quickly for gist and then to go through it in detail in pairs, making notes in answer to the questions. Ask if Gary Lineker's qualities are the same as the ones they thought of after reading the newspaper headlines.

Exercise 3 Study the words.

KEY

1 boast 2 make a point of 3 send off 4 foul 5 swear

GRAMMAR REVIEW

Remind students that *concession* means the same as *contrast* and that clauses of concession are sometimes called *contrast clauses*. Point out how a concession clause introduces something that contrasts with the main clause by using the conjunctions listed in the Review box. Explain that the choice of conjunction influences the way the clause is contructed. e.g:

1 *Although it was intensely hot in the desert during the day, it was quite cold at night.*
2 *Despite the intense heat in the desert during the day, it was quite cold at night.*

Work with the whole class and ask individual students to complete the sentences with the different conjunctions and write these on the board. Then ask if students can make the rule for each conjunction.

KEY

1 *Despite/In spite of* being young,
2 *Despite/In spite of* the fact that he's young,
3 *Although/Even though* he's young,
4 *Despite/In spite of* his youth,

RULES

Although and *even though* are followed by a subject + verb; *despite* and *in spite of* can be followed by a gerund (*-ing* form), a noun or *the fact that* + clause.

Exercise 4 PRACTICE

Students work individually or in pairs. Check by asking different students round the class to produce the four different versions.

KEY

1 In spite of his youth, In spite of being young, Despite the fact that he is young, Even though he is young
2 In spite of a full time job, In spite of having a full time job, Despite the fact that she has a full time job, Even though she has a full time job,
3 In spite of a poor background, In spite of coming from a poor background, Despite the fact that he comes from a poor background, Even though he comes from a poor background,
4 In spite of his injury, In spite of having an injury, Despite the fact that he has an injury, Even though he has an injury,
5 In spite of his illness, In spite of being ill, Despite the fact that he was ill, Even though he was ill,

SUGGESTED LESSON BREAK

Exercise 5 VOCABULARY

Read aloud the sentences with compound adjectives in the examples and ask individual students to make the compound adjectives 1-9 and write them on the board. Ask individual students round the class to see if they can use some of the adjectives to describe someone they know. Alternatively, ask students to give examples of behaviour which typifies these characteristics, e.g: *Someone who always wears smart, expensive-looking clothes* (well-dressed); *someone who always smiles even when things go wrong* (good-humoured).

KEY
1 bad-tempered 2 fun-loving 3 well-meaning
4 good-looking 5 hot-blooded 6 well-dressed
7 broad-minded 8 good-humoured 9 big-headed

STUDY POINT

Ask students to read the notes in the Study Point silently. Ask them to look back at the text on the previous page and to note the overall structure of it, i.e. how many main points are made (four) and how they are introduced (*First of all, Secondly, Another thing, Finally*). Ask students to read out the other three topic sentences in the text.

KEY
1 He is much more open-minded than other football stars.
2 Another thing that makes him different from other footballers is his sense of fairplay on the field.
3 Finally, you get the impression that Lineker is a human being with human emotions like anybody else.

After each topic sentence has been found, ask a different student to give the development sentence or sentences.

Exercise 6 PRACTICE

Students might like to base this on a famous singer or to use an imaginary one. If they prefer, they can base it on an actor or actress.

WRITING

Exercise 7 Before you write

Students form groups and discuss famous people from different fields. Each group should 'shortlist' about three people and try and think of at least three reasons why these people deserve the title. Individual members of the group can decide which of these people to write about in their composition.

Exercise 8

Read through the writing plan highlighting the linking phrases. Remind students how important it is to get into the habit of making organised notes before they write. These can be written as topic sentence headings followed by some development ideas, e.g:

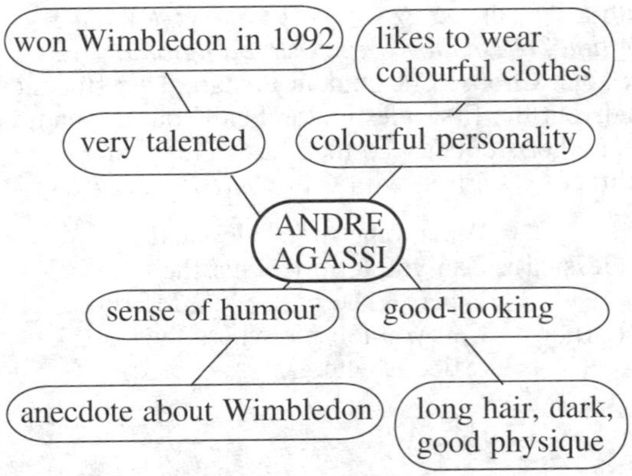

Try to set aside time so that students can complete the whole writing in class.

EXTRA ACTIVITIES

1 Who is it?

This activity is linked to the composition which students have written in Exercise 8. Ask different students to read out their descriptions without revealing the identity of the person they have written about. The other students have to guess the identity of the person who has been described.

2 *In spite of*: a famous personality activity

Write a list of famous personalities, living or dead, on separate pieces of paper so that there is one for each member of the class. Each student picks a name at random and has to prepare a sentence about that person using *In spite of* and an appropriate construction, e.g:
Marilyn Monroe: *In spite of being called the most beautiful woman in the world, she was never very secure.*
President Clinton: *In spite of his election promises, he still hasn't managed to improve the US economy.*
Paul McCartney: *In spite of his age, he sings almost as well today as he did twenty years ago.*

UNIT 10 An unusual job

Suggested lesson break: after Exercise 6

BACKGROUND NOTES
Chanel and Yves St Laurent: Two famous French fashion designers who have perfume and fashion houses named after them.

Exercise 1 Before you read

Before asking the 'Before you read' questions, ask students to scan the page of text. First ask them where they think the text originates from (it is taken from the women's section of a serious British newspaper called *The Guardian*). Also ask how they would categorise it, e.g: is it a news item, a fashion story, a sports story or a special feature article? Finally ask students what they think the article is going to be about and to explain the meaning of *private eye* (another name for a private detective).

Ask the questions to the whole group. With the first question, elicit names of well-known fictional detectives from the students such as Inspector Maigret, created by the French crime writer, Georges Simenon, Miss Marple and Hercules Poirot, created by Agatha Christie and Philip Marlowe in Raymond Chandler's novels. Discuss what image private detectives have in books and on TV.

Exercise 2 READING

Students read the text through once, noting down any difficult words or expressions. Students might think various features of the article unusual, for example that the agency is run solely by women and only recruits women; or that physical strength is not an essential attribute of a good detective.

Exercise 3 Read and answer.

Students read through the questions and read any relevant parts of the text again. Ask them to cover the text or close their books while they give the answers so they are not tempted to 'lift' sentences from the text.

Exercise 4 Study the words.

Spend some time discussing the words and how else they may be used. Take the opportunity to check on any other words or expressions in the text that students are still not sure of.

KEY

1 whiff 2 top-to-toe 3 bulk 4 tricky 5 leaked
6 to pose as 7 jerky 8 dart

Exercise 5 SPEECHWORK

After doing the exercise, point out the variations in spelling of the /ə/ sound in the words they have written.

Play the tape again for students to repeat the words. Ask students to find a few more examples of polysyllabic words in the article and to say which syllable(s) in each word has the /ə/ sound.

TAPESCRIPT AND KEY

mistaken announce arrival private secretary
director distraction happened movement
photograph sudden opposite

Exercise 6 Talk about it.

Conduct the discussion with the class as a whole. Extend the discussion, if you wish, by asking: *What sort of questions might be asked in an interview for a private detective's job? What sort of test or task might be set to see if the person is suitable?*

SUGGESTED LESSON BREAK

GRAMMAR REVIEW

Ask students to work through the tasks individually. Remind them that the opposite of *must* is not *mustn't* but *needn't*, and that *doesn't/don't have to* mean the same as *needn't*.

KEY

To be a good private detective
Group 1: a) you must be intelligent. d) you've got to be intelligent. e) you have to be intelligent.
Group 2: b) you should be intelligent. g) you ought to be intelligent.
Group 3: c) you needn't be intelligent. f) you don't have to be intelligent.

What's the difference in meaning?
Note that in some contexts, British people use *must, have to* and *have got to* interchangeably, e.g: *That must be the postman/That's got to be/has to be the postman*. However, there are certain contexts where one usage is more appropriate than the others.

Sentence a) implies that it is the speaker's usual routine to get up early.
Sentence b) implies that the speaker is required to get up early by an 'outside force' beyond the speaker's control, i.e. work.
Sentence c) implies that there is a special reason why it is necessary for the speaker to get up early tomorrow morning, but that it is not necessarily a routine.

Explain that *must* is often used to express a personal decision based on a sense of obligation, duty or necessity and that the auxiliary *must* is often stressed in this context, e.g: *I must phone my mother this afternoon.*

Exercise 7 PRACTICE

Note that more than one answer is appropriate in some cases.

KEY

1 must/ought to 2 have to/'ve got to 3 don't have to 4 ought to 5 has to 6 have to/'ve got to 7 don't have to 8 ought to

Exercise 8 VOCABULARY

KEY

Adjective	Abstract noun
dedicated	strength
enthusiastic	energy
resilient	ambition
responsible	stress

After students have completed the exercise, do some pronunciation work on the adjectives and pronouns and ask students to note the main stress on each word. Ask if they can make a sentence with each new word in the chart.

Exercise 9

KEY

Adjective endings	Noun endings
-ive: intuitive	-ion: intuition, dedication, ambition
-ed: dedicated	
-ic: energetic, enthusiastic	-th: strength
-ious: ambitious	-y: energy
-ible: responsible	-sm: enthusiasm
-ful: stressful	-ence: resilience
	-ity: responsibility

Noun endings: -ment, -ness, -sion, -or, -ance, -age
Adjective endings: -ant, -ible, -ial

Ask if students can think of words ending in these other noun and adjective endings, e.g: *movement, happiness, tension, doctor, importance, hostage, extravagant, possible, special.*

Exercise 10 PRACTICE

It may help students first to rank order the quantity expressions in terms of intensity *(an enormous amount of, a great deal of, lots of, a lot of, considerable, plenty of).*

SUGGESTED ANSWERS

2 A doctor works under a great deal of stress.
3 Social work demands an enormous amount of resilience.
4 A train driver's job involves considerable responsibility.
5 A labourer's job requires a lot of strength.
6 You need plenty of/a great deal of dedication to be a private detective.

Exercise 11

Ask students to name the different jobs portrayed in each picture.

KEY

1 a traffic warden 2 pilots 3 an architect
4 a miner 5 a teacher of very young children
6 a ballet dancer

Ask students to describe what each job involves and then suggest what qualities and skills are needed.

POSSIBLE SUGGESTIONS

traffic warden: vigilance, honesty, etc.
pilot: precision, concentration, etc.
architect: imagination, able to think laterally, etc.
miner: physical toughness, patience, etc.
teacher: dedication, imagination, etc.
ballet dancer: stamina, suppleness, etc.

LISTENING

Exercise 12 Before you listen

Open the discussion to the pros and cons of working long hours. Mention the motivation behind working late, the effect on one's domestic and social life, etc.

Exercise 13

Play the tape through twice and check the questions afterwards.

TAPESCRIPT

(From *You and Yours,* Radio 4 3.3.92)

1 I'm a Civil Rights lawyer and on average I'd work about seventy hours a week and, added to that, a couple of hours over the weekend. Personally, I wouldn't be prepared to take less time over a set of papers than I currently do because I would regard myself as being professionally compromised.
2 I start work in the office at about 8.15 and continue until 9, 9.30. It's probably one of the features of the lifestyle of working in London in the City. We're relatively well-paid in the jobs that we do and I think it's expected and therefore it should be done.
3 I've got meetings to prepare for the next day, the next week, client reports to get done. You only get those done when the telephones stop ringing and that is normally not until 5 o'clock.

EXTRA ACTIVITIES

1 Job interviews

Divide the class into groups of four or five. Write a list of some jobs and professions on separate strips of paper or card and distribute one to each group. The group should make a list of the qualities and qualifications needed for the job and think of a list of suitable questions to ask in an interview. Write the list of all the jobs on the board and ask students to choose which of the jobs they wish to be interviewed for. (They may not apply for the job which has been discussed in their own group). The members of each group form an interviewing panel and interview candidates for the job, using the questions they have prepared. Tell the candidates that they can make up information about themselves and their background if they wish. The groups should reveal their preferred candidate at the end.

2 For and against

Imagine that your government has asked the people to comment on a proposed law which will make illegal the use of telephone 'bugging' devices (hidden microphones which enable people's telephone conversations to be intercepted and recorded), hidden long-range cameras, and access to private personal data on computer files (e.g: medical records, credit card records and bank account information). It is also proposed that surveillance by private detectives should be outlawed. In groups of four or five, think up arguments either supporting or disagreeing with this proposal.

CHECK 2 Units 6-10

(For advice on handling this section, see the notes for Check 1 Units 1–5)

KEY

Ex.1

1 lip chin cheek eyelash forehead
2 ponytail plait fringe chignon bun
3 velvet silk cashmere woollen cotton
4 tall skinny broad-shouldered stocky overweight

Ex. 2 1 enormous brown eyes 2 a smart cashmere coat 3 long red hair 4 an ugly black dog 5 short curly hair 6 old blue denim jeans

Ex. 3

1 She arrived at the party in white pyjamas and slippers.
2 We saw a boy with red hair running down the street.
3 He got married in a smart grey suit and a green silk tie.
4 A tall woman with long blonde hair entered the compartment.
5 A young music student in her early twenties won the song competition.
6 At the end of the corridor there is a room with a small green door.
7 When I got home there was a man in an army uniform waiting for me.
8 I remember my first maths teacher was a man with a small beard and bright blue eyes.

Ex. 4 1 have you known 2 have you been cooking 3 has taken 4 has been learning 5 have you been doing 6 have already made 7 've been reading, haven't finished

Ex. 5

1 Could you possibly call back in a few minutes?
2 Is it all right if I leave my bags here for a moment?
3 Would you mind very much moving your car?
4 Do you mind if I turn the television on?
5 Would you mind very much looking after my cat for a week?

Ex. 6

1 Is it all right if I open the window (a bit)?
2 Would you mind looking after my suitcase today?
3 Do you mind if we watch another channel/switch over to another channel?
4 Could you possibly give me some extra milk?
5 Would you mind typing an important letter for me?

Ex. 7

1 Can you tell me where the British Airways check-in desk is?
2 I wonder who the manager is?
3 Do you know if the 9.30 train for Oxford is running on time?
4 Could you tell me if anyone left a parcel for me this morning?
5 Have you any idea what I did with my reading glasses?
6 Could you give me some idea how long this meeting is going to take?
7 Do you know if the old lady has found her cat yet?
8 Have you any idea why there isn't anyone at the reception desk?

Ex. 8 1 looking for 2 mind 3 look after 4 Mind your own business 5 make up your mind 6 look 7 look like 8 never mind 9 look it up 10 Look out

Ex. 9 1 Although the weather is awful, ... 2 In spite of his poor health/being in poor health, ... 3 Even though they don't speak the language, ... 4 Despite not studying very hard, ... 5 In spite of not having a job, ... 6 Even though she is young, ...

Ex. 10 1 open-minded 2 warm-hearted 3 hard-working 4 bad-tempered 5 fun-loving 6 good-looking 7 well-dressed 8 big-headed

Ex. 11 1 must/have to/should 2 don't have to/needn't 3 have to 4 mustn't 5 shouldn't/mustn't

Ex. 12 1 had to 2 don't have to 3 'll have to 4 have to 5 didn't have to 6 I'll have to 7 have had to

UNIT 11 Coincidences

Suggested lesson break: after Exercise 6

BACKGROUND NOTES

Canadian Rockies: part of a chain of high mountains which stretch down through the western side of North America from Alaska to New Mexico. In the USA they are called the Rocky Mountains.

National Park: an area of great natural beauty or of special interest in terms of wildlife, which is officially designated by governments as a public or national park, e.g. Yosemite National Park in California, USA.

Exercise 1 Talk about it.

Ask students to read the dictionary entry for *coincidence* and see if they can think of an equivalent word in their own language. Tell a story about a coincidence that has happened to you to prompt students to tell you about their own experiences.

Exercise 2

Ask students to look at the picture story and read the captions. In pairs, they should try to link the captions into a coherent story about a coincidence. Choose a pair and ask them to tell you the story between them.

SUGGESTED STORY

James and Chris were close friends at school. However, when they were about fourteen, James and his family moved away from the area and went to live in another part of the country. Gradually Chris and James drifted apart. Ten years later, Chris got married and he and his wife decided to spend their honeymoon in Canada.

They were staying for a few days at a campsite in a National Park in the Canadian Rockies. Imagine their surprise when Chris discovered that the people in the next tent were his old school friend James and his wife!

READING

Ask students to look at the picture and ask: *What's the girl doing? Do you think she's good at playing the piano? Why do you think so? What sort of mood do you think she is in?*

Exercise 3 Guess the meaning and Exercise 4

Ask students to read the text, guessing the meaning of the words as they read. They should then put the events in order. Check this by asking different students to read the sentences in the correct order.

KEY

1 Hester and Alison studied the violin at school and became friends.
2 The two friends drifted apart.
3 Hester eventually came to London but was unable to find work.
4 She decided to go back to Scotland.
5 She was playing the piano because she was depressed.
6 She heard someone playing the violin in the flat above.
7 Alison was the violinist in the flat.
8 Alison helped Hester find a job.

Ask students to close their books and retell the story in their own words.

GRAMMAR REVIEW

Ask students to read the information and answer the questions individually.

KEY

Verb tenses:1 = past continuous 2= past simple 3 = past perfect simple

Ask students to find examples of these tenses in the text.

Ask students to describe what is happening in Pictures 1 and 2 and then to match the sentences. Picture 1 = b, Picture 2 = a

While or *when?*

1 I was having dinner *when* the doorbell went.
2 *While/When* I was having dinner, the doorbell went.

Explain that *while* is only used with continuous activities and is therefore not possible in Sentence 1.

Exercise 5 PRACTICE

KEY

1 While I was painting the ceiling, I spilt some paint on the floor.
2 While I was watching the news, the TV broke down.
3 While I was making the bed, a spider fell onto my pillow.
4 While I was chewing a piece of meat, my tooth fell out.
5 While I was making a phone call, someone stole my wallet.

Explain that the *while* clauses can also be placed at the end of the sentence and ask one or two students to give you some sentences with the *while* clause in this position, e.g: *The fire alarm went off while we were doing our exams.*

Exercise 6

Ask students to look at the sentences in list B and read the example. Explain that students need to use their imagination.

SUGGESTED LESSON BREAK

In order to refresh students' memories of the use of *while* and the past continuous, ask them to think of their own activities over the past twenty-four hours and to give you a sentence using *while.*

Refer back to the story about Hester and ask a student to read the sentence in the first paragraph beginning with *On her last day...* . Ask students to name the tense *had been staying* (past perfect continuous).

GRAMMAR FOCUS

Explain that this tense is often used to describe background activities in relation to an event in the past, e.g: *I had been living in the USA for three years when I met my boyfriend.* This tense frequently occurs with words like *live, work, study, stay* and *feel.* Ask students to find another example of this tense in the text.

Read the information from the Grammar Focus box aloud and ask students to make a sentence of their own using this tense. Alternatively, ask them to answer questions like: *Why were his hands dirty? Why were her eyes red? Why was he out of breath? Why was he arrested?* (to elicit *Because he'd been working in the garden,* etc.)

KEY

What's the difference in meaning?
In Sentence 1 it was still snowing when the speaker looked out of the window, in Sentence 2 it had stopped snowing when he/she looked out of the window.

Exercise 7 PRACTICE

KEY

1 He'd been running in the park.
2 She hadn't been feeling very well.

3 No, they'd been planning to do it for some time.
4 She'd been lying in the sun all day.
5 He'd been drinking and driving.

Exercise 8

Ask students to work in pairs to find the answers using the tenses suggested.

KEY
1 They had studied the violin together.
2 They had drifted apart./Hester had been living/staying in London.
3 Because she had been unable to find work.
4 Because she had been feeling depressed.
5 Because they hadn't seen each other for eight years/since they were teenagers.

Exercise 9 WRITING

Ask students to turn to the first page of Unit 11 and remind themselves of the coincidence that happened to Chris and James. Tell them to write about the coincidence using a selection of past tenses including more details as they go along. Write the first few sentences on the board using students' suggestions.

SUGGESTED EXPANDED VERSION
When James was at school, he was very close friends with Chris. They'd been at school together for about nine years when James' parents decided to move to London. Although they wrote occasionally to each other, James and Chris gradually drifted apart. Many years later, Chris got married to a girl he'd been going out with for some time. As they had saved up enough money, they decided to go to Canada for their honeymoon. While they were touring the Canadian Rockies, they decided to stop at a campsite in a National Park. Imagine Chris' surprise when he discovered that his old school friend James was in the next tent! James had also just got married, and not only that, he and his new wife had been touring the Rockies on their honeymoon!

EXTRA ACTIVITIES

1 Find an explanation

Imagine you lent your house/flat to a group of students for the weekend. When you arrived back you noticed that:
- the ceiling in the sitting room was dripping wet.
- most of the sitting room furniture was in the garage.
- the kitchen door was off its hinges and leaning against the wall.

Students have to think of an explanation for the situations using the past perfect or past perfect continuous. They should start their explanations with *I expect someone/they'd (been)* ... .

2 Continue the story

Write some 'story openers' (see below) on strips of paper and put them into a box. Students sit in a circle. One of the students picks a story opener and reads it out. The rest of the students must make a sentence in turn round the group to make a story.

SAMPLE STORY OPENERS:
It was the last day of our holiday ...
It was my first day at work ...
We had decided to go shopping in town ...
We had been given some tickets for a big pop concert ...
It was cold, dark night ...
We had just moved into a new flat ...
It was the first time we had ever been in the mountains ...
We had never been to the USA before ...
We had been given a kitten for Christmas by a good friend

UNIT 12 Street violence

Suggested lesson break: after Exercise 5

BACKGROUND NOTES
Gateshead: a city on the north-east coast of England, near Newcastle-on-Tyne.

Exercise 1 About you

Use the questions as a general warm-up. If it appears that some students have some detailed experiences to relate, you may like to return to these later in the lesson, after some of the language work has been covered.

LISTENING

Exercise 2 Before you listen

Encourage students to use dictionaries for this pre-listening activity. Ask them to read aloud the example sentences for the words they look up.

The text

Ask students to read the introductory text. Check that they understand the meaning of *intervene, coach* and *subsequently*. Ask them to paraphrase the phrase *you could risk becoming a victim yourself.* Now ask students to discuss what they think happened to Stephen Marriott.

Exercise 3

Ask students to read through the multiple choice questions and make sure they understand any new words, e.g: *punch, twist, serve* (a prison sentence), *fine* (v).

Play the tape, pausing at intervals for students to note or circle the correct answer.

TAPESCRIPT

LINK: And now the third programme in our series 'What would you do?' Today we look at the way people respond to street violence. Would you go to help someone in trouble in the street? Of course most people would say yes, but it isn't as easy as that as Stephen Marriott, a 32-year-old football coach, found out one cold night in Gateshead.

WOMAN: Stephen, you were the victim of an attack in the street once, weren't you?

SM: That's right, yeah. A couple of years ago now.

WOMAN: What happened exactly?

SM: Well, I was walking home one evening, it was about 10.30, I suppose, when I heard someone screaming and I saw these two teenage lads kicking an old man on the ground.

WOMAN: So you went to help?

SM: That's right. In fact, there were two other men walking past at the same time but they didn't do anything. Just walked past. I couldn't believe it. Anyway, I shouted at the two lads to stop but they just said 'Push off!' or words to that effect. So I went to help the old man and one of them hit me over the head with a brick.

WOMAN: Didn't that knock you out?

SM: Well, nearly. I think I was only half conscious. Then they grabbed my arms and cut my face with a piece of broken glass. Then they ran away.

WOMAN: It all sounds absolutely horrific. Wasn't there anyone around to help you?

SM: No, it all happened so fast. So, anyway, I lay there. I didn't feel a thing at the time. I remember that. Then I told the old man to get away.

WOMAN: He was still there, was he?

SM: Yes, but he could walk so he went off and then I went into a pub to ask for help to get to the police station. I only realised later that I was covered in blood. Several people ignored me but in the end a woman gave me a lift to the police station, which was very good of her.

WOMAN: How badly were you hurt?

SM: Well, I had to have several stitches in my head and on my face . I was in a pretty bad state - you know - mentally for quite a time. Couldn't sleep, had nightmares and all that. And of course I'll always have a scar on my face.

WOMAN: Did the police catch the boys in the end?

SM: Yes, one got two years in prison and the other got fifteen months. But they only served part of their sentences. I see them on the streets occasionally and, well, it makes me very bitter.

WOMAN: Do you regret what you did? Going to help the man?

SM: Yes, I do. I think if I saw that sort of thing happen again, I'd just walk by, ignore it. But then you never know, do you, what you'd do when the time comes?

Ask students how Stephen Marriott feels about the incident now, and what he said he would do in the future.

Exercise 4 Study the words.

Students work individually or in pairs to explain the expressions.

KEY

1 Go away! 2 took me in her car 3 quite badly hurt and shocked 4 one was sent to prison for two years 5 he only stayed in prison for part of the time 6 when you find yourself in a certain situation

Exercise 5 Read and think.

Use the questions as a prompt for a general discussion of the incident. The listening text may prompt other similar stories about unfair sentences. Allow the discussion to develop if time allows.

SUGGESTED LESSON BREAK

GRAMMAR FOCUS

Refer students back to the introductory text and point out the sentence *I was walking home when I heard someone screaming and saw two teenage boys kicking an old man.* Ask the 'What's the difference in meaning?' question.

KEY

In the first sentence the person carried on screaming; in the second sentence the person only screamed once.

Read through the rest of the information with students. Ask them if they can make other sentences using the verbs of perception and a gerund or infinitive. Give a few sentences for them to say if they are right or wrong, e.g: *I heard the door bang shut.* (right) *I saw the old man sit comfortably in a rocking chair.* (wrong) *I heard the window breaking.* (wrong) *I noticed a man wearing white jeans and a red coat.* (right) *I smelt some sausages cook in the kitchen.* (wrong)

Exercise 6 PRACTICE

Students work individually to complete the sentences.

KEY

1 walk 2 shouting 3 break 4 burning 5 grab 6 sleeping

Exercise 7

Ask students to spend a few minutes preparing the account. They may make notes to expand the prompts if this helps them.

Ask different students to tell the story, allotting a short section each so that they get practice in extended speaking. Make notes of any recurring errors, especially in tense usage.

Exercise 8 Talk about it.

Divide students into groups to discuss the situations. Point out that they should use the second conditional in their suggestions, i.e. *I'd …/I wouldn't …* . However, it is more important to concentrate on the content of their answers than on their structural accuracy. You may like to make a note of any problems with the second conditional and revise the rules for it briefly afterwards. This structure, and extensions of it, will be practised in depth in Unit 22.

Exercise 9 VOCABULARY

Choose some volunteers to come to the front of the class and mime as many of the words as possible to illustrate their meaning. Then ask the students to work out the exercise in pairs.

KEY

1 pat 2 squeeze 3 punch 4 stroke 5 shake
6 slap 7 wave 8 grab 9 grip

Spend some time investigating other contexts for using these words. Ask them what other things they would pat, shake, grip, wave, etc.

Exercise 10 WRITING

If some teachers feel that their students were quite fluent at recounting the incident and do not need this extra reinforcement, they can move on to the next writing exercise.

Exercise 11

Ask students to say what is happening in the photograph and where it is taking place. Help students create the details of the story by asking (or writing on the board) the following prompt questions: *Where had you been? What had you been doing? Where were you going? What time of day was it? What sort of neighbourhood was it? Why were you walking alone? Did you notice anything unusual before the person snatched your bag? How did you react? What did you do afterwards? What effect has it had on you?*

EXTRA ACTIVITIES

1 A ghost/horror story

Students work in groups to create a ghost story. This might involve situations like spending the night in an old deserted house, being lost in a remote part of the countryside or taking a walk in a cemetery. The story should include as many of the verbs of perception as possible.

2 Project: street crime

Students collect information outside the lesson in order to make a five-minute presentation about street crime and violence in their area. This information might be in the form of incidents and articles collected from current newspapers (either from their own newspapers or from British newspapers), interviews between the local police and some residents, as well as statistics and magazine pictures about street crime.

UNIT 13 Arrangements

Suggested lesson break: after Exercise 6

BACKGROUND NOTES

Erasure: a pop duo whose speciality is to imitate the Swedish '70s pop group, Abba.
*phantasmagorical***:** the adjective from *phantasmagoria,* a confused, dreamlike changing scene of different things, real and/or imagined.
Hammersmith Odeon: Once a cinema in West London, it is now a well-known venue for pop and jazz concerts.

Ask students to look at the picture and to quickly describe the people and where they are.

Exercise 1 LISTENING

Ask students to read the questions before playing the tape. Students should make notes of their answers.

TAPESCRIPT AND KEY

JACK: Are you doing anything this evening? I wondered if you'd like to come out for a meal?
HANNAH: I'm afraid I can't. I've got a photography class.
JACK: Oh, yeah. I forgot. What about tomorrow, then? Shall we meet in town and have lunch together?
HANNAH: No, tomorrow's no good, either. I'm going to Brighton to see my sister. I'm leaving on the ten o'clock train.
JACK: How long are you staying?
HANNAH: Just for the weekend. I'll be back on Sunday afternoon.
JACK: O.K. I'll give you a ring then. Maybe we can do something in the evening. Perhaps go to the cinema or something?
HANNAH: Yes, Sunday evening sounds fine. Anyway, what are your plans for the weekend?
JACK: I'm going to do some studying tomorrow and then I think I'll sleep all Sunday morning! By the way, I'll give you a lift to the station tomorrow if you like.
HANNAH: Oh, thanks. That's really kind.

Exercise 2 COMMUNICATION FOCUS

Ask students to note down or underline the expressions in the Communication Focus box which are used in the dialogue.

Go through the questions and sentences in the Focus box, practising the intonation of each chorally and individually. Use backchaining (i.e. building up sentences backwards for choral repetition) to practise any sentences which are causing problems, e.g: *evening... something in the evening... you'd like to do something in the evening... Maybe you'd like to do something in the evening.*

Exercise 3 PRACTICE

To guide students with their conversations, suggest the following situation:

Student A: you would like to invite someone in the class to the cinema or out for a meal. Select some suitable expressions from the Communication Focus box and note down a couple of different activities and days to suggest to your partner, B.

Student B: You must turn down at least two different days or times (with reasons) before accepting an invitation.

Write the following skeleton dialogue on the board:

A: *Are you ... ? I wondered if ...*
B: *No, ... no good, I'm afraid. I ...*
A: *Oh, that's a pity. What about ... ?*

GRAMMAR REVIEW

Introduce the Grammar Review by making true sentences about yourself similar to those in the Review box, e.g: *I'm going to do some gardening this weekend. I'll mark your homework this evening*, etc. Ask students to look at the Grammar Review box and work through the exercises individually. Then ask them to make different sentences relating to their own activities and plans.

KEY
Which tenses are used?
1 Present continuous 2 Future with *will* 3 Future with *will* 4 *Going to* future 5 Future with *will*

Which sentence?
a)4 b)2 c)3 d)5 e)1

What's the difference in meaning?
Sentence a) indicates a sudden decision or an offer, Sentence b) indicates an intention which has been formed at some point in the recent past.

Exercise 4 PRACTICE

Write the following skeleton exchange on the board to help students with their pair work:

A: *What are you doing next week?*
B: *Well, on Monday I'm ...ing and on Wednesday evening I'm ...ing but, apart from that, I'm not doing anything. What about you?*

Tell any students who do not have diaries to invent some imaginary plans for next week. Go round and listen to the students' conversations making sure they use the present continuous, not the *will* future.

Exercise 5

Ask students to use real-life plans for the future. Use the example in the Students' Book to work T-S with a student, checking the use of tenses.

Exercise 6

Students work in pairs or individually.

SUGGESTED ANSWERS
1 I know, I'm going to buy a new one in the sales. (intention)
2 Yes, I'm catching the 4.55 to Liverpool. (definite arrangement)
3 Yes, I'll have the fish, please. (decision)
4 No, it'll be ready in twenty minutes. (prediction)
5 I'll do it if you like. (offer)
6 Don't worry, I won't forget to send you one this time. (promise)

SUGGESTED LESSON BREAK

Exercise 7 READING

Ask students to read the letter first before reading the questions which precede it. Check the content of the letter by asking one or two comprehension questions, e.g: *What did Sharif do last weekend? What was Steve's invitation? Why did Sharif refuse it? When does he say he will contact Steve again?*

Note that the expression *driving my grandparents across to Paris* means that Sharif is going to take his car to France either by ferry or through the Channel Tunnel.

Now ask students to look at the questions relating to the letter and discuss the answers with the class as a whole.

KEY
1 - the letter starts with *Dear* followed by a first name, and ends with *Yours* and a first name.
- the address of the receiver is not included above the salutation *Dear ....*
- the style of the letter is informal: use of short forms, and informal words like *thanks* and *anyway*.

2 Three. The first one refers to the last time the people met and thanks the receiver for his hospitality; the second contains the purpose of the letter, which is a polite refusal to an invitation with an explanation; the third rounds off the letter with a polite wish and a promise to write again.

3 He signs off with *Yours*. Other ways are: *(Lots of) Love from* (often between women or between men and women); *Yours ever* (slightly more formal); *Cheers!* (often between men); *All the best*.

STUDY POINT

Go through the Study Point with the students. Ask them to say which categories occur in the letter (It opens by referring to the last time they met and closes with a promise and a polite wish).

Exercise 8 PRACTICE

First ask students to divide the expressions between opening and closing expressions, and then to match each of them where possible with the appropriate category in the Study Point. When they have done this, they should copy them down under the different headings in their notebooks.

KEY
Opening expressions:
It was great to see you again last week. (refers to the last time you met)
Sorry I haven't written earlier/for so long but ...
Thanks so much for your last letter ... (refers to a letter recently received)
What a surprise to hear from you after so long! (refers to a letter recently received)
I received your letter this morning (refers to a letter recently received)
I was very sorry to hear that ...(refers to an event which has made you write)

Closing expressions:
I'll send you a postcard. (promise)
Write soon! (friendly command)
Get better soon. (friendly command/polite wish)
Don't forget to call me/write to me. (friendly command)
Please give my regards/love/best wishes to ... (friendly command)

Exercise 9 WRITING

Start the letter on the board with the help of students. Discuss how many paragraphs they are going to write and suitable opening and closing phrases. Students write the letter for homework.

Exercise 10 ROLEPLAY

Ask students to read their respective role cards and help them with any explanations. Use the information in the Background Notes to explain the poster. Ask students to spend a few moments preparing their roles, referring to the Communication Focus and the Grammar Review for guidance on expressions and tenses.

Ask a couple of pairs of students to perform their roleplay in front of the class. Note down any serious errors for feedback later.

EXTRA ACTIVITIES

1 Grammar quiz

Write ten numbered sentences on the board all of which incorporate an aspect of the future tense, some of which are incorrect. Students have a time limit to note down which of the sentences are incorrect and what the correct version should be. Go through the sentences with the class afterwards. Students get one mark for identifying the incorrect sentence and one mark for supplying the correct version. The student who gets the most marks wins.

EXAMPLE SENTENCES
(Incorrect sentences marked with a X)
1 I'll telephone you tomorrow.
2 Don't worry. I am sending you a postcard. X
3 As soon as I will hear from him I will tell you. X
4 It'll be Easter soon.
5 I'm afraid I won't come to your class next week. X
6 I hope you shall get better soon. X
7 I'll help you with your essay if you like.
8 We are redecorating the kitchen next year.
9 I am not here next week as I will go back home to see my parents. X
10 Look at those clouds. It is raining soon. X

2 Arranging a class social event

In groups or as a whole class, students must arrange a suitable time and place for a class social event which is convenient for everyone.

UNIT 14 Embarrassing moments

Suggested lesson break: after Exercise 4

Exercise 1 Talk about it.

Open the lesson by relating an embarrassing incident that happened to you recently. (Invent one if necessary). Ask students what sort of situations they think are embarrassing. Write some of these on the board. Then put students into small groups to discuss the list of embarrassing situations in the book and to decide which two or three they think are most embarrassing.

After a few minutes' discussion check by asking for feedback from the groups. Elicit if any of the students have actually experienced any of these embarrassing moments.

Exercise 2 LISTENING

Ask students to read through the *True/False* statements and to try and guess what the incident was about. Write the following questions on the board: *Where was Richard going? Why? Where was his son at the time? What did Richard buy? What happened?*

Play the tape straight through to the end. Check the answers to the questions on the board and then go through the *True/False* statements. When the answers have been checked, play the text once more.

TAPESCRIPT
I had to go shopping the other day to get a present for a friend of mine and I went into one of the big department stores, I can't remember which one, M & S or somewhere like that and I took Joe with me in the pushchair and we were just kind of wandering around and I was looking at various things and I suddenly saw this … this pile of rather nice silk scarves which I thought would do, and in fact I chose one and Joe was asleep in the pushchair, at least I thought he was asleep. But anyhow, I bought one of the scarves and went along to the cash desk, paid for it, etcetera, and I was just leaving the shop when, literally as I was going through the doors, one of the security guards came up to me and said 'Excuse me sir, have you paid for everything?' And of course I said 'Yes, I have' and I was busy getting a receipt out of my … my pocket when he went … he walked over to the pushchair and put his arm down the side of the pushchair and there … there was another red silk scarf.
Well, I don't know how it got there. I mean, I assume that Joe, who wasn't asleep … pretending to be asleep, knowing him, had picked it up while I was paying for the scarves or while I was choosing one. He must have just picked it up and stuffed it down the side. I was so embarrassed because I could tell that the guard didn't believe me. I mean, I said that's what I thought had happened but he just had that kind of look in his eye that says, you know, 'I don't believe you,' so I had to … I just had to convince him, which was quite difficult. I think … I think in the end he did believe me but even so, it was just so embarrassing. And in the very end I gave the scarf back. Obviously I didn't have to pay for it, and he let me go.

Exercise 3 READING

Ask students to look at the introductory paragraph to the article 'What a cat-astrophe'. Ask in what sort of publication they think the article appeared. Ask them to read the questions and the article. As the text is fairly simple, set a time limit for the reading. Ask them not to look words up in dictionaries at this stage but to note down any difficult words which they cannot guess, e.g: *ranks as, impress, salmon, mousse, entire*. To check comprehension, ask different students to use the questions as prompts to retell the story.

Exercise 4 About you

Allow the conversation to embrace all cooking disaster stories, embarrassing or otherwise.

SUGGESTED LESSON BREAK

GRAMMAR REVIEW

Go through the tasks with the class as a whole.

KEY
The sentences all contain nouns which in many contexts do not have a preceding article (*lunch, home, school*).

Other words which only take an article in certain contexts are: *college, university, church, hospital, market, prison, breakfast, lunch, tea, dinner*.

What's the difference in meaning?
Sentence 1 describes a general situation; the person has had an accident or is ill in some way and as a result has gone to hospital for treatment. The particular hospital is not important.
Sentence 2 implies that the person went to a particular hospital which has been previously referred to, but not necessarily for medical reasons.

Exercise 5 PRACTICE

KEY
1 to bed 2 to hospital 3 at work 4 at university 5 to school 6 to prison 7 to church 8 at home

Exercise 6 VOCABULARY

Draw students' attention to the following two sentences in the text:
There were fish bones all over the floor.
I suppose it wasn't such a bad evening all in all.

Ask students to paraphrase the meaning of the expressions with *all* (*all over* = everywhere on the floor, *all in all* = on the whole/generally). Then ask students to match the expressions with *all* in the box with the correct definition from the list.

KEY
1 all in all 2 all over 3 all in 4 (to be) all the same to 5 all along 6 all of a sudden 7 (to be) all in favour of 8 once and for all

Exercise 7

KEY
1 all along 2 once and for all 3 all in favour of 4 all of a sudden 5 all in 6 all over 7 all in all 8 all the same to

Ask students to try and use the expressions in sentences of their own.

STUDY POINT

Ask different students to find and read out the relevant sentences in the 'What a cat-astrophe' text which contain the adverbial phrases. Write these on the board as they give them to you. Ask: *Which of these appear at the beginning of a sentence or main clause? (in fact, to my horror, needless to say, in the end)*

Which occur at the end of a sentence? (all in all, in future).

Explain the following points:

1 Position
The adverbial expressions can all occur either at the beginning, in the middle or at the end of a sentence. The one exception is *to my horror*, which cannot come at the end of a sentence.

2 Use of commas
If the adverbial expression occurs at the beginning of a sentence, it is usually followed by a comma, e.g:
In fact, I was quite looking forward to it.
If it occurs in the middle, it has commas on either side, e.g:
I was, in fact, quite looking forward to it.
If it occurs at the end of a sentence, a comma usually precedes it, e.g:
I was quite looking forward to it, in fact.
The only exception to the last rule is the phrase *in the end* and *in future* which do not usually have a preceding comma.

Write a few sentences on the board and ask students to insert the adverbial phrase in brackets in three different positions. e.g:

I haven't finished it yet. (needless to say)
He was very ill. (in fact)
I decided not to go. (in the end)

Exercise 8 PRACTICE

Students work individually to complete the paragraph. Check that students understand the meaning of the following words in context: *stretched, hopelessly, furious, explode, pretty* (= rather), *promised myself.*

KEY
To my horror, in the end/needless to say, Needless to say, In fact, All in all, in future

Exercise 9 WRITING

If some students find it hard to think of a situation, prompt them with a situation or location, e.g: in a restaurant, in a shop, on the street, at a party, at school, in the sports centre. Failing this, students can write about a difficult situation or problem which they managed to solve.

Go through the text 'What a cat-astrophe' to show how its structure reflects the paragraph plan in this exercise. Remind students of the tenses which relate to each paragraph.

Ask students to make notes according to the paragraph prompts given in their books. Go round and check these notes, pointing out any mistakes and suggesting improvements. Students can write the account for homework.

EXTRA ACTIVITIES

1 Jigsaw text

Write or find a text of approximately three paragraphs about an embarrassing incident. Photocopy each text so that there is one per group of five or six students. Cut each text into strips and put them jumbled in envelopes to distribute to each group. The groups then compete to piece the text together in the shortest time.

2 Word-making

Write the word *catastrophe* on the board and see how many words of three or more letters the students can make from it.

3 Dialogue construction

Students work in pairs to write a conversation, about anything they like, which includes at least six of the expressions with *all* from the unit.

UNIT 15 Memories

Suggested lesson break: after Exercise 7

BACKGROUND NOTES
Eleanor Farjeon (1881-1965) was an English writer of plays, poetry and short stories mainly for children. The best of her poetry is contained in two collections, *Silver-Sand and Snow* (1951) and *The Children's Bells* (1957).
Christy Brown (1932-1981) overcame his crippling handicap of cerebral palsy to become one of Ireland's foremost artists by teaching himself first to paint and then to write with the toes of his left foot. He wrote without self-pity and his autobiography, first published in 1951, is full of wit and cheeky humour as well as rage and frustration.
bilberries: blue-black berries which grow on low, bushy plants on hillsides and in high woods in Northern Europe.
Percy Sledge: a black American soul singer famous in the 1960s and 70s

Exercise 1 Before you read

Use the questions as a general lead-in to the lesson. If students have problems using the verb *remember* followed by a gerund, refer them to the relevant section of the Grammar Focus on the last page of Unit 15.

LITERATURE

Explain to the students who Eleanor Farjeon is (see Background Notes). Ask them to look at the title and the illustration and to guess what the poem is about and what sort of things the little girl is likely to remember.

Exercise 2

Possible rhyming words are: *be, me, he, she, tea, three, we, pea, see, sea, tree, knee, bee, agree, key.*

Accumulate all the students' suggestions on the board. Don't worry if they have not got all the right ones e.g: *knee, tree, three.* They should be able to guess these from context when they see the gap in the poem. Finally, ask students to read the poem and try to complete the lines.

Exercise 3

Play the tape so that students can check their suggestions.

KEY

me, tree, knee, tree, three, me, tea, tree, me, see, knee, tree, be, me, me, see

Exercise 4 Read and answer.

Ask the questions to the class as a whole.

Exercise 5 STYLE

Check that students understand the difference between rhyme and rhythm and point out their spelling. Ask the questions to the class as a whole.

SUGGESTED RESPONSES

The words *I remember* are repeated at the end of the first line of each verse and the vowel sound /iː/ as in *me*, *tree*, etc, is often repeated at the end of the second and third line. The sound /əʊ/ occurs at the end of most verses.

The rhythm seems very simple, childlike and regular. The repetition of *I remember* gives a certain hypnotic effect. The repeated use of *me*, *tree*, etc, makes the poem sound childlike.

Exercise 6

Spend a few minutes discussing the general content of the poem. Ask if anyone has ever eaten bilberries and where they grow. Ask if they have any idea in which country the scene took place. Students can discuss the questions in groups. Collect some of the responses after a few minutes.

Exercise 7 SPEECHWORK

Give an example of a word containing the sound /əʊ/, e.g: *boat*. Ask students to find words with this sound in the poem (*ago, road, old, know, won't*). The three different spellings for the sound are *o*, *oa* and *ow*.

Play the tape for students to write the words.

TAPESCRIPT

snow stone road go float ago below row photo alone

KEY TO SPELLING PATTERNS

ow: snow, below, row
o + consonant + *e*: stone, alone
oa: road, float
o: go, ago, photo

SUGGESTED LESSON BREAK

Exercise 8 VOCABULARY

Tell students they need only look at the definitions of words they are not certain of (although it can be quite useful to read the ones they know too). Students should do the exercise individually. After checking the exercise, ask different students to make the sounds.

KEY

1 sing 2 scream 3 shout 4 cheer 5 cough 6 cry 7 hum/whistle 8 whistle/hum/sing 9 whisper 10 howl/scream

Spend a few minutes talking about the words. Ask students if they can think of other sentences and contexts to use the words in, e.g: birds sing, babies cry rather than scream, etc.

Exercise 9 LISTENING

Introduce the context of the listening text, giving an example of something that prompts your memory, maybe an old tune or something in your wardrobe. Introduce the expression ... *reminds me of* ...

Students copy the table into their books. Play the tape, pausing after each speaker for them to write notes. Tell them not to bother with any detail but to listen for gist. Explain that the first speaker is American and the third speaker is Scottish.

TAPESCRIPT

1 Whenever I smell freshly baked bread it reminds me of my childhood. When I was young my mother always used to bake bread every day. She doesn't any more but I remember we used to come in from playing in the evening and there was always this lovely smell of freshly baked bread in the house. Wonderful!

2 There's a piece of music which I hear occasionally on the radio and it always sets me off. It's a song from the sixties called 'When a man loves a woman' by Percy Sledge and it reminds me of the first girl I ever went out with. Very romantic!

3 In the back of my cupboard in my bedroom I've got an old train set. I remember getting it as a birthday present from my grandfather when I was eight. He's dead now but it was the best present I'd ever had. I don't play with it now of course and Mum wants to me to give it away. She says: 'You're grown up now. Surely you don't want to hang on to that old train set?' But I want to keep it because it reminds me of my grandfather.

4 There's a special poem by Keats about autumn - you probably know it, it's very famous - and whenever I see it in a poetry book it always reminds me of school and my English teacher. This was one of her favourite poems and she used to love the sound of her own voice. She used to recite this poem frequently in class and I can see her now, rolling her eyes and using her special reading voice.

LITERATURE

Read the introduction to Christy Brown aloud to the students. Ask them to look up *cerebral palsy* in a dictionary. Ask if any of the students have ever seen the film *My Left Foot* or heard of Christy Brown. If anyone has, they can tell the rest of the class briefly about it.

Exercise 10 Guess the meaning.

Ask students to listen to read the account of how Christy Brown learnt to write with his foot, guessing the meaning of the words as they read.

Exercise 11 Read and answer.

Ask students to ask and answer the questions alternately in pairs. Alternatively, ask students to cover the text and use the questions to give an oral summary of the text.

GRAMMAR FOCUS

Read through the explanations with the students. (If the first section has already been dealt with in an earlier part of the lesson, move straight on to *would* and *used to*). Refer to the Christy Brown text to show students how *would* is used for past habits and activities. Try and get students to make sentences of their own after each example sentence.

Exercise 12 PRACTICE

Students write the sentences in class. They need not complete the full sentence, provided they have the first part correct.

KEY

1 I remember being frightened of the dark ...
2 I remember her bringing me a glass of milk ...
3 I remember him taking the dog for a walk...
4 I remember my mother eating a whole box ...
5 I remember collecting shells from the beach ...

WRITING

Exercise 13

Tell students about a childhood friend of yours as an example to set their thoughts in motion. Students can write this paragraph in class. It doesn't need to be more than a few sentences long but point out that they should use *used to* or *would* if appropriate.

Exercise 14

Ask students to discuss in pairs before they start in order to get some ideas flowing. Go round the pairs helping with new expressions and vocabulary. Encourage them to use the structures practised in the unit. A paragraph will probably be sufficient in length.

EXTRA ACTIVITIES

1 A poem I like

Ask students to find a poem in English which they like and to bring a verse or two to read to the class. Students work in groups. In turn, each student reads out their selected piece of poetry and the other students have to say what it is about and, if they can, who it is by.

2 Memory prompts

This is a chain activity which requires the students to use their imagination. Start the chain by suggesting something evocative like 'freshly ground coffee', 'Michael Jackson's album *Thriller*', 'the sound of church bells', 'waves breaking on the sea shore', etc. The next student has to give a sentence saying what the word or phrase reminds them of or makes them think of, e.g:

T: Freshly ground coffee
S1: Freshly ground coffee reminds me of a holiday I once had in France.
S2: France makes me think of garlic.
S3: Garlic reminds me of snails.
S4: Snails reminds me of a field in the country. etc.

CHECK 3 Units 11-15

(For advice on handling this section, see the notes for Check 1 Units 1–5)

KEY

Ex. 1 1 were you doing 2 was watching 3 switched 4 watched 5 went back 6 did you do that? 7 realised 8 had left 9 had been working 10 went 11 happened 12 got 13 rang 14 answered 15 looked 16 was 17 was lying 18 looked 19 had been lying 20 had hit 21 could 22 was

Ex. 2 1 playing 2 win 3 cry 4 playing 5 burning 6 crawling 7 slam 8 fall

Ex. 3 1c 2a 3b 4c 5a 6b 7c 8b

Ex. 4 1 school 2 work 3 the church 4 prison 5 the University 6 home 7 the hospital 8 breakfast, bed 9 hospital

Ex. 5 1 all along 2 all of a sudden 3 all over 4 all in favour 5 once and for all 6 All in all

Ex. 6 1 waving 2 shout 3 squeeze 4 stroke 5 gripped 6 cheered 7 whisper 8 shake 9 slapped 10 howling

Ex. 7 1 used to 2 would 3 used to 4 didn't use to 5 Did you use to 6 did he use to 7 would 8 used to

Ex. 8

1 She can remember hating ...
2 She can remember not liking ...
3 She can remember being stung ...
4 She can remember not wanting to ...
5 She can remember falling ...

UNIT 16 A place to eat

Suggested lesson break: after Exercise 6

BACKGROUND NOTES
Edward Hopper: a US painter, (1882-1967). His paintings of New York in the 1930s and 1940s capture the loneliness and the empty glamour of city life. 'Nighthawks' is one of his most famous paintings.
O'Rourke's Diner: an example of a typical modern diner in Connecticut, USA
Bill Bryson: an American writer and journalist who was born in 1951 in Des Moines, Iowa, USA but now lives in the north of England. His travel book *The Lost Continent,* which describes a journey across the USA to his father's birthplace, established his reputation as a humorous writer.

Exercise 1 Talk about it.

Use the questions to start a general discussion about diners and other similar eating places. Ask if any of the students have ever been to a real diner in the USA and what they think is the main difference between a diner and an ordinary café or restaurant. You may like to extend the discussion into considering what sort of eating places suit different moods and situations.

READING

Ask students to look at the photograph next to the 'American Diners' text and ask: *What signs indicate that diners are not sophisticated places to eat?*

Exercise 2 Guess the meaning.

Ask students to read the text and guess the meaning of the words listed. They should also underline any words they are not sure of, but do not encourage using dictionaries at this stage.

Check the meaning of these words when students have finished reading. Explore other contexts for some words, e.g: *to waver* when making a decision; *exotic* locations, language, food, smells; *to wipe* a table, your brow, the floor; the *counter* of a shop. If students want to know the meaning of other words or expressions, direct them to Exercise 4 first to see if they are covered in that exercise.

Exercise 3 Read and make notes.

Ask students to read the text again and make notes about the Y Not Grill under the two headings, 'Good points' and 'Bad points'.

Exercise 4 Study the words.

KEY
1d 2e 3f 4b 5c 6a

Exercise 5 Read and think.

Put the questions to different students in the class.

SUGGESTED RESPONSES
1 The name of the diner was 'the Y Not Grill' and presumably was short for 'The Why Not Come in Grill'. The author and his friends secretly called it 'The Why not Come in and Get Food Poisoning Grill', to reflect the standard of food at the diner. (British often make word puns by using single letters of the alphabet and numbers to stand for words, e.g: Y B Sad? = Why be sad? IOU = I owe you, CU tomorrow = See you tomorrow, CU2 night = See you tonight.)
2 He used to feel frightened because she was so rude and she used to shout at her customers and pretend not to hear the orders.

Exercise 6 LISTENING

Ask students to look at the photo of the Hard Rock Cafe in London and ask if they have ever been there or to a branch of a Hard Rock Cafe in their country. Go through the headings and try to get students to predict some of the answers, e.g: the type of food, the type of people and music, what the decor is like and so on.
Play the tape, pausing in parts for students to note down the answers. Do not expect students to get all the names of the other locations (the man mentions eight, of which six are in the USA).

The following pop groups and singers are mentioned: Chuck Berry, Bo Diddly, Elvis Presley, Guns and Roses (American); the Beatles, (British); U2 (Irish)

TAPESCRIPT
I = interviewer, M = manager

I: The Hard Rock Cafe is one of the best-known theme restaurants in London. How long has it been open?

M: The original Hard Rock Cafe opened in London on June 14th 1971.

I: And what was so different about it at the time it opened?

M: There really wasn't any place to get American-style food, (meaning good hamburgers and barbecued ribs and barbecued pork sandwiches) things like that, in London at the time. It's hard to believe now but there wasn't any place to find those things then and it was combined with the whole idea of, like, rock and roll at the time, based on a typical American sort of truckstop cafe. And it really was unique and that is one of the secrets of its great success.

I: So what kind of clientele, what kind of customers did it originally bring in - the truck drivers?

M: No, originally we had a lot of local English people and a lot of musicians, because they liked the fact that it was relaxed, that it was a lot of fun, that it was a lot of good music being played and that it had a good atmosphere. The … It became a tourist attraction in later years, but originally it was a lot of local people.

I: And now you've been open a good many years, what sort of things have changed? Is your menu still offering the same sort of food, do you still have the same sort of music, still the same sort of people?

M: The basic spirit of the place hasn't changed. The menu has expanded slightly, while still remaining true to the American cuisine base. We've added a lot of vegetarian items, and some more modern items. But the biggest change has been a lot of vegetarian food. The music - we still play rock music, but obviously rock music's changed, so we play, you know, some of the old music. You'll still hear Chuck Berry and Bo Diddly and Elvis and the Beatles, but you'll also hear Guns and Roses, and U2 and some modern, you know, some more modern rock music. Our customer base has probably widened a lot. We get everyone in there from, you know, grandmas, babies, up to, you know kids, lots of celebrities, lots of musicians and actors and stuff – very, very broad clientele base.

I: The Cafe in Park Lane isn't the only one, is it? How many other Hard Rock Cafes are there throughout the world?

M: We've got about twenty of them now, there's about twenty of them worldwide.

I: Was the Park Lane one the first one?

M: Yes, that was the original one. London was the only Hard Rock for, I guess, about six or seven years.

I: And whereabouts in the rest of the world are you?

M: We have … we've just opened in Berlin and Paris. We've …we are opening in Atlanta in the States very soon. We've Cafes in Orlando, Washington' D.C., Boston, New York, lots of them, Dallas.

I: And is it the same kind of character for every one of them, or does each one have its own theme?

M: Each … each Hard Rock has got its own personality and style. There's a lot of things that are common to all the Hard Rocks. They're all based on the London one - the brass, the dark wood, the wooden floors, the checked tablecloths, that's the same in all of them, the sort of colours and the logo and the menu's very much the same.

I: Whenever I've driven past there, there has always been a queue in Park Lane. But do you in fact suffer when times are bad?

M: We're very fortunate in that we suffer less than any other restaurant - definitely in this country, and probably in the whole world from any sort of economic recession because going to the Hard Rock is a special thing. It's like, a lot of people might decide that they're going to cut down eating out, but they won't cut down going to the Hard Rock – it's too much fun.

SUGGESTED LESSON BREAK

Exercise 7 Talk about it.

Students discuss the picture, barbecue cooking and the problems of barbecue cooking. List on the board some of the things that can go wrong. Then ask students to read the Tips and see if any of their problems are mentioned and any tips given on how to avoid the problem. Do not draw attention to the structures used yet. Explain any new words, e.g: *coals, stick, herbs, sprinkle.*

Exercise 8

Ask students to read the text again and sort the tips into two columns under DOs and DON'Ts.

KEY

DOs
Always wait until the coals are white hot before starting to grill.

Make sure you brush the grill with oil before placing the meat on it, otherwise the meat will stick to the grill.

For a real outdoor flavour, sprinkle some fresh herbs on the meat just before grilling.

Enjoy your barbecue!

DONTs
Never rush a barbecue!

Don't brush too much oil on the meat or the meat will catch fire and burn.

Make sure you don't put salt on the meat before grilling or the juices will run out as it cooks.

Be careful not to put too much meat on the barbecue at one time.

Ask students if they agree with the Tips or not, and if they can think of any other tips to add to the list.

GRAMMAR FOCUS

Draw students' attention to the structures used in the Tips by asking them to do the first activity in the Grammar Focus box.

KEY

a) *Always* + imperative, *Make sure you* + verb phrase, a simple imperative on its own
b) *Never* + imperative, *Don't* + imperative, *Make sure you don't* + verb phrase, *Be careful not to* + verb phrase

Read the note to the students. Note that the rule illustrates the most frequent usage but British speakers do sometimes interchange *otherwise* and *or* with positive instructions, e.g: *Make sure you wear a coat otherwise/or you may catch cold.*

Exercise 9 PRACTICE

Students work individually to complete the exercise in class.

KEY

1 or you'll/you may feel sick 2 otherwise the police will stop you 3 or it'll shrink
4 otherwise you'll get sunstroke 5 otherwise we/you may not (be able to) get in 6 or it'll go sour
7 or someone might break in and steal them

Exercise 10 VOCABULARY

Students work in pairs to complete the exercises.

KEY

The brackets indicate that the process is not usually associated with this type of food.

boil: milk, water, fish, vegetables, potatoes, egg
bake: fish, vegetables, potatoes, bread, cake
fry: steak, fish, vegetables, potatoes, bread, egg
steam: fish, vegetables
roast: (vegetables), potatoes
grill: steak, fish, (vegetables)
barbecue: steak, fish

grate: potato, cheese, apple, onion
peel: potato, apple, onion
chop: (potato), (apple), onion
grind: coffee
slice: potato, cheese, apple, onion

Students can discuss in pairs the way they like their food prepared.

Exercise 11 WRITING

Students divide themselves into groups according to which situation they want to write about and have a 'buzz' session to collect ideas. In the case of the recipe, some groups may want to write about the same dish. Go round and help groups with any words they may need. Explain that they must try and use some of the structures from the Grammar Focus. If possible, give photocopies of any recipes you may have in English to help those who have chosen Question 1.

Help students who have chosen the video situation with any useful words, e.g: *focus, charge the battery, spare batteries and cassettes, tripod/a camera stand, to pan from left to right, close-up, zoom in/out.*

EXTRA ACTIVITIES

1 Project: Your ideal café

Students imagine that they have been asked by a firm of architects to make suggestions for an ideal café. In groups, they choose a city and a site, the exterior and interior decor, a theme, the type of food, drink, clientele and music, the opening hours, the name and any other details.

2 Class recipe book

This is an especially interesting project with a mixed nationality class. Students cooperate to make a class recipe book either to give to friends or to sell for charity. The whole class together decide on the broad contents of the book and choose one or two students to be responsible for collecting and editing the recipes. Other students can be encouraged to draw sketches or collect pictures to accompany the recipes. This is a project that can extend over a period of time.

UNIT 17 The telephone call

Suggested lesson break: after Exercise 5

BACKGROUND NOTES

'The telephone call': The text is the first page of a six-page short story which continues the same stream of consciousness from beginning to end. The 'story' does not resolve itself. At the end, the woman is still counting the seconds and waiting for the phone to ring.

LITERATURE

Ask students to read about Dorothy Parker and to look at the picture which accompanies the text. Ask them what details in the picture suggest that it is set in America and that it is not a modern-day setting.

Exercise 1 Read and think.

Set students a time limit for reading the text and ask the 'Read and think' questions of the class as a whole. If students wish to know the answer to Question 3, refer to the Background Notes.

Exercise 2 Read and act.

Refer back to the relevant parts of the text and give an example of the first possible exchange. Set students to write their version in pairs, then select a couple of conversations to read out loud.

SUGGESTED TELEPHONE CONVERSATION

SHE: Could I speak to Mr Walt Kruger please?
HE: Speaking.
SHE: Oh, er, it's Doris here.
HE: Oh. Doris. Hello, Doris.
SHE: I know I shouldn't phone you at work but ...
HE: That's all right.
SHE: But I haven't spoken to you for three days.
HE: Look, Doris, I can't say very much here in the office.
SHE: How are you?
HE: I'm fine. Fine.
SHE: I'm not bothering you, am I?
HE: No, of course you're not. But I am rather busy at the moment.
SHE: Are you? I'm sorry. When can I talk to you?
HE: I'll call you at five o'clock, darling.
SHE: Oh ... all right.
HE: Goodbye, darling.
SHE: Goodbye, Walt.

Exercise 3 Talk about it.

Discuss the questions with the whole class.

Exercise 4 STYLE

Explain that the expression 'stream of

consciousness' is used in literature when thoughts and feelings are expressed exactly as they pass through a person's mind rather than being ordered in a way that usually appears in novels.

The 'stream of consciousness' here enables the reader to share the woman's tension and emotion in a vivid, realistic way.

Exercise 5 WRITING

Students work individually to write the paragraph.

SUGGESTED PARAGRAPH

'Here we are, then. Number 63. Please, let them like me. Susan said they were very nice and that they were bound to like me and that I shouldn't feel nervous. She told me not to worry about what to wear. But perhaps I should have worn a suit? At least I've brought some flowers. They were very expensive. But what if they don't like carnations? What if her mother's allergic to flowers? No, it'll be all right. O.K. Here we go. I'll count to three and then press the bell.'

SUGGESTED LESSON BREAK

GRAMMAR REVIEW

Ask students to work through the exercises on their own.

KEY

What are the actual words of the speaker?

1 'I'll phone you.' 2 'How are you?' 3 'Don't worry.' 4 'I spoke to the police yesterday.' 5 'I have to go tomorrow.'

In reported speech, the verb tense moves 'one step back' into the past, e.g: the present simple moves to the past simple; the past simple moves to the past perfect, etc.

Will becomes *would; must* and *have got to* become *had to*.

Time adverbials usually change, e.g: *tomorrow* becomes *the following day; next week* becomes *the following week; yesterday* becomes *the day before*.

What's wrong with these sentences?

1 The object pronoun has been omitted. (*He told me/them,* etc)
2 The actual question in a reported question takes the form of a statement, not a question, i.e. the verb follows the subject. The correct sentence here should be *I asked him how much it cost*.
3 *Told* is used for reported instructions, not *said*.

Exercise 6 PRACTICE

KEY

1 She asked if this/it was the right way to the station.
2 He said he wouldn't be able to come to the meeting next/the following week.
3 She asked when Jim had to go.
4 He told her he had to go by six o'clock the following/next day.
5 She asked me if I could help her to lift this/the box.
6 She said she had left her dictionary at school.

Exercise 7 ROLEPLAY

Make sure that students work in groups of three and that everyone knows which role, A, B or C, they are. Tell students to read their roles. Student A in particular must prepare what to say. Explain that the roleplay falls into two parts.

In part 1, Student A talks to Student B on the telephone. Student B must pay attention to what A says. Student C has no role in this part so all Cs should withdraw or leave the room for the first part of the roleplay.

In part 2, Student C returns and Student B reports the telephone conversation to him/her. Allow enough time for all students to play the role of Student B.

To help students, put the following skeleton conversations on the board:

PART 1

/phone rings/

A: *Hello. It's Marcus here.*
B: *Oh, hello Marcus.*
A: *Is Jenny there?*
B: *Well, she's busy at the moment getting the glasses ready. Can I give her a message?*
A: *Yes, listen, I'm afraid I'm still at home.*
B: *Oh no! Why?*
A: ...

PART 2

C: *Who was the telephone call from earlier?*
B: *Oh, it was from Marcus.*
C: *Oh, what did he want?*
B: *He said he was still at home and that he wouldn't ...*

Exercise 8 LISTENING

Play the tape of the conversation, pausing slightly after the 'bleeps' for students to give the correct verb of reporting.

TAPESCRIPT AND KEY

NICK: Hello?
ERIC: Hi, Nick, it's Eric here. Sorry I didn't phone you last night. /bleep/ (*apologise*)
NICK: That's O.K. Listen, I've got a problem with my bike. It won't start.
ERIC: Shall I come over and have a look at it? /bleep/ (*offer*)
NICK: That would be great. Thanks.
ERIC: No problem. What about coming over now? /bleep/ (*suggest*)
NICK: Er ... I wouldn't come just now, if I were you.

/bleep/ (*warn*) I've got all my relations here.

ERIC: Oh, that doesn't matter, does it?

NICK: No, not really. Except that I'm supposed to be entertaining them.

ERIC: Don't worry. I won't stay long. /bleep/ (*promise*) I'm sure I'll be able to fix the bike in no time. I expect the tank's empty, knowing you.

NICK: No, it's something else. I'm not that stupid.

GRAMMAR REVIEW

Because this task is a lengthy one, it is best to divide students into six groups so that each group deals with only one category. Students may use a dictionary for this task.

KEY

1) tell (+ object pronoun), agree, explain, advise, point out, suggest, complain, promise, warn (+ object pronoun), insist, recommend, admit
2) tell, advise, warn (+ not to), invite
3) offer, agree, promise
4) suggest, admit, recommend
5) accuse (+ object pronoun) + of, apologise + for, insist + on
6) offer, tell, explain (something to me) , point out (something to me), promise

Point out the note about the negative and ask students to provide different negative sentences with each verb.

Exercise 9 PRACTICE

If time is short, set the exercise for homework. Draw students' attention to the time phrase in Question 2 that will need changing.

KEY

1 She warned Jenny not to lean out of the window.
2 He apologised for not phoning the night before.
3 They promised not to stay too long.
4 She accused John of not reporting the accident to the police.
5 The doctor advised him/her not to eat so much red meat.

Play the tape of the dialogue from Exercise 8 again. Pause at the end of each 'bleep', leaving enough time for students to give the reported sentence each time.

KEY

Eric apologised for not phoning Nick the night before/last night.
Eric offered to come over and have a look at it/ the bike.
Eric suggested coming over now/then.
Nick warned him not to come over just then.
Eric promised not to stay long.

Exercise 10 LISTENING AND WRITING

Play the tape for each message separately. Students should note down the important points to report in a written message. To give them some help, write the following reporting verbs on the board:

Message 1: apologise, suggest, say
Message 2: offer, tell, promise

Obviously, the versions of each message given in the key are full versions in order to provide written practice of the reported speech verbs. If there is time, students can write more realistic, condensed messages.

TAPESCRIPT

1 Hi. This is David. I'm phoning about that job in the States. Sorry I didn't get in touch before. Anyway, I suggest you write to the American Embassy for their list of addresses. I hope I'll see you sometime next week. Cheers.

2 Hello, Carol. This is Jenny speaking. Would you like a lift with me and Mike to the concert in Bath next weekend? Don't worry about tickets, we'll be able to get them there. I'll phone you again on Friday night - I promise! Bye!

KEY

1 David phoned about the job in the States. He apologised for not getting in touch before. He suggested writing to the American Embassy for their list of addresses. He said he hoped he'd see you some time next week.

2 Jenny phoned and offered you a lift/asked if you would like a lift to the concert in Bath next weekend. She told you/said not to worry about the tickets as they/you would be able to get them there. She promised to phone again on Friday night.

EXTRA ACTIVITIES

1 Jigsaw telephone conversations

All students write a brief telephone conversation between two people, A and B, about any subject they like. They then write out the conversation omitting all the B lines. They should put their initials at the bottom of the conversation so that they can be identified later. The 'gapped' conversations are then collected, jumbled and redistributed among the class. Students have to try and complete each other's conversations.

2 A hitchhiker story

Students have five minutes to write a story about a hitch-hiker bringing in at least eight different reporting verbs from the Grammar Review as possible.

UNIT 18 Any ideas?

Suggested lesson break: after Exercise 4

BACKGROUND NOTES
karaoke: a machine which plays recorded music that people can sing to. Most of the songs are very well-known. The words are written on a screen or in a book which the 'singer' sings while the backing music is played. Karaoke was introduced from Japan and became very popular in British pubs and American bars in the 1990s.

Exercise 1 Talk about it.

Ask students to look at the photograph and ask the questions. Ask any other questions you feel may be appropriate, e.g: *Could this photograph have been taken in your country? If not, why not? Have you ever been to an open-air concert? Where do you go to meet friends in the evening? What sort of places do you go to if you want cheap evening entertainment?*

Exercise 2

Students should choose to work with someone they know reasonably well out of class. They should look at the list of activities to choose those five which they think their partner likes doing best. If they like they can add other activities which are in vogue at the moment.

Students then check with each other to see if their guesses were right. Go round and listen to the post-activity discussion and check that students are producing accurate sentences, e.g: *No, I much prefer ...ing to ...ing.*

Exercise 3 LISTENING DIALOGUE

Have a brainstorming session with the students to see how many ways of making suggestions they can think of (without looking at the Communication Focus box). Refer them to the dialogue and explain that many of the expressions for making and responding to suggestions are missing. Obviously in many of the contexts more than one expression is possible.

When students have looked through the whole dialogue and guessed what might be in the gaps, play the tape, pausing at the relevant parts for them to hear (or note down) the missing words. If you do not like students to write in their books, ask different students at random to repeat the missing words.

When students have completed the dialogue, play it again without stopping, encouraging them to speak (quietly) at the same time as the voices on the tape.

TAPESCRIPT AND KEY

DEREK: I've got to entertain my Canadian cousins on Saturday evening. *Where do you think* I should take them? Any ideas?
GAIL: You *could always* take them to a film.
DEREK: *Isn't that* rather boring? They can go to the cinema at home.
LEA: Well, *I can recommend* a restaurant that's quite fun. It's called Banana Joe's. It's decorated like a jungle and the waiters all wear fake leopard skins.
GAIL: That sounds interesting.
DEREK: I'm afraid *I'm not very keen* on theme restaurants but I suppose my cousins might like it. O.K. That's *quite a good idea*. But *what shall I* do with them afterwards?
GAIL: Well, if you like discos, you *might like* Buzz. It's supposed to be very lively.
DEREK: I can't stand discos. Anyway, it'*ll be* very crowded, *won't it*?
GAIL: Probably. All good discos are. *How about* taking them to a karaoke bar?
DEREK: A what?
GAIL: A karaoke bar. You know, a bar with karaoke machines. They give you the words and you sing into a microphone with backing music.
LEA: It's great fun, honestly. But you have to be prepared to let your hair down.
DEREK: Mmm. *I'm not sure.*
LEA: Oh, come on, Derek! Don't be so boring!
GAIL: Yes, it's about time you did something exciting in your old age, Derek!

Ask if any of the students have ever sung to a karaoke machine or been to a karaoke bar or pub. Ask them to tell the rest of the class how it felt and whether it was fun or embarrassing. If students are interested, discuss the concept of theme restaurants and the latest disco and café fashions in their country today.

Exercise 4

Students work in pairs to make questions for the answers.

KEY

1 What has Derek got to do on Saturday evening?
2 What does Gail suggest doing?
3 What is Banana Joe's like?/What does Banana Joe's look like?/What is special/different about Banana Joe's?
4 Where does Gail suggest that he takes his cousins after Banana Joe's?
5 Why does Lea tease Derek?/ Why does Lea think Derek is boring?

SUGGESTED LESSON BREAK

COMMUNICATION FOCUS

Divide the class into pairs and ask each pair in turn to read out a three-line exchange from the Focus Box, taking a line from each of the three sections. Student A reads one of the requests for suggestions in the first section, Student B responds by choosing one of the suggestions from the second section and Student A then chooses one of the responses from the third section, e.g:

A: Where do you think I could take them?
B: What about taking them to a film?
A: That's not a bad idea.

Work on the intonation if it sounds flat. Now ask the next pair to do the same, choosing different exponents this time. Encourage them to choose different activities (i.e. not just going to a film. Students can refer to the list in Exercise 2 for ideas.) Continue until all the examples from the box have been chosen. (This will mean repeating some from the first section)

Exercise 5 PRACTICE

Divide the students into groups of four or five. Read the situation aloud and go through the list of activities and the prices. Read the example exchange with one of the students and encourage them to use some of the expressions from the Communication Focus box in their discussions if possible.

Set a time limit of 5-10 minutes for their discussion, and then ask one person in each group to act as a reporter for their decisions. Make sure that each group has kept within the budget.

GRAMMAR FOCUS

Refer back to Gail's last line in the dialogue: *It's about time you did something exciting in your old age.* Ask them to say what tense is used in the clause following *It's about time* (the past tense). Ask if the speaker is referring to the present or the past (the present). Now ask students to read the note in the Grammar Focus box.

Exercise 6 PRACTICE

Encourage students occasionally to make questions rather than statements, e.g: 3 *Isn't it about time you washed those jeans?*

KEY

1 It's about time you gave up smoking/cut down on your smoking.
2 It's time you took some exercise.
3 It's about time you washed those jeans.
4 It's high time you took a holiday.
5 It's about time you went to see a doctor about that cough.
6 It's high time you went to bed.

Exercise 7 LISTENING

Give students time to read the situation and explain that they are going to have to note down all the times of the films as they hear them in order to make their choice.

Play the tape without pausing. Students then work in pairs to compare notes and decide on an appropriate time and film to see, giving their reasons. Check round the class to see if they have come to the same conclusion.

TAPESCRIPT

Hello. This is the MGM Cinema, Chelsea. Here are details of our programmes until Thursday the 5th of March.
Screen 1: *Ninja Warriors* Certificate PG at 1.30, 4.10, 6.50 and 9.25
Screen 2: *Basic Attraction* Certificate 15 at 2.30, 6.10 and 9.10
Screen 3 in the afternoon: *Snow White and the Seven Dwarfs* Certificate U at 2.10, then: *Love Hurts* Certificate 15 at 5.10, 7.25 and 9.40
Screen 4 /fade/

KEY

The logical choice would be *Basic Attraction* at 6.10 which finishes just before 9.10.

Exercise 8 WRITING

Tell students to use the decision made in the previous listening exercise as the basis for their note. Tell them to complete the note in class, giving them a time limit.

EXTRA ACTIVITIES

1 Problem solving situations

Students form groups to make suggestions and find solutions to the following situations:
- how to educate young people at school against misuse of drugs
- how to get rid of the pigeons in city centres
- how to increase security in educational institutions
- how to decorate your classroom for a theme party
- how to attract people to a new arts centre off the beaten track
- how to persuade people to be more environment-conscious

2 Find your partner

Write a selection of sentence starters and corresponding sentence endings on different pieces of paper. The sentences should be taken from the Communication and Grammar Focus, and broken at a suitable place, e.g:
Where do you think // I should take them?
What shall I // do with them afterwards?
Where do you suggest // going to eat?
Why don't we // take them for a meal?
It's high time // you had a holiday.

Try and make sure that there is only one possible sentence ending. This can sometimes be done by splitting the sentence in a particular way, e.g: *That's not a // bad idea. That // sounds fun.* (With a large class, sentence openers from previous lessons can be used e.g: *This is the first time // I've been in a helicopter.*)

Jumble the papers and give one to each student. Ask a student who has a sentence opener to read out her/his words. The student who thinks she/he has the concluding words reads out her/his strip of paper. The activity continues until every sentence opener has been completed.

UNIT 19 A film review

Suggested lesson break: after Exercises 4 and 5

BACKGROUND NOTES
The photographs The film scenes are, from the top: *Alien 3*, a science fiction horror film, with Sigourney Weaver and the Alien; *Robocop*, a police action thriller; Laurel and Hardy, film comedians, in an early 1930's Hollywood comedy; Harrison Ford in the adventure film *Indiana Jones and the Temple of Doom*
Spielberg: Steven Spielberg, a highly successful Hollywood producer and director.
Michael Douglas: an American actor who became famous in the 80s and 90s for his roles in *Romancing the Stone, Wall Street, Fatal Attraction* and *Basic Instinct*.
black comedy: an amusing film, play or story based on the unpleasant side of human life.

Exercise 1 VOCABULARY

Students work in pairs or groups to choose a title for each category. The groups then put forward their suggestions so that the class can draw up a list of top three titles for each category. If they like, students can add extra categories, e.g. musicals, action films, dance films, classic films, political thrillers, war films, martial arts, courtroom dramas.

Do some pronunciation on the film categories to make sure students know where to put the main stress.

Exercise 2 About you

Students discuss the first two questions in pairs. Ask the last question to the class as a whole, relating it to the headings listed in Exercise 3. Ask: *Do you choose a film because of the type of film, the director, the actor, the critics' review, etc.? How important do you think the reviews are to the popularity of a film?*

Exercise 3 READING

Ask students to skim-read the film review quickly and find the information.

Check the information and ask students which words gave them the clue to the last question.

Exercise 4 Guess the meaning and Exercise 5

Ask students to reread the text, paying attention to the details. They should guess the meaning of the words as they read and note *True* or *False* to the statements in Exercise 5.

Discuss the words in 'Guess the meaning' and try and get students to use some of them in sentences of their own.

SUGGESTED LESSON BREAK

STUDY POINT

Ask students to work through the task individually. Note where the main mistakes occur and spend some time showing the difference in usage between the different words using the notes below.

KEY
1 a. *In the beginning* can only be used as a phrase on its own. It cannot be used with *of*.
2 b. *In the end* here is a summing up phrase meaning 'after considering everything' or 'finally'. *At the end* describes a point of time as opposed to *at the beginning*.
3 a. *First* is an enumerator and used to indicate the first item in a list, e.g: *First we went to see the Eiffel Tower, then we went on a boat trip up the River Seine. At first* means 'at the beginning'.
4 b. *Afterwards* is an adverb like *then*. *After* is a preposition and has to be followed by a noun, a gerund or a clause. (c.f. *beforehand* and *before*)
5 b. *After everything* cannot be used in this context, only in sentences like *He always smiles after everything he says. After all* in this context means 'against all expectation'.

Exercise 6 PRACTICE

KEY
1 At first 2 afterwards 3 at the end 4 In the end 5 after all 6 at the beginning

Exercise 7 SPEECHWORK

Compare the spellings with /f/ sounds in the students' own language. Give students two minutes to write down as many different words as they can with the four different spellings (*f, ph, gh* and *ff*).

Play the tape once for students to copy down the words and again for them to repeat the words after they have checked the spelling.

TAPESCRIPT AND KEY
orphanage telephone fiction staff phrase fantastic photograph fantasy laughing offer coughed philosophy

Exercise 8 WRITING

Go through the categories briefly. Explain 'message' (important, main idea or moral that the film is trying to put across). In pairs, students settle on a film and discuss it under the categories listed. If necessary, let students ask other students in the class for any details or information they may require. Help them with any new words or expressions. Students who cannot think of a film may like to write about a TV programme.

Exercise 9

Ask students to read the openers and say which introduce positive reviews and which introduce negative ones. They may like to think of other suitable openers. They should use the *'Cross My heart'* review as a model and their own notes from Exercise 8.

EXTRA ACTIVITIES

1 Project: This month at the cinema

Students produce an up-to-date film magazine in English. This can contain one or two long reviews (based on Exercise 9) and various 'thumb-nail' reviews using the categories from Exercise 1. They can also list the top ten films with their personal five star rating. Some students may like to write news flashes about film stars and news of future films.

2 Give us a clue

In groups, students take turns to mime a film title for the other students in their group to guess within a time limit of one minute.

They can use certain fixed gestures used in mime games to indicate certain information, e.g: showing fingers to indicate the number of words in the title, showing fingers on the forearm to indicate the number of syllables in a title, holding the hand to the ear to indicate 'sounds like' or 'rhymes with', holding the thumb and forefinger to indicate a small 'grammar-like' word such as *a/an* or *the*.

UNIT 20 Romantic fiction

Suggested lesson break: after Exercise 6

Ask students to look at the covers of the paperbacks at the top of the page and say what they have in common (they are all classed as romantic fiction). Ask students on what occasions, if at all, they might read this sort of book.

Exercise 1 READING

Before asking students to read the extract, ask them if they can suggest the important ingredients of a romantic plot, e.g: pretty heroine, handsome hero, etc.

Ask students where they think the article may have appeared. Read it aloud, glossing any difficult words or expressions, e.g: *outside forces, internal conflict, united, identify with, genuinely, estranged.* Ask if students can name a romantic story or a film in which these ingredients are reflected (e.g. *Cinderella*).

Exercise 2 LITERATURE

Ask students to read the information about Charlotte Brontë and find out the answers to these questions: *How many brothers and sisters did she have? How many of them were writers? What were the names of the other sisters who wrote? Which of her family died young? Why is 'Jane Eyre' so famous?*

Exercise 3 Listen and answer.

Explain that students are going to hear a summary of the story of *Jane Eyre*. Ask them to read the list of questions in their books before playing the tape. If any students have read *Jane Eyre*, ask them if they can tell the class the answers before listening to the tape.

The tape can then be played for students to check if their fellow-students' information was right. Write the following names on the board before you start the tape: *Jane, Rochester, Thornfield Hall, The Reverend St John* /ˈsɪndʒən/ *Rivers* and pre-teach *governess* and *telepathic*. Play the tape a couple of times if necessary.

TAPESCRIPT

Jane Eyre is an orphan. After her parents die, she is put in the care of her aunt. She has a very hard and difficult upbringing, and eventually becomes a governess at Thornfield Hall where she is given a job of looking after the daughter of a certain Mr Rochester. Mr Rochester is a classic hero from romantic fiction. He's dark and very angry-looking and has a bad temper but at the same time he is very attractive. In spite of Jane's plainness, Rochester is fascinated by her. He finds her witty and full of spirit. Gradually, he falls in love with her and Jane falls in love with him. Everything looks as if it's going to be happy but at the very last moment they are prevented from marrying when it is revealed that Rochester's wife is not only alive, but she's also mad, and living in the attic rooms of Thornfield Hall.

Jane runs away and nearly dies out on the moors. Luckily, she is rescued by the Reverend St John Rivers, and later, although she is still in love with Rochester, she agrees to marry Rivers and go with him to India. She is stopped from doing this by a telepathic message from Rochester. Jane returns to Thornfield Hall to find that the house has burnt down, and that Rochester is sad and deeply depressed. He had tried unsuccessfully to save his wife from the fire, and during his attempt he had been blinded and permanently injured by the fire.

Exercise 4

Ask students to read the extract from the end of *Jane Eyre*. Tell them to note down any words they are not sure of, but not to use dictionaries yet. Ask a student afterwards to briefly summarise what happened. Then ask different students the questions in Exercise 4.

Exercise 5 Read and describe.

The questions in the book should encourage extended answers from the students.

SUGGESTED ANSWERS
Jane: she is quite plain to look at, quite small with small fingers. She is witty, brave and capable of strong feelings and loyalty.
Rochester: he is dark and bad-tempered but very good-looking. He is a large man and capable of strong passion.
The dog, Pilot: he is old but friendly, and loyal to his master.
The room: it is big, dark and gloomy. It has an open fire surrounded by a mantlepiece. The room is rather cold as the fire is nearly out.

Exercise 6 Think about it.

On a more light-hearted note, students may like to suggest a famous contemporary actor and actress for the parts of Jane and Mr Rochester in a new film. To encourage discussion you may want to write a list of five possible people for each part.

SUGGESTED LESSON BREAK

Exercise 7 Study the words.

Give students a few minutes to match the words to the definitions. Help slower students by telling them to look only at definitions which relate to the same part of speech as the word in the list, e.g: verb, noun or adjective.

KEY
curl up: *phr v* (I) to lie comfortably with arms and legs drawn close to the body
gather: *v* (T) to pull around or close to something
bound: *v* (I) to move along quickly by jumping or leaping
prick up: *v* (of an animal) to raise the ears so as to listen attentively
sigh: *v* (I) to let out a deep breath slowly and with a sound, usu. expressing sadness, tiredness or satisfaction
grate: *n* the bars and frame which hold wood, coal etc. in a fireplace
gloomy: *adj* almost dark, esp. in an unpleasant way

Talk about other uses of each word, e.g: a person can *curl up* on a sofa or bed with a book; you can *gather* people together, *gather* information, *I gather* can also mean 'I understand'; *gloomy* can refer to the weather, to predictions, to moods; you can *sigh* with boredom, with exasperation, with sadness, with pleasure; people can metaphorically *prick up their ears* when they hear something that interests them.

Exercise 8

Help students by directing them to the part of the text in which each of the words appear.

KEY
1 neglected 2 leaning 3 trodden on
4 imperiously 5 seized 6 entwined

Exercise 9

KEY
hand, heart, rib, head, ear, lip, eye, brain, finger, arm, shoulder, neck, waist

Exercise 10 VOCABULARY

As a form of check, ask students to mime the actions as well as give the phrases.

KEY
1 clap their hands 2 snap your fingers 3 poke someone in the ribs 4 shrug their shoulders
5 close your eyes 6 nod your head

Exercise 11

Younger students may want to give sound effects to accompany their answers.

KEY
a dog barks, a horse neighs, a wolf howls, a cow moos, a lion roars, a sheep bleats, a snake hisses, an owl hoots, a cat miaows, a hen clucks, a bird chirps

You may like to point out that many of these verbs can be used of people as well, e.g: he *barked* the orders, the crowd *roared* with approval, the crowd booed and *hissed* when the performer arrived late, she *hooted* with laughter, she was in a very *chirpy* (bright) mood.

Exercise 12 WRITING

This can be prepared orally round the class to help those students who find it difficult to use their imagination.

Exercise 13 About you

These questions can serve as a general 'wind down' to the lesson. Students ask and answer them in pairs to save embarrassment in case some students are non-readers. You may like to extend the discussion into other areas, e.g: *Is there an equivalent of romantic fiction for male readers? Do you think different sexes have different tastes?*

Exercise 14 Talk about it.

Use the chart to stimulate a general class discussion. Ask students if they can think of any explanation for the figures. Is it just a question of the richer countries reading more? Is it to do with the cost of books? Ask if they are surprised at the position of their own country on the list. Do their own reading habits bear this out?

EXTRA ACTIVITIES

1 Reading survey

Students prepare a questionnaire to find out information about books and reading habits from people in, say, their apartment block, another class, the teachers, their family or their circle of friends. The questions can be based on those in Exercise 13 'About you'. Other questions can be added to find out about favourite authors, favourite books as a child, etc.

2 Animal sounds: noughts and crosses

Draw a box three squares by three squares on the board. In each square, write the name of one of the animals listed in Exercise 11. Divide the class into two teams, Team A using noughts and Team B using crosses.

One person from Team A starts by choosing one of the animals in the squares, e.g: *cow* and says the sound associated with it. If it is correct, the team wins a nought in that square. A person from Team B now chooses another animal and says the appropriate sound to win a cross in that square. The aim of the game, as in noughts and crosses, is to hinder the other team from getting three noughts or three crosses in a row, either vertically, horizontally or diagonally.

3 Memory test

At a later stage you may want to type out the *Jane Eyre* extract leaving gaps in various places and give students photocopies. Students compete individually or in pairs to see who can complete the text the fastest. (Obviously they must be told not to look at the text in their books.) It is up to you to decide how much you wish to omit in each gap.

CHECK 4 Units 16-20

(For advice on handling this section, see the notes for Check 1 Units 1–5)

KEY

Ex. 1 1d 2f 3e 4b 5a 6g 7c

Ex. 2 1 Boil 2 Fry 3 Grill 4 Grind 5 Peel 6 Grate 7 Bake 8 Chop 9 Slice 10 Roast

Ex. 3

1 Mike accused Clive of taking the money.
2 Tom invited Gill to come/go sailing at the weekend.
3 Gerry apologised to Mrs Prentice for being late.
4 The young woman offered to help the elderly man to carry his bag/offered to help carry the elderly man's bag.
5 Carol agreed to take on another assistant/agreed that she should take on another assistant.
6 Della thanked Sally for the lovely flowers.
7 The man warned me not to park my car in front of his gate again.
8 Chris advised Nigel to get a good solicitor as soon as possible.

Ex. 4

1 'Could you water my plants for a week?'
2 'Which is the best way to drive to Portsmouth?'
3 'I'm going to hand in my resignation next month.'
4 'How much did your new guitar cost?'
5 'I'm sorry but I'll have to leave the staff meeting a bit early tomorrow.'
6 'I think I left my watch in a locker in the changing room yesterday.'
7 'I've already told the police about the break-in.'

Ex. 5 1 recommend 2 might like 3 don't you 4 couldn't you 5 you could

Ex. 6

1 It's time we went home.
2 It's time I bought a word processor.
3 Isn't it time your cousin started looking for a job?
4 It's time the government did something about it.
5 Isn't it time the children chose something serious to read?

Ex. 7 1b 2a 3c 4b 5c

Ex. 8 1 fold your arms 2 clap your hands 3 shrug your shoulders 4 hold your nose 5 snap your fingers 6 close your eyes 7 prick up your ears 8 raise your eyebrows

Ex. 9 1 barked 2 chirping 3 hiss 4 clucked 5 roared 6 hoot(ing) 7 moo

UNIT 21 Money matters

Suggested lesson break: after Exercise 7

BACKGROUND NOTES
The photograph: a busker or street entertainer entertains passers-by in central London.
Keith Waterhouse: (b. 1929) a well-known British author, TV scriptwriter and journalist noted for his humorous writing.
J. Paul Getty: (1892-1976) an American billionaire philanthropist who lived in England for part of his life. He became very rich through oil.

Exercise 1 Talk about it.

Ask students to look at the picture and to describe the scene. Introduce the word *busker* (a street musician who plays in order to earn money. The verb is *to busk*). Ask where buskers usually like to perform. Explain the difference between a *beggar* (*to beg*) and a busker. Depending on the answer to the last question in this section, ask students what sort of things they *do* consider mean.

Exercise 2 Before you read

Find out if students are familiar with all the words in the list. They will probably need to use a dictionary for words like *stingy, thrifty* and *spendthrift.*

KEY

Positive: generous, careful, (extravagant), thrifty

Negative: overgenerous, mean, miserly, (extravagant), stingy, spendthrift

Point out the use of *over* to suggest criticism, e.g: *overuse, overrate, overlarge*. Explain that *thrifty* is the opposite of *spendthrift*, and that *spendthrift* is similar to *extravagant* but is more negative in tone.

To test if they have understood the meaning of the words, ask how they would describe:

- someone who, after a trip costing £3, gave a taxi driver a tip of a) 10p b) £1
- someone who, when invited to dinner at a friend's house, brings a) nothing b) a dozen red roses
- someone who checks every single item on his or her bank statement every month in case the bank has made a mistake?

Make sure students do not take the question *Which words would you apply to yourself?* too seriously.

READING

Ask a student to look at the article and see if someone can explain the phrase *a mean streak* (*a streak* = a character quality which is different from other character qualities, usually in a bad way, e.g: *a stubborn streak, an aggressive streak*). Write the word *economy* on the board and ask a student to use it in a sentence. Show how it can be used to describe the financial situation of a country, e.g:*The economy is in a bad/healthy state*. It can also be used to mean *a saving* and can be used in the plural form as well, e.g: *We've had to make some serious economies in our budget for next year*. The verb *to economise* means *to make economies*. Ask students to look at the cartoon and to describe the scene.

Exercise 3 Guess the meaning.

Ask students to read the text to themselves, guessing the meaning of the words in the list as they read. They should also underline any other words they have not understood. Many of these will be focused on in the unit but there are other words and expressions in the text which may need explanation, e.g: *applies to, buy up, presume, special offer, coupon, discount, affect, run out on them*.

Exercises 4 and 5

Students work in pairs to complete these comprehension tasks.

Exercise 6 Study the words.

Ask students to work individually and see how fast they can complete the exercise.

KEY

1f 2g 3a 4e 5d 6b 7c

Ask students if they can think of: something material or an opportunity they have squandered recently; something they like to hoard; something that they have allowed to accumulate over the years; something that they try to recycle in the home.

Exercise 7 About you

Ask students if they sympathise with Keith Waterhouse's views, or whether they find them exaggerated. Ask if they can identify any mean streaks in their own behaviour. The questions can be asked in pairs in class or answered for homework.

SUGGESTED LESSON BREAK

Exercise 8 VOCABULARY

Students can use dictionaries if they wish. Do the exercise either as an individual or a class oral activity depending on the pace of the lesson.

KEY

generosity, envy, extravagance, meanness, obsession, intelligence, jealousy, tidiness, selfishness, loyalty, imagination

Check with students that they know where the main stress fall in the adjective and noun forms. *Generous* and *imaginative* are the only two which involve a change in stress in the noun form (generOSity, imagiNATion). Ask students to copy down these words into their vocabulary notebooks.

Exercise 9 LISTENING

Before playing the tape, look at the questions and discuss the important qualities to look for in a friend. Start making a list on the board. Ask students also to consider the other two questions: the basis of a good friendship (i.e. who make the best sort of friends) and the sign of a good friendship. Ask also if any of them have experienced a relationship or friendship which has been damaged by arguments involving money.

After discussing these questions for a few minutes, play the tape and ask students to make notes to see if the people on the tape share their opinions.

TAPESCRIPT

WOMAN 1: How would you, how would you describe your best friend?

WOMAN 2: Um, I suppose someone to listen to me, as much as I would listen to them. Not necessarily when things are bad but just generally … an ear.

MAN: Kind of supportive.

WOMAN 2: Yes, yes, and loyal – someone I know wouldn't say to the three of you … .

WOMAN 1: … what you had told them … honest.

WOMAN 2: Yes, yes.

WOMAN 1: You want an honest opinion back, don't you, when you've said things? You don't want someone just to agree with you all the time.
MAN: That's got to be the most important thing in friendship, honesty, I would have thought. And having a good time, I think … I mean a laugh, having fun.
WOMEN: Someone who has a sense of humour.
MAN: Yeah, if you share a sense of humour with someone, that's half the battle really, isn't it, don't you think?
WOMAN 1: Yes, it's everything.
WOMAN 2: It's terribly important.
WOMAN 1: Someone who's going to stick with you through thick and thin. Loyalty is very important, isn't it?
WOMAN 2: Yes.
WOMAN 1: To see you through things.
MAN: Sure.

MAN: I think one of the most important things with friendships is shared experiences, I mean someone that you're the same age as, someone you've gone to school with, you have a history together. And that can be wonderful, and no matter how much your life changes since leaving school, whatever, there's always that there, do you find that?
ALL: Yes.
WOMAN 2: You can grow away completely and still say 'Do you remember that day?'
MAN: But on the other hand I also think there's something intrinsic about good friendship and even if you don't see this person for ten years, you know you can pick up where you left off. But it's really sad if you hang around with someone for a year or two and you're great buddies and then years later it's gone, you know what I mean, that sort of temporary thing?
ALL: Yeah.
MAN: And you don't feel you can phone them up, after not seeing them for a while, whereas true friends – no matter how long it is since speaking to them, you feel you can, just get in touch.
WOMAN : Schoolfriends are like family …

STUDY POINT

Read out the list, giving examples of each noun-preposition combination in context. Some teachers may want to dictate the examples for students to write down, e.g:

for: a reason for changing jobs; a demand for more staff, a request for money; a need for more time; an opportunity for discussion; a hope for the future
about: an obsession about tidiness; an idea about a present; a complaint about the food; an opinion about capital punishment
in: a rise/fall in temperature; an increase/decrease in the number of people out of work; an improvement in staff relations
of: the cause of the accident; the result of the test
to: a solution to the crossword; an answer to your question; an invitation to a party; an attitude to (or towards) crime
with: her relationship with an Irishman; in connection with the robbery

Alternatively, ask students to study the list and note down in their books any combinations which they are not sure of. Stress that these nouns should be learnt together with the preposition.

Exercise 10 PRACTICE

Do the exercise with the class as a whole. Ask one student to read the original sentence and another to read the reconstruction of it.

KEY
1 There has been a big rise in the number of people out of work.
2 There is no need for any more staff.
3 We must try and find a solution to this problem.
4 She has a good relationship with her boss.
5 We have received a complaint about the prices.
6 Do you know the cause of the fire?

Exercise 11 PHRASAL VERBS: Money and spending

Students work in pairs to complete the exercise. Explain that they may have to change the verb form of some of the phrasal verbs.

KEY
1 pay in 2 paid off 3 live on 4 pay for 5 live off 6 saving up for 7 pay back 8 run out of

Afterwards, ask them to say which of the phrasal verbs are transitive and can take an object in two positions (Type 1) and which can only take an object after the phrasal verb (Type 2).
Type 1: pay in, pay off, pay back
Type 2: live on, pay for, live off, save up for, run out of

Exercise 12 Talk about it.

Divide students into pairs or groups. Explain what a proverb means and refer to the first example. Ask a student if a similar saying exists in their own language. Ask them to work through the list of proverbs, explaining to each other in their own words what they mean, or, in a monolingual class, thinking of an equivalent saying in their own language.

Students then choose one of the sayings with which they agree or disagree strongly and think of examples. Before starting the discussion, sort out which student is going to speak about which proverb, and whether their opinion will be 'for' or 'against'. If possible, select one person to speak for, and another to speak against the topic. It is highly probable that some of the sayings will invite no disagreement, e.g: 4 and 6. Encourage students to be anecdotal and to give examples, e.g:

STUDENT A
I don't agree with Number 5 'Lend your money and lose a friend'. I think it's a sign of a good friendship that you can lend money to a friend without worrying, and that you feel you can borrow it too. I remember once last Christmas when I had ...

STUDENT B
Well, I think you're wrong. I think you are asking for trouble if you lend money to a friend. A friend of mine once wanted to buy a ...

EXTRA ACTIVITIES

1 Plan an extravagant party

Students imagine they have been given an unspecified amount of money to throw a party for their friends. Students work in groups and plan an extravagant party. After ten minutes, groups come together to share their ideas. The class can vote on the party they would most like to attend.

2 The meanest person in the world

The object is for each student to give an imaginary (and amusing) example of what 'the meanest person in the world' does at different points of the day. Students sit in a circle and S1 starts:

S1: The meanest person in the world always gets up after eight o'clock because it saves putting on an electric light.
S2: He measures out his toothpaste so that he only uses a centimetre at a time.
S3: When he has a shower, he turns it off while he soaps himself in order to save water.
(... and so on right through the day)

UNIT 22 Would you do it?

Suggested lesson break: after Exercise 5

BACKGROUND NOTES
The photo: in some Northern European countries, e.g: Finland, Sweden and Russia, it is customary to take a dip in the lake after having a sauna (steam bath). In the middle of winter, this usually means breaking a hole in the ice to do so.

Exercise 1 Talk about it.

Ask students to discuss the photograph and use the Background Notes for explanation if necessary. Ask if there is any similar tradition in their own country. (e.g. In Brighton on the south coast of England some people traditionally swim in the sea on Christmas Day.) In answer to the last question *Would you do it?*, students may just give *Yes/No* answers. If students expand on the answers, check how accurately they use the second conditional in their replies. This will indicate how much remedial work is needed on the basic form of the second conditional, before moving to the Grammar Focus.

Exercise 2

Ask different students to read the bubble captions aloud. Ask which one they agree with most. If they are inclined to agree with the person who would only do it for a very large sum of money, ask what figure they would settle for.

GRAMMAR REVIEW

Work through the examples with the whole class.

KEY
b) suggests that the possibility of being paid is greater.

Which of the following sentences mean the same?
a) and b) mean the same. Point out that *unless* means *if ... not*. However, *unless* is used in preference to *if ... not* when the speaker wants to stress a condition or issue a threat.

Exercise 3 PRACTICE

Students work individually. Obviously, some students will disagree about the likelihood of some events compared with others. If some of their categorisations seem odd, check by questioning them carefully.

KEY
a) the weather is fine, you wake up early tomorrow, you decide to go to the cinema at the weekend, you have some money to spend at the end of the month, you are bored this evening
b) you speak fluent Russian, you become Prime Minister of your country, you are able to take a holiday abroad next week

Exercise 4

Students can now work individually making first and second conditional sentences, using the situations in Exercise 3.

Point out that they must change *you* to *I*, where relevant.

Exercise 5

Ask students to try and imagine the situations in which each sentence is spoken.

KEY
1 unless 2 unless 3 If 4 Unless 5 If

SUGGESTED LESSON BREAK

GRAMMAR FOCUS

Read through the notes in the Grammar Focus box to illustrate the meaning of *if* and *even if*. Point out that *provided* is often used on its own, and that there is no difference in meaning between *as long as* and *provided that*. If students should ask, point out that it is also correct to say *providing (that)*. However, to avoid confusion, it is advised to concentrate on one option only at this stage.

In a monolingual class, draw comparisons with the students' own language so that they fully understand the nuances of meaning between *if, even if, provided* and *unless*.

Exercise 6 PRACTICE

Students complete the exercise in pairs.

KEY
1 as long as 2 unless 3 even if 4 as long as
5 even if 6 Unless 7 Even if

Ask students to make sentences of their own using the different conjunctions.

SUGGESTED LESSON BREAK

Exercise 7 READING

Ask students to read the text, guessing the meaning of the words listed. Encourage students to share their knowledge of the words with each other. After they have read the text, ask students to cover it, and see if they can remember 'the seven opportunities' and the sum of money that might be offered.

Exercise 8 Think about it.

Students form groups to discuss each opportunity. Read out the exchange first to give them guidance as to the sort of language you want them to use. Go round and listen, making notes of any persistent errors. Ask someone in each group to be prepared to report back the outcome of the groups' discussion on any or all of the points.

Exercise 9 WRITING

Ask a student to read the extract from the letter. Then ask them to discuss in pairs what the person replying might be concerned about, e.g: it's uncertain whether s/he would or wouldn't have a job when s/he got there; maybe it would be difficult to get into the country without a guarantee of a job, especially if s/he didn't have much money. Maybe the person is also concerned about accommodation. Perhaps s/he would come on condition that s/he was given a letter guaranteeing a job, and that accommodation was provided.

Students may suggest other worries. Discuss how these might be expressed in a letter. Encourage students to use the second conditional by prompting sentences like: *I'd like to come as long as ..., I wouldn't come unless ..., If I knew ..., If they could ...* .

Students can start the letter in class and complete it for homework. Point out it can be a short letter, simply to express concerns and lay down certain conditions.

EXTRA ACTIVITIES

1 What's it worth?

Students together as a class think of a list of interesting challenges, similar to those in the reading text. Each student makes a chart, with the list on the left and three columns on the right with differing amounts of money, e.g:

	£10	£50	£100	etc.
1 make a speech in front of 1,000 people?				
2 take part in a TV dating game?				
3 swallow a raw egg?				
4 dive from the top diving board of a swimming pool?				
5 dye your hair purple?				
6 shave all your hair off?				
etc.				

Students try and find out the minimum amount of money that their partner would do the 'dare' for, e.g:

S1: Would you make a speech in front of 1,000 people for £10?
S2: No, I wouldn't.
S1: Would you do it for £50?
S2: No, I wouldn't. I'd do it for £100. What about you?
S1: I wouldn't do it for under £1,000.

2 Life questions

Dictate or distribute copies of the following life questions for students to discuss in groups.

1 For a million pounds would you be willing never again to see or talk to your best friend?
2 Would you rather live in a democracy where your political leaders are incompetent and dishonest, or in a dictatorship where the leaders are talented, efficient and well-meaning?
3 If your friends were prepared to tell you truthfully what they really thought of you, would you want them to?
4 If someone offered you a potion to give you (and only you) eternal youth, would you take it?
5 Would you accept a job at five times the normal salary for that job as long as you never reveal anything about the job to anyone you know?

UNIT 23 Holiday blues

Suggested lesson break: after Exercise 7

BACKGROUND NOTES
Aegean Sea: an arm of the Mediterranean Sea, off south-east Europe, between Greece and Turkey. It is full of islands and is a popular holiday destination.

READING

Ask students to look at the title of the magazine feature and ask what sort of warnings may be relevant in connection with going on holiday with a 'best friend'.

Exercise 1 Guess the meaning.

Ask students to read the text and find out what happened between the writer of the letter and her friend Catherine on holiday in Greece. Ask them to guess the meaning of the words listed and note down any other words and expressions they are not sure of. Ask a series of simple comprehension questions, e.g: *Where did they go? When? How long for? What would Catherine do all day?*

Exercise 2 Read and think.

Students discuss the questions in pairs.

Exercise 3 Talk about it.

Ask students to suggest a list of possible holiday companions and write them on the board, e.g: your brother/sister; your best friend; your parents; a party of school friends; friends from work; your boy/girlfriend; your aunt/uncle and cousins; a group of unknown people.

Discuss with the whole class who they think the best holiday companions would be.

Exercise 4 DIALOGUE

Ask students to read the dialogue and find out what happened to Don (he got sunstroke on the first day of his holiday). Check that students understand *ice pack* and the expression *It serves him right.* Ask: *What did Don do wrong?*

Exercise 5 LISTENING

Tell students to copy the chart into their books and to complete it while you play the rest of the dialogue on tape. Play the tape again to check that the students understand *tropical fruit, pineapple, to go for,* and *bit of a nightmare*. Ask students where they think the people went for their holiday and then find out if any of the students have ever suffered from sunstroke and if they know what the best treatment for it is.

TAPESCRIPT
MIKE: But you were all right?
KATE: Yes, you know me. I love the sun.
MIKE: What about the rest of the holiday?
KATE: Very good. We thought the people were just fantastic.
MIKE: What about your hotel?
KATE: Oh, it was fine, very comfortable. Don didn't think much of the pineapple for breakfast. But then he never did go for tropical fruit. I loved it.
MIKE: Did the flight go all right?
KATE: No, it was a bit of a nightmare. We weren't very impressed with the charter company. But on the whole the holiday was fine.

COMMUNICATION FOCUS

Read out the sentences for choral practice. As you do so, point out that certain words can be emphasised by stress to give a stronger impression of approval, e.g:

I was VERY impressed by the hotel.
I thought the people were fanTASTic.
I LOVED the tropical fruit.

When expressing disapproval, the use of intonation with a fall-rise pattern is important in certain statements, e.g:

I wasn't very impressed by the travel arrangements.

I didn't think the beach was very good.

He didn't think much of the breakfasts.

VOCABULARY

Exercise 6

Do this as a class exercise and ask students to use a dictionary to check the opposites of the starred words.

KEY
1 noisy 2 dirty 3 inexpensive/cheap
4 unfriendly 5 inefficient 6 uncomfortable
7 tasteless 8 small/cramped 9 unexciting/dull/boring 10 disorganised

Exercise 7 PRACTICE

Show how the example works by asking one or two students to do the first two or three items. Encourage them to alternate the phrases used. After giving the correct sentence, ask them to say the sentence again, this time faster and more fluently.

If time allows, discuss with the whole class any disappointing holiday experiences people have had, where things did not meet expectations.

SUGGESTED LESSON BREAK

GRAMMAR REVIEW

Students work through the Grammar Review individually, completing the three tasks. Give an example of the past form of the verbs in the second task.

KEY

What's the difference in meaning?
Sentence 1 refers to the present or immediate future; Sentence 2 refers to an incident in the past where the person regrettably did not see a doctor.

What's the past form?
ought to have taken, should have done, should have gone, ought to have brought, should have driven, should have written

Which sentence is correct?
a)

Remind students that *should* and *ought to* mean the same.

Explain that the simple form of the modal *should* is used to criticise a completed activity, e.g: *You should have bought a larger size.* The continuous form is used when the activity or event in question took place continuously over an extended period of time. It shares the same time aspect as the past continuous tense, e.g: *You should have been wearing seatbelts.* i.e. You weren't wearing seatbelts (when something unfortunate happened).

Exercise 8 PRACTICE

Tell students to work in pairs. Remind them that the first sentence must be a simple form of the modal, and the second sentence must be a continuous form.

KEY

2 I shouldn't have gone out. I should have been revising.
3 She should have taken more care (of it). She shouldn't have been wearing it.
4 She shouldn't have gone shopping. She should have been working.
5 I should have remembered what happened. I should have been taking notes.

STUDY POINT

Go through the sentences with students, pointing out the prepositions in the phrases *because of, owing to* and *in general*. Draw comparison with similar expressions in the students' own language if possible. Give more examples to show how the expressions are used in context.

To give students extra practice, write a few sentences on the board for them to link in different ways, e.g:

Cause and effect: There was a storm./We couldn't go out on the boat.
Qualifying a statement: He's not a very experienced captain./They have managed to win a number of matches.
General statement: There are one or two boring moments in the film./It is quite entertaining.

Exercise 9 WRITING

Ask students first to work individually to complete the report extract. Point out that sometimes more than one expression is possible.

KEY

On the whole; As a result/Consequently; because of; Nevertheless/Having said that; Having said that/Nevertheless

Now ask students to write about one of their own holidays. Tell them to mention other aspects besides travel arrangements and the hotel. They can do this in class, if time is available, or for homework.

EXTRA ACTIVITIES

1 The ideal holiday

Write the following list of 'holiday features' on the blackboard. Students have to rate the items on the list on a scale of 1-5 according to their importance to them. Bring the class together to decide on the top five features which make an ideal holiday.

good companions
exciting nightlife
being in another country
comfortable accommodation
clean beaches and good swimming
beautiful scenery
plenty of sun
being on or near water
cheap travel
meeting lots of new people
plenty of things to do
good food and drink
good shopping
peace and quiet

2 What went wrong?

Divide the class into teams of equal number. Students sit next to other members of their team. Make 'result cards' (see list below) on separate pieces of card or paper so that you have a duplicate set for each team. Distribute these among students so that they have one each. Tell students to place them face down until their turn comes in the game.

At the word 'Go!', students in each team take turns to read out the 'result' on their card for the student sitting next to them to suggest what should or shouldn't have been done, e.g:

S1: I got sunstroke.
S2: You should have worn a hat/You shouldn't have sat so long in the sun. I've lost my hotel key.
S3: You should have …

The teams work through all their members simultaneously. The winners are the first team to work through all their 'result cards'.

RESULTS

1 I feel sick.
2 My money's been stolen.
3 My back's terribly sunburnt.

4 I've gone deaf in one ear.
5 I've lost my hotel key.
6 I've got to pay excess baggage.
7 There was no vegetarian food on the flight.
8 I ran out of money.
9 I don't speak the language and can't order a cup of coffee.
10 I've got a headache.

UNIT 24 Fire! Fire!

Suggested lesson break: after Exercise 4

BACKGROUND NOTES

The Great Fire of London: The fire was such an important historical event that it is referred to with capital letters (c.f. The Great Plague, The French Revolution)

King Charles II: (1630-1685) son of King Charles I, who became king of England, Scotland and Ireland after the English Civil War ended in 1651.

St Paul's Cathedral: a fine cathedral in central London built (1675-1710) by Sir Christopher Wren.

The River Thames: the main river flowing through London. It was once a very busy waterway. The section of the river from its mouth to the City of London was lined with docks and warehouses and was central to the economy of the country.

The Great Plague: a very infectious disease that produced high fever, swellings on the body and, ultimately, death. It swept through Europe and parts of Asia in the 14th and 17th century. It was also called 'the Black Death'.

Baker Farynor: Apart from military titles and certain professions, it is not usual to put a person's job in front of their surname. In the text in this unit, it is a stylistic device to remind the reader about the background of the person who started the fire.

Exercise 1 Talk about it.

Open the lesson by relating an incident that you (or someone you know) has been involved in, thereby prompting students to come up with incidents of their own.

Note down any words to do with fire as they come up in the conversation, e.g: *match, strike, spark, singe, burn, flame, put out, alarm, extinguish, damage, smoke, fume, spread.*

READING

Ask students if they know anything about the Fire of London, e.g:. when and how it started. Ask: *Why do you think a fire in 1666 was so damaging?* Ask students to describe the scene in the picture and ask if their own town or country has suffered any major fire disaster.

Exercise 2 Guess the meaning.

Ask students to read the text, guessing the meaning of the words in the list. They should also note down or underline any other words they are not sure of. These will probably include words from Exercise 3.

Exercise 3 Study the words.

Ask students to find all the words in the text and then work in pairs to order them. Check the answers with the whole class. Point out that *conflagration* would not normally occur in everyday speech.

Ask them which words can occur as nouns and verbs (*spark, fire, blaze, flame, flicker, burn*).

KEY
Nouns: a, f, b, e, c, d
Verbs: b, c, a

Exercise 4 Answer the questions.

Either students can work in pairs or the teacher can ask the questions of the whole class. Ask students to close their books so that they are not tempted to read from the text.

Chose a few students to give an oral summary of the story to practise extended speaking.

SUGGESTED LESSON BREAK

Exercise 5 SPEECHWORK

Play the tape and ask students to repeat the examples (*next question, stand clear)* as they hear them. Ask them to read aloud the words and phrases listed in the book and then play the tape for them to compare their pronunciation.

Play the tape again for students to listen and repeat, then ask them to try and make a sentence to include each of the phrases, e.g: *When we got there the snow had almost gone.*

GRAMMAR REVIEW

Go through the questions with the whole class.

SUGGESTED ANSWERS
What are the actual facts?
Fires were uncommon. People were not alarmed.

What tenses are used?
The past perfect is used in the *if* clause. *Would have* + past participle is used in the main clause.

Transform the sentence.
If he hadn't come home early, he wouldn't have noticed the fire.

Point out that other modals, e.g: *might(n't) have* and *could(n't) have* can be substituted instead of *would(n't) have*. Mention also the possibility of

mixed conditionals if the main verb is the verb *to be*.
e.g. *If we hadn't noticed the fire, we would all be dead.*

Exercise 6 PRACTICE

SUGGESTED ANSWERS
2 people would have been more alarmed.
3 the fire wouldn't have spread to the west.
4 the firefighters hadn't smashed the waterpipes and cut off the water supply.
5 more people would have died.
6 the firefighters hadn't knocked down buildings to make firebreaks.
7 the slums of central London wouldn't have been destroyed so quickly.

GRAMMAR FOCUS

To revise the use of *I wish* and *If only* with the past perfect and the simple past, give the following situations (or other ones relevant to you and your situation):

I spent all my money last week and now I've got none left. I wish I hadn't spent it all.
Ask: *Did I spend it all? Are we talking about the present or the past?*

My apartment is rather small. I wish I had a bigger one.
Ask: *Have I got a big apartment? Are we talking about the present or the past?*
Ask students to read the examples in the box.

KEY
Sentence a) refers to the past; Sentence b) refers to the present.

Exercises 7 and 8 PRACTICE

Ask students to work in pairs, with one student writing the answers to the exercises.

KEY
Exercise 7
2 If only John was here.
3 If only I didn't live in London.
4 If only it wasn't raining.
5 If only you could remember her name.

KEY
Exercise 8
2 If only I'd/we'd taken it more seriously.
3 If only they'd told me earlier.
4 If only the fire hadn't spread to the warehouses.
5 If only we hadn't smashed the waterpipes.

LISTENING

Exercise 9 Before you listen

With the students' help, list some common causes of fire on the board and, as you do so, introduce vocabulary like: *frying pans, stove, cigarette ends, arson, lighted matches*. Discuss with the class what you should and shouldn't do in case of fire. Students will probably be able to suggest things such as keeping low on the ground and not opening doors and windows, but try and elicit from them the reasons for this.

Exercise 10

Before playing the tape, explain that the man who is speaking uses quite formal-sounding words. Write these on the board and explain what they mean, e.g:

disposal of cigarettes = putting/stubbing out cigarettes
electrical appliances = electrical equipment/ gadgets
alert everybody = call everybody
retrieve possessions = collect personal possessions
unattended = with no one in the room
extinguished = put out

Ask students what the civil organisation for fighting fires is called in Britain (*the Fire Brigade*).

Play the tape, pausing for students to make notes at the end of each section. The tape will probably have to be played at least twice for students to be able to pick up the detailed information. Other words which may cause difficulty are: *vapour, tumble drier, susceptible, huddling up, arson, trapped, temptation* and *wiring*.

TAPESCRIPT
I = Interviewer, F = Firefighter
I: Can you first of all tell me what are the main causes of domestic fires?
F: Yes. One of the main causes of domestic fires is the careless disposal of cigarettes, pipes, etcetera. Another one of the main causes is cooking appliances - someone's left the cooking oil on a gas or electric cooker and the vapour catches light whilst unattended. And that can be quite frightening. Electrical appliances is another major cause of fire. By that I mean such things as hair driers, they are used quite regularly, tumble driers and washing machines. Electrical heaters naturally pose a problem in themselves. During the winter months, the old people, very susceptible - huddling up towards the fire to keep warm and sometimes the clothing or blankets they have wrapped around them catch light. That is of concern to us in the winter. Another major cause and cause for concern to us is children playing with matches, and another one would be where older persons play with matches i.e. arson. This is another major cause of fire.
I: If you've been unfortunate enough to have a fire break out in your house, what do you advise? What are the things you should do and what are the things you shouldn't do?
F: The first thing to do is to alert everybody in the house by shouting quite clearly and loudly the words 'Fire!'. You should then shut the door on the fire and get everybody out and call the Fire Brigade. If you are trapped within a fire then one should keep

very low so that you can get below the smoke and try and get to a window or a door.
There is always a temptation to try and fight the fire. This can be done if the fire is in its early stages and we can't really describe each condition to say what are the early stages. But what one shouldn't do is to go back into the house to retrieve possessions, handbags, etcetera. The advice that we give is to shout, to get out and not go round opening doors and windows unless necessary. By opening more doors and windows then you're actually providing oxygen to the fire which will feed the fire and make it worse.

I: What precautions should we take to prevent fires happening?

F: We should ensure that cigarettes have been extinguished safely into ashtrays and not left balancing on the edge. We should not smoke in bed because that is a danger place that we fall asleep with a cigarette. We talked about cooking appliances - we should never leave a cooking pan unattended. Electrical appliances, they should be checked regularly. We should check plugs on a regular, perhaps three monthly, basis to make sure that the wiring is not becoming loose. Children with matches - children must be taught from an early age the dangers of fire. Temptation shouldn't be left in front of the children. Matches and lighters should be removed … kept in a high place.

Exercise 11 Talk about it.

See if students can guess the meaning of the proverbs and idioms. Refer to similar ones in the students' own languages if you can. Ask if students can give an example of situations when they might use each of them.

EXTRA ACTIVITIES

1 Find your partner

Write a number of third conditional sentences in large handwriting on separate strips of paper and tear each in half into two clauses, e.g: *If I hadn't run out of money//we could have taken a taxi.* or *I would have been extremely angry if//he hadn't turned up.* (The *if* clause can come either at the end or at the beginning). Jumble the strips and distribute them round the class so that each student has half a sentence.

Ask students to read out the first half of a sentence and the student who thinks he or she has the second half has to read it out. Occasionally more than one alternative may be possible.

2 Song: *London's burning*

The following traditional children's song has its origin from the Great Fire of London. The words can be copied onto the board and students may like to sing it. It is usually sung as a 'round'.

UNIT 25 The Verger

Suggested lesson break: after Exercise 7

Ask students if they have ever heard of Somerset Maugham (pronounced /mɔːm/), and if they know anything about the sort of books and stories he wrote. Ask them to read the short introduction 'About the author'. Explain *shrewd* (intelligent, showing good practical judgement).

LITERATURE

Refer to the glossary to explain what a verger is. Ask students to look at the illustration and ask: *When do you think the story takes place? How can you tell?* (the style of man's clothes, the old briefcase). *In which country or town do you think it is set? What do you think the story will be about?* (Money? Church life?)

Read the introduction aloud to the students to set the context to the story. Explain *vicar* and *a month's notice*.

Exercise 1 Guess the meaning.

Play the tape or ask students to read the story quietly to themselves, trying to guess the meaning of the words in the list and noting down any other words or expressions they do not understand, e.g: *abstainer* (someone who doesn't drink alcohol at all), *latitude* (freedom), *come-down* (a fall in social status), *move with the times* (be modern and keep up with the latest fashions), *takings* (earnings), *a rough idea* (some idea), *disarming* (gaining trust especially through friendliness).

Exercise 2 Read and choose the best answer.

Students read through the questions and reread the relevant parts of the text.

KEY

1c 2a 3c 4b 5b

Exercise 3 Read and think.

Ask students to discuss the questions in pairs or groups.

SUGGESTED ANSWERS

In what way would you say Albert had good business sense?
He spotted a need and acted on it promptly; he bought the shop before he left his job at the church; he saw an opportunity and expanded on it; he gave personal time and attention to all of his shops.

What is ironic about his story?
He was able to be so successful and make so much money as a tobacconist and newsagent without being able to read and write, and yet it was this very lack of ability that lost him his job as a verger, an unskilled job, in which the need to read and write was not so important.

Exercise 4 Read and analyse.

Ask students to work individually.

KEY

1 a shop 2 setting up a shop to sell tobacco and sweets 3 the shop 4 setting up in business as a tobacconist and newsagent 5 his ten shops 6 the week's takings 7 the money he had on deposit (the thirty thousands pounds) 8 sign some forms 9 read and write my name

Exercise 5 Study the words.

KEY

(Line numbers given in brackets)

1 reflectively (15) 2 do very well (19) 3 making money hand over fist (37) 4 anxiety (57)
5 a troubled look (61) 6 distinguished (62)
7 a trifle sharply (72) 8 extraordinary (80)
9 obstinate (83) 10 amassed (88)

Exercise 6 SPEECHWORK

Refer students back to the expression *a rough idea* and point out the pronunciation of the *ough* in *rough*. Ask what other words students know which are spelt (though not necessarily pronounced) in this way.

Draw students' attention to the words in the book and ask them how to say the words. Play the tape for the students to check their pronunciation. Pay special attention to the differentiation between *through* /θruː/ and *thorough* /ˈθʌrə/.

Exercise 7 STYLE

Ask what students noticed about the style of writing in the story and what sort of things indicate that it is slightly 'old-fashioned' in style. Elicit one or two of the more formal words in the story, e.g: *amassed*, and ask students to give an informal equivalent. Students then do the exercise individually.

KEY

1e 2h 3i 4b 5g 6n 7f 8l 9c 10j 11m 12a 13d 14k

SUGGESTED LESSON BREAK

STUDY POINT

Refer back to the examples in the story: *a little shop to let that looked as though it would exactly suit him* and *The manager stared at him as though he were a prehistoric monster*. Explain that it is also possible to use *as if*. Ask the students to read through the notes in the Study Point.

Some British speakers use *like* instead of *as if/as though* in the same context, e.g: *She looked as if she was going to cry/She looked like she was going to cry*. At this stage it is probably best to avoid this complication.

Exercise 8 PRACTICE

KEY

1 as if/though she was going to burst into tears.
2 as if/though they had a secret to hide.
3 as if/though I was going to be sick.
4 as if/though they were having a row.
5 as if/though she was mad.

Exercise 9 VOCABULARY

Remind students of the words and expressions to do with money which occurred in Unit 21 and revise these briefly. Explain that the words in the box are also to do with money but have more to do with business and finance. Then ask students to work individually or in pairs to complete the paragraph.

KEY

set up in business, run a business, for let, bank loan, interest rate, make, invest, takings

Encourage a general discussion about famous people who have set up in business and either been very successful, or lost money. If students are interested, this can extend to a discussion of the current interest rate in their country and how easy it is to get an overdraft, a bank loan or a mortgage on a home.

LISTENING

Exercise 10 Before you listen

Ask students if they remember where the 1992 Olympics were held (Barcelona) and whether their country/ies won any medals. Explain that Britain won very few gold medals, one of which was in a speed cycling event, the 4km pursuit, which involves two competitors racing each other round a track. This particular achievement was interesting in that the record was beaten so convincingly. The reason for this is ascribed to the design of the bicycle that the cyclist, Chris

Boardman used. The bicycle was designed by Lotus, the racing car manufacturer.

Draw a picture of a bicycle on the blackboard and get students to name a few basic parts, e.g. *frame, wheel, spokes, handlebars, chain, mudguard, saddle, gears*. Ask students to look at the picture of the bicycle in their books and to say what makes this bicycle different from other racing bikes they have seen. (The frame looks different, the 'fork' is not made of a circular metal tube but something much flatter, there are no spokes on the back wheel).

Exercise 11

Play the interview question by question, going back to check any difficult parts before going on to the next question. At the end you can play the whole tape through and ask students just to listen with their books shut. Some words and expressions which may need preteaching or writing on the board are: *carbon fibre, steel tube, airflow, latch on to it, registered, interested in backing it, picked up on it, wind tunnel, not a desperately realistic price* and *rosy future.*

TAPESCRIPT

I = Interviewer, M = Mike

I: Tell me, Mike, how is the bike different from other bikes of its type?

M: Well, if you imagine the normal bicycle. Everybody's seen a bicycle. It's a collection of round steel tubes, two wheels, mounted in a fork at the front. Now the Lotus is, first of all, a monocoque. That means it's one single form. So instead of having the individual tubes, you've just got one smooth shape. I mean, an electric guitar is probably the nearest shape to it, and that allows for a much better air flow and an easier bicycle to construct.

I: And what is it actually made of?

M: It's made of carbon fibre. Carbon fibre is basically expensive black glass fibre.

I: Is it much lighter?

M: Yes, carbon fibre, if you analyse strength and weights and everything, is the strongest, lightest structural material in the world that we can use.

I: And obviously this makes it a much faster bike. How much faster was it for Chris when he was riding in the race?

M: Well, the test, the early test in the wind tunnel and subsequent tests by the rider suggested it was worth ten to twelve seconds over that four and a half minute period, the four kilometre ride in comparison to a traditional tubular steel bicycle.

I: But if the bicycle was so good, why didn't people latch on to it earlier? I mean I understand that this is not ... this hasn't been a new item for you, that you thought of it some time ago. Why did it take so long before they caught on to this?

M: Well, as you said, the original design goes back to December '82 when I registered the design for the original carbon fibre moulded bicycle. I took the bicycle to various cycle shows, I raced it. It was seen by everybody within the cycle industry and, I mean, nobody said it wasn't any good but really nobody was interested in backing it and taking it any further and really nothing happened.

I: But eventually somebody was interested. It was Lotus, wasn't it?

M: That's right, it was Lotus who were on my doorstep. A friend of mine, Rudi Toman, who both rides bicycles and drives racing cars for Lotus borrowed the bicycle, took it into work one day and that's the beginning of the end, as it were. They just loved the bicycle.

I: And the story goes from there.

M: That's right. They picked up on it. They knew how to make it. They knew how to improve it. So the bicycle became much better as a result of going to Lotus than it could ever have done if it had stayed in the cycle trade as such.

I: It sounds as if Lotus and yourself must have put a lot of money into the development of the design. Is that right?

M: Well over the years I haven't counted, because it's my hobby and you spend all you've got in your pocket on your hobby. Lotus again, I suspect, have spent between fifty and a hundred thousand, probably on the entire development - wind tunnel research, the whole lot, yes.

I: But that's not what the bike would cost to make. I mean, how much would the bike that he cycled and won in the Olympics cost to produce?

M: If you wanted one of those bicycles at the present, because the production techniques are very unsophisticated in terms of volume, ten to fifteen thousand pounds, you know, which is, you know, not a desperately realistic price for a bicycle. At the end of the day, once the bike is a production bicycle, then three thousand, which is, you know, a lot for a bicycle, but that's what good bicycles cost today, so that's entirely realistic.

I: So it's a very rosy future for Lotus, you feel?

M: The potential is there, yes. There are still lots of problems to solve - engineering, design problems to make it a practical bike without spoiling its appearance and production problems because it's such a new design it needs new processes.

I: And do you reckon it will make you a millionaire?

M: I don't particularly want it to. I mean, I'm satisfied it's won the Olympics. I gave up worrying about money long ago. Yes, it will probably make me rich if they sell a lot of bicycles.

EXTRA ACTIVITIES

1 Memory test

Select a passage from the story, e.g: lines 24 - 40, and write it out again with certain words missing for students to complete. Make sure that all books are closed first. These can be photocopied and given out to each pair. Give students a time limit and see which pair can complete the text most accurately in that time.

2 Success story

Ask students to do some research to find a 'success story' which has been in the news in recent years in their country. It could be a story about a new type of shop, bicycle, car, kitchen gadget, health food or anything else they can think of. Students should prepare a report outlining where the idea originated, how it developed, how the business started, who financed it and what were the stages towards its success.

CHECK 5 Units 21-25

(For advice on handling this section, see the notes for Check 1 Units 1–5.)

KEY

Ex. 1 1 jealous 2 selfish 3 generous 4 extravagant 5 loyal 6 obsessive 7 stingy 8 envious

Ex. 2

1	uncomfortable	comfort
2	tasteless	taste
3	disorganised	organisation
4	inefficient	efficiency
5	unexciting	excitement
6	unimaginative	imagination
7	unintelligent	intelligence
8	careless	care/carefulness

Ex. 3 1 in 2 with 3 for 4 of 5 about 6 in 7 to 8 with 9 for 10 to

Ex. 4 1 'll/will wake up, shout 2 left, would you do 3 telephone, will be able to 4 would go, wasn't/ weren't 5 peel, 'll take 6 wouldn't work , paid 7 'll enjoy, like 8 wouldn't stand, was/were

Ex. 5
1 provided that there was someone with me.
2 even if I had an instructor with me.
3 provided that we just went to the cinema.
4 provided that the pay was very good.
5 even if the business was likely to make money.

Ex. 6 1 provided 2 as long as 3 unless 4 even if 5 provided

Ex. 7
1 I was very impressed with the Chinese gymnasts on television last night.
2 I didn't think much of England's performance in the World Cup match.
3 I wasn't too impressed with the new Ferrari.
4 They/The travel company should have given us back the air fare/our money.
5 He shouldn't have been riding his bicycle at night without any lights.

Ex. 8
1 You should have written to them immediately.
2 You should have read the small print before signing the contract.
3 She shouldn't have been listening to us while she was pretending to study.
4 You shouldn't have mixed it with water instead of milk./You should have mixed it with milk instead of water.
5 I should have checked the oil before leaving.
6 He shouldn't have been smoking in bed.

Ex. 9
1 Owing to the high interest rate, people are falling into bad debts.
2 The train was very crowded, but on the whole we had quite a comfortable journey to Moscow.
3 Owing to pressure from the public, the government was forced to change the laws about shop opening hours.
4 She fell and twisted her ankle. Consequently, she couldn't play in the hockey match.
5 Factories in many parts of the country are cutting back their production. As a result, skilled workers are losing their jobs. (or) As a result of factories cutting down, skilled workers ..
6 Because of the large number of complaints the company had received about him, he lost his job as a travel representative.

Ex. 10
1 If I had known that Hungarian was going to be so difficult, I would never have started to learn it.
2 If he hadn't used his credit cards so much, he wouldn't have been/wouldn't be so badly in debt.
3 What sort of career would you have had if you had left school at sixteen?
4 I would have helped Mary with the barbecue if she had asked me.
5 What would you have done if the fire had spread to the stairs?
6 Sally would have married Peter if he had proposed to her.
7 You would have got your money back if you had kept the receipt.
8 If Sheila had known that the brakes were faulty, she wouldn't have bought the car.
9 I would have been here earlier if I hadn't missed the bus.
10 I don't know what I would have done if Alan hadn't arrived with his car.

Ex. 11
2d I wish we had a balcony.
3e If only I didn't have such big feet.
4a If only I'd looked after it better.
5c I wish I'd asked for her telephone number.
6b I wish I was/were able to sing.
7f If only I'd worn/was wearing more comfortable shoes.

Ex. 12 1 as if 2 like 3 -- 4 as if 5 like 6 as if 7 as if 8 -

UNIT 26 Tomorrow's world

Suggested lesson break: after Exercise 6

BACKGROUND NOTES

The illustration: This montage was the illustration which accompanied a major article in the British national Sunday newspaper, *The Independent on Sunday*. The article was titled 'How long have we got?'. Some of the images are ambiguous and it might be interesting for the students to try to interpret them. The illustration

shows a domestic cat (= mankind? endangered species?) parachuting into a world which seems on the verge of destruction. On the globe the cat is surrounded anti-clockwise by:
-a pile of motorcars in the USA (= overcrowding of cities, air pollution, destruction of the environment, materialism, unhealthy lifestyles, etc)
-burning rainforests in Latin America and a painting of clouds in the sky (= damage to the ozone layer, changing climate, global warming?)
-overpopulation in the African continent (= famine, poverty, disease, civil war, corruption)
-factories and houses all over Europe, Russia and Scandinavia (= pollution, over-urbanisation, destruction of the environment?)
billion: one thousand million (1,000,000,000)

Exercise 1 Talk about it.

Ask students to look at the picture and say what they can see in it and what significance they think the images have.

Discuss the questions and list any new vocabulary on the board as it comes up. Students may want to list other serious world problems they are worried about, e.g: unemployment, civil war, racism, recession, etc.

Exercise 2 VOCABULARY

Practise the pronunciation of the multi-syllable words so that students know where the main stress falls. Point out the pronunciation of *drought* /draʊt/, *resources* /rɪ'zɔːsɪz/ and *species* /'spiːʃiːz/.

KEY
1 acid (rain) 2 famine 3 overpopulation 4 drought 5 natural resources 6 pollution 7 endangered species 8 (nuclear) waste

Exercise 3

KEY
2 In order to protect elephants, which are an endangered species.
3 Because of drought.
4 Because of famine and drought.
5 In order to reduce/avoid overpopulation.
6 Because of nuclear waste.
7 Because of acid rain.
8 In order to reduce/avoid pollution.

READING

Draw students' attention to the topic of overpopulation and ask them which countries/ cities are suffering from this problem.

Ask: *Which cities in the world have the largest populations at the moment?* Refer students to the chart headed 'The expanding cities' contained in the article 'Population fears' and ask which facts and figures they find most interesting/surprising.

(Note: The chart, which is taken from a national newspaper, uses the alternative spelling of São Paolo i.e. São Paulo.)

Ask students to make a list in pairs of what they think are the consequences of overpopulation for the world as a whole and what can be done to reduce it. Collect their ideas on the board.

Exercise 4 Read and analyse.

Ask students to read the introduction to the text (in bold type) and the first paragraph and to complete the graph.

KEY
1950: 2.5 billion
1992: 5.4 billion
2025: 8.5 billion
2050: 10 billion

Exercise 5

You may like to divide the reading of the text into four sections, corresponding to the headings for note taking. (Section 1: paragraph 2, Section 2: paragraphs 3, 4 and 5, Section 3: paragraph 6, Section 4: paragraphs 7 and 8.)

Divide students into four groups and allot each group a section to read. Tell students that they may use a dictionary if they wish, but they should be prepared to summarise the content of their section in their own words for the rest of the class.

After they have all finished reading and made notes, select a good student in each group to summarise the section she/he has read. The others in the same group can assist where necessary.

When the whole text has been summarised, ask each group to say which words in their portion of the text were new to them. Pool these on the blackboard and make sure all students are familiar with their meaning. Point out those words which are of general importance.

Exercise 6 SPEECHWORK

Refer back to the spelling and pronunciation of *resources* mentioned in Exercise 2. Ask students to read out the words listed in their books. Afterwards, play the tape for students to check their pronunciation.

KEY
source, pour, your, mourn

Finally, ask if students can think of any other words with this spelling.

SUGGESTED LESSON BREAK

GRAMMAR FOCUS

Ask students to look at the first paragraph of the text again and to tell you what tense (apart from the present, past and future simple) is used and ask them to find another example of that tense in the text (paragraph 4: *we will have used up*).

Explain that the tense relates to the future but has a sense of completeness about it. Contrast the two sentences:

1 *We'll redecorate our house in 1995.* (i.e. We have decided to start redecorating in 1995. There is no indication as to how long it will take.)
2 *We'll have redecorated our house by 1995.* (i.e. It is fixed that before the beginning of 1995 the decoration will be complete. It may or may not have already started at the time of speaking.)

Read through the notes in the Focus box with the students and do some choral repetition of the contracted form, e.g: *it'll have reduced by, I'll have finished it.* Give examples of sentences in which the prepositions *in* and *by* are used with a future time adverbial, e.g:

We will have used up the entire reserves in four years' time.
We will have used up the world's energy resources by the year 2025.

Ask what the negative of this tense would be. (*won't have* + past participle)

Exercise 7 PRACTICE

KEY

1 They will have finished the new motorway by the end of the year.
2 There's no point coming next week. We won't have completed the work by then.
3 In six months' time I hope I will have found somewhere to live.
4 By the year 2000, most car owners will have changed to unleaded petrol.
5 I still won't have finished my education in five years' time.
6 This time next year we will have elected a new Prime Minister.

Ask students to make statements about themselves or their own countries beginning with the following phrases:

This time next week/month/year...
In ... years' time
By the year ...

Exercise 8

Ask students to look at the figures for the population increase in China. Read out the example, giving the two alternative lead-ins to the sentence provided. You may also like to add a statement reflecting the numerical rise between 1970 and 1988, using the past tense, e.g: *Between 1970 and 1988 the population increased to 1,244 million from 925 million. In 2010 it will have increased to 1,595 million* (or *by another 351 million*).

Discuss with students if they feel that any of the statistics seem unlikely and whether any political/economical/scientific developments since their publication in 1990 have made or will make any significant difference to them.

Exercise 9 LISTENING

Refer students to the statistics on the number of motor vehicles in the previous exercise. Ask if they have any idea how many cars are on the road in their country every day. Do they know of any plans to ease traffic in cities? What do they think can be done? List a few of their suggestions on the board.

Explain that students are going to listen to a news programme in which a conservation expert is giving his opinions on car pollution on the telephone. His voice has been directly recorded from the phone.

Play the tape in short sections to enable students to summarise what the man says under each section. Words which may cause problems are: *global warming, unacceptable, approach, congestion, tackle the problem, establish a maximum ceiling, pedestrian, subsidies/subsidise, allocate, perceptions, privilege, overwhelming extent.*

Teachers who have access to three cassettes may like to split the listening into three parts so that different parts of the class listen to the different parts of the recording. Students then join up, one from each group, and the activity works as an information gap exercise.

TAPESCRIPT

I = Interviewer, S = Steve

I: And now to talk to us about car pollution, we have Steve Elsworth on the line. Hello there, Steve. Can you give us your views?

S: Most of the global environmental problems which we face at the moment are caused by too many people doing the same activity, and this is certainly true of the car. At the moment, there are about 450 million cars in the world and they're increasing at the rate of one car per second coming on to the world's roads. By the year 2010 the number of cars on the road will have doubled and because of the impact of cars, firstly on air pollution and secondly as contributing to global warming, we believe that something has got to be done to slow this rate of growth or the environmental consequences will be disastrous. I think that the personal use of the car, in ten or fifteen years' time will have become as unacceptable as smoking is in public places.

In the UK the government is taking an unusual approach. It's not going to do anything about traffic congestion. It has estimated that in twenty years the amount of traffic on Britain's roads will have increased by between 80 and 140%. And they believe that that's the reality and there's nothing they can do about it. Whereas, in fact, in other countries they are beginning to tackle the problem and they are trying to establish a maximum ceiling for traffic above which it's regarded as being unacceptable. And if you look at some of the big cities in Europe, they'll have become car-free within five or ten years. I know that Amsterdam is going to become car-free, Vienna is going to become car-free, Frankfurt is experimenting with it and certain cities in Italy, too.

The problem with traffic and transport is that it's a very long-term problem and I think that there'll have to be two or three different mechanisms by which we try and solve the transport crisis. The first one is that we need to redesign our city centres to make them pedestrian areas and not allow cars into the middle of city areas. This will force the introduction of a better public transport. And cities will also become nicer places to live without the car. The second one is that we'll have to change the financial subsidies which we give to private transport. Huge amounts of money are allocated to road building, to subsidise car factories to subsidising oil imports and that will have to change. And the third thing which I think is that we will have to change people's perceptions. In ten or fifteen years' time people's ideas of travelling will have changed completely, I think. People will no longer believe that it's their right to drive cars around in millions all over the country and that it's a privilege and a pleasure and that people will still be able to drive their cars but not to the same overwhelming extent that they do at the moment.

Exercise 10 Talk about it.

Point out to students that the accent is on achievement, or possibly lack of achievement, by the year 2025 (hence the future perfect tense) rather than what will be happening in the year 2025.

EXTRA ACTIVITIES

1 Me and my future achievements

Students copy the following chart:

ME	in 2 months' time	in 2 years' time	in 10 years' time
education			
work			
travel			
home			

Ask students to write as many predictions as they can in the four areas according to the three time frames suggested. (They may add different areas and change the time frames if they wish), e.g: *In two months' time I'll have finished this English course./ In two years' time I'll have started at university.* Ask students to read out their entries.

2 Tomorrow's world: project

Students can prepare and assemble their own collage to illustrate 'Tomorrow's world'. They can take pictures from magazines and write a caption and a factual statement about the future to accompany each picture. This may take a number of weeks while pictures are selected and captions written.

UNIT 27 Visions of the future

Suggested lesson break: after Exercise 4

BACKGROUND NOTES

The Great Pyramid: The pyramids in Egypt were the burial sites of the kings of Egypt. The Great Pyramid of King Cheops (2680BC) is the largest pyramid ever built and is one of the Seven Wonders of the World.

Aztec Temple: the Aztecs were an American Indian tribe who lived in Mexico and were conquered by the Spanish in 1519.

Exercise 1 Talk about it.

Discuss the picture with students and elicit what they know, if anything, about Virtual Reality. Introduce the words *helmet* and *screen*. Find out if any students have seen or used a VR set and ask them to explain how it works and what the person sees.

Exercise 2 READING

Ask students to read the text in three sections of two paragraphs at a time, noting down any words or expressions they find difficult. After everyone has finished reading each section, ask individual students to tell you any words they have noted. Explain these and then ask other students to try and interpret them in their own words. Collect new words on the board as you work through the sections. After reading the complete text, work with the whole class to extract the answers to the comprehension task and write the notes on the board.

KEY

Virtual Reality

1 You have to wear a helmet and a special glove.
2 You are surrounded by a 3-D computer-generated screen.
3 You can see things from different angles
4 You can move around.

Exercise 3 Read and answer.

Students complete the answers to the two questions individually.

Exercise 4 Study the words.

KEY
1 amazing/exotic 2 clumsy 3 manipulate
4 miniature 5 potential 6 damaging 7 mimic

Spend a few minutes discussing the usage of each word.

Exercise 5 Talk about it.

Ask students to form groups and discuss the questions. Ask them to make a list of five other uses they can think of, as well as a 'pleasure trip'. Collect the ideas from each group at the end of the discussion.

(For more detailed work on the uses of VR, see Extra Activity 1 below.)

SUGGESTED LESSON BREAK

Exercise 6 PHRASAL VERBS: *pick*

Refer students back to the sentence in the third paragraph of the text: *'You can 'look behind' computer-generated objects, pick them up and examine them ...'*. Ask them if they can think of any other uses of the phrasal verb *pick up* or if they can think of any other phrasal verbs with *pick*. Then ask students to do the exercise.

KEY
1 at 2 up 3 out 4 up 5 on 6 up

Ask students to say in which of these sentences the verb cannot be separated from the preposition (*pick at, pick out, pick up* (of a film), *pick on*).

Ask them to rephrase Sentence 2 so that the preposition is next to the verb.

STUDY POINT

Ask students to read through the information in the box. Explain the meaning of the prepositions:
- *By* usually answers the question *How...?*
- *Instead of doing this, do that* means 'Although you normally do this (or 'Although you are doing this now'), I want you to do that'.
- *She did this without doing that* means 'She did this but she didn't do that' with the implication that the action is somewhat unusual.

PRACTICE Exercise 7

Working with the whole class, ask individual students to join the sentences. Explain that the completed sentences 4, 5 and 6 sound better if the parts are reversed.

KEY
2 He went out without taking any money with him.
3 We got to the station just on time by taking a short cut.
4 Why don't you help me instead of complaining?
5 Guess how much I paid for this jacket without looking at the price tag.
6 He damaged his eyes by working too long at his computer screen.
7 She made a speech without looking at her notes.

Exercise 8 VOCABULARY

First ask students what sort of gadgets they have in their homes. List these on the board and then ask students to work in pairs to match the two lists, A and B, in their books.

KEY
portable television, video recorder, electric toothbrush, sound system, personal stereo, food processor, exercise bike, coffee machine, tin opener, juice extractor

Exercise 9 SPEECHWORK

KEY
Adjectives: portable, electric, personal
Nouns used as adjectives: video, sound, food, exercise, coffee, tin, juice

Play the tape for students to note the stressed words.

TAPESCRIPT
PORTABLE TELEVISION VIDEO recorder
ELECTRIC TOOTHBRUSH SOUND system
PERSONAL STEREO FOOD processor
EXERCISE bike COFFEE machine TIN opener JUICE extractor

KEY
Equal stress on both words: portable television, electric toothbrush, personal stereo
Main stress on first word: video recorder, sound system, food processor, exercise bike, coffee machine, tin opener, juice extractor (i.e. all those with nouns used as adjectives).

Play the tape again so students can repeat the words.

Exercise 10 LISTENING

Explain that students are going to listen to an interview with a young couple who are discussing which of their gadgets they like and don't like and why. Play the tape once only and say that you just want students to listen for gist. Tell them that the information doesn't necessarily come in the same order as the headings.

TAPESCRIPT
INTERVIEWER: Have you got a lot of gadgets in the house?
DAVE: Yes, far too many. And none of them are much use.
LOUISE: Oh, that's not true. What about my electric toothbrush? I certainly wouldn't want to live without that.
DAVE: Oh, yeah, OK, that is a good one, yes.
LOUISE: I mean it's wonderful now. When I go to

the dentist she says 'Your teeth are so much better, so much cleaner,' and I say, 'I know, it's the electric toothbrush, you see.'

DAVE: I agree. The electric toothbrush is good.

LOUISE: And there's another thing that's proved useful, and that's the food processor.

DAVE: You reckon?

LOUISE: Yes. It saves so much time, especially when it comes to soups. You can do them in no time at all, just throw everything in, press the button and woof, it's all done in a second.

DAVE: I wish you'd use it more often to make pancakes, though.

LOUISE: What's stopping you from using it to make pancakes? Anyway, talking of favourite gadgets, what about you and your video recorder?

DAVE: Well, yeah, I have to say I think that's one of the best inventions ever. I don't know how I managed without it.

LOUISE: Dave's always watching old videos.

DAVE: Yes, I have to admit, though, that it's an awful waste of time, very dangerous. I've got all these films and football matches piled on shelves ...

LOUISE: ... that you feel you've got to watch.

DAVE: Yeah, I know. It is a bit of a time waster, but I like it.

INTERVIEWER: So, is there any gadget you don't like?

LOUISE: Yes, come to think of it, the juice extractor.

DAVE: Oh, yeah, what a useless present that was! It makes nice fruit juice, but what a palaver, all those bits you have to take apart and clean, and all you get is a thimbleful of juice. It's more trouble than it's worth, isn't it?

LOUISE: We never use it now. Do you remember the time when I forgot to clean it and all the fruit skins went bad inside?

DAVE: Oh, yes, I do ...

Exercise 11 Talk about it.

Ask students which of the gadgets from this unit they would like to have if they could afford them and which they wouldn't like to have and why.

EXTRA ACTIVITIES

1 Virtual Reality: the benefits

Students form groups to make a list of possible educational uses of Virtual Reality. They should think of all the school subjects, e.g: history, geography, art, biology, etc, and think of one way in which VR would improve the knowledge of that subject.

2 The *without* game

Students give each other instructions to perform actions including a *without* ... restriction. e.g: Draw a picture of a house without lifting your pencil; Answer questions in a interview without saying 'yes' or 'no'; Stare at another person for one minute without blinking; Speak for one minute on a subject without stopping or hesitating, etc. Students should each try to think of a similar instruction of their own.

UNIT 28 Valley of the kings

Suggested lesson break: after Exercise 4

The texts

Write the word *archaeology* on the board and say the word out loud. Ask if any of the students can explain in English what it means. Ask students what famous archaeological discoveries they know about and if there are any archaeological sites in their country.

Find out if any of the students have ever been on an archaeological dig and, if so, where it was and what they had to do. Try and elicit words like *dig, clean* and *record* (v).

Ask students to read the short texts at the top of the page while you write the following questions. Then ask: *What and where is the Valley of the Kings? Who was Tutankhamun? How long must you stay if you want to join the dig in Luxor? What sort of work are you expected to do? What hours do you work? What other activities and trips are there? Do you have to pay for your own accommodation and food?*

Exercise 1 LISTENING DIALOGUE

Ask students to cover the words of the dialogue and to listen for the answers to the following questions as you play the tape: *What is Julie planning to do for the summer? What is Dan planning to do? What illness do they mention?*

Play the tape a first time to check these questions. Then tell students to follow the text while you play the tape a second time. Pause to explain any colloquial expressions students are not familiar with, e.g: *Just think, No such luck, worse luck.*

Check through the *True/False* questions with the class as a whole.

Ask students which words or sentences in the dialogue confirm their answers. Give a brief explanation of the future continuous tense and how it is used, but leave detailed discussion and practice until later in the lesson.

Exercise 2 SPEECHWORK

Write the words *archaeology* and *archaeological* on the board and ask different students to pronounce them. Point out how the main stress shifts to another syllable for the adjectival form. Explain the rule, that adjectives ending with the suffix *-ical* have their main stress on the syllable before the suffix, e.g: *TOPic/TOPical, psyCHOlogy/psychoLOGical.* Ask students to take turns to read the words in the list aloud, then play the tape for checking.

COMMUNICATION FOCUS

Go through the table of responses with the students. When it comes to the negative responses, you may like to point out that although *I think not* and *I expect not* are possible responses, the other versions *I don't think so* and *I don't expect so* are more common. Draw comparisons with the students' own language if possible.

Practise the responses chorally and individually to make sure that students are saying them correctly with a fall-rise intonation pattern, e.g:

I don't think so.

Exercise 3 PRACTICE

Do the exercise with the whole class. Accept the alternative suggestions in brackets provided that students can give a suitable context.

KEY
1 I hope not. (I hope so.)
2 No, I don't think so.
3 I'm afraid so.
4 I think so. (I don't think so.)
5 I expect so.
6 I'm afraid not.
7 I suppose not.

Follow up this exercise with a few questions about the weather, travel, the weekend, e.g: *Do you think it'll rain tomorrow? Are you going abroad this summer? Are you going away this weekend?*

Exercise 4

With the class as a whole, ask students to give you some examples for each category and write these on the board, e.g.

Famous person: Bill Clinton
Sporting event: next year's Wimbledon; the next World or UEFA Cup
Political event: your next election, etc.

Ask students to discuss these while you go round and listen.

SUGGESTED LESSON BREAK

GRAMMAR FOCUS

Ask students to find examples of different ways of expressing the future in the dialogue, e.g:

Present continuous: *Are you going away in the summer?/I'm going on an archaeological dig.*
Future with *will: Won't it be great?*
Going to future: *You're not going to catch malaria, are you?*
Future continuous: *This time next week we'll be doing our exams; we won't be working in the heat of the day; apparently we'll be going to other places as well; I'll be filling shelves in our local supermarket.*

Ask if they can explain why the future continuous is used where it is and not the simple *will* future .

Present the two sentences a) and b) from the Grammar Focus box. Ask students first to explain the difference in meaning between them and then to match them with either Sentence 1 or 2.

KEY
a2 b1

Ask students to read through the explanations and examples in the rest of the box.

Point out that although the present continuous for future use can often be used as an equivalent of the future continuous (e.g: *What are you doing for Christmas/What will you be doing for Christmas*?) the future continuous must be used with certain future time adverbials, i.e: *this time next year, in two years' time.* You cannot say: ~~*I'm working in France this time next year.*~~

Exercise 5 PRACTICE

Ask different students to ask you the two first questions to check that they are producing the correct tense. Set them to work in pairs. Tell students to remember their partner's answers so that they can report back, e.g: *Luisa will be going to her grandparents' for Christmas./Gianfranco will be spending his summer holiday working in his father's shop.*

Exercise 6 LISTENING

Make sure students listen to the whole of the conversation once before trying to frame any answers. In many cases, it is the following response which gives the clue to the question. Play the tape a second time, pausing to ask individual students to provide a suitable question, using one of the verbs in the box.

TAPESCRIPT AND KEY
JULIE: I'm really pleased. I've been accepted to go on an archaeological dig.
STUDENT: (leave) *When will you be leaving?*
JULIE: At the beginning of July. On the fourth, actually.
STUDENT: (go) *Where will you be going?*
JULIE: To Luxor in Egypt.
STUDENT: (do) *What will you be doing?*
JULIE: Digging and drawing and labelling. All that sort of thing.
STUDENT: (work) *How long will you be working every day?*
JULIE: About six hours, from dawn until about two in the afternoon.
STUDENT: (sleep) *And where will you be sleeping?*
JULIE: In tents, I think. We have to take sleeping bags.
STUDENT: (earn) *How much will you be earning?*
JULIE: Nothing. It's voluntary work.
STUDENT: (come back) *When will you be coming back?*
JULIE: In time for college, I expect.

Exercise 7 VOCABULARY

Ask students to tell you what Julie's last response was in Exercise 6 (*In time for college*) and also to find a couple of expressions with *time* in the dialogue in Exercise 1 (*this time next week, not all the time*).

Do the matching exercise with the whole group.

KEY

1e 2f 3b 4c 5g 6a 7d 8h

Give extra practice of these expressions by writing the gapped sentences below on the board. Alternatively, read them out with a tap on the desk at the point in the sentence where students are to supply the expression.

1 We can't go through passport control together, we have to go through ... (*one at a time*)
2 I hope we get there ... to get a good seat. (*in time*)
3 ... I wonder if I'm doing the right job but when I see the finished product I realise I am. (*At times*)
4 I've told you ... to put the milk back in the fridge! (*time after time*)
5 Why do you keep complaining ... ? (*all the time*)
6 There's no sugar left so you'll have to do without it ... (*for the time being*)
7 I hope the train's ... . I don't want to hang about on the platform in the cold. (*on time*)
8 ... I thought he was lying but then I realised he was telling the truth. (*For a time*)

Now divide the *time* expressions among students and ask them to make sentences of their own.

Exercise 8 WRITING

Remind students of the layout and presentation of formal letters by referring back to Unit 5. Before they write, ask students to work briefly in pairs to plan realistic details of their journey, e.g: the name of the airline and flight number, and also to think of effective ways of being recognised at an airport.

EXTRA ACTIVITIES

1 How well do you know your partner?

Students form pairs. The teacher writes on the board five or six different times of the day, e.g: 7 a.m., 9 a.m., 12 noon, 6 p.m., 10 p.m. Students copy these down and then make notes against each time saying what they think their partner will be doing at these times the following day. When they have completed them, they read them out for their partner to confirm or correct as appropriate.

2 Write a dialogue

Students write a dialogue on a suggested topic, e.g: weekend activities, plans for holidays, future work plans, etc. Their aim is to build into the dialogue as many of the conversational responses from the Communication Focus box as possible without sounding stilted. The conversation must contain at least five or six exchanges between the speakers. Students read their completed dialogue aloud.

3 Wordmaps

Students take a multi-syllable word similar to those in the Speechwork exercise and see how many words they can derive from it, using a dictionary if necessary, e.g:

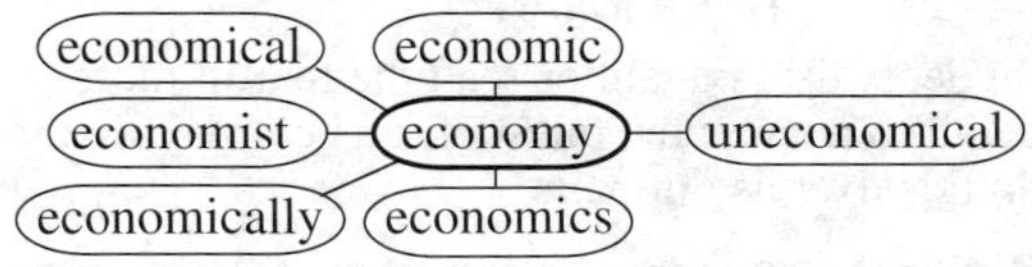

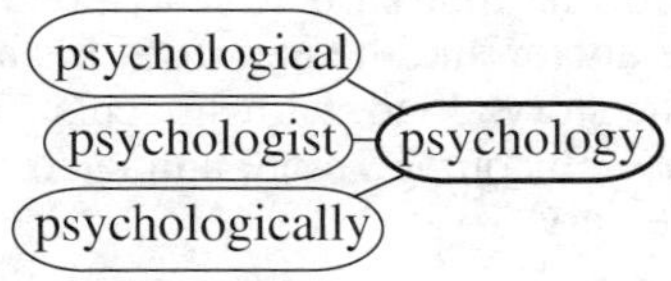

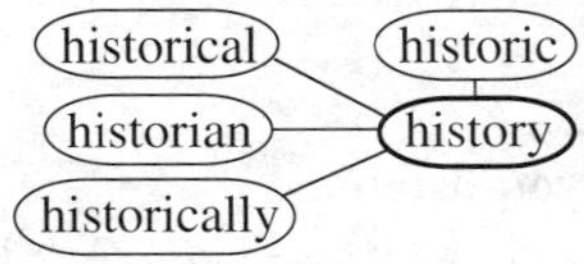

UNIT 29 Compassion circuit

Suggested lesson break: after Exercise 5

Exercise 1 About you

Ask the questions to the whole group. Refer to any films and books that have featured robots. Ask if students know of any industrial uses of robots. Ask what they think might be sinister or menacing about the idea of having a robot in the house.

Exercise 2 Before you read

Give some examples of sentences with the word *circuit* in them to illustrate all the different meanings of the word as they are given in the dictionary entry.

Ask students to look at the picture to make the decision about the meaning of *circuit* in this story (a complete circular path of an electric current).

Exercise 3 LITERATURE

Ask students to say what they think the title means in relation to a robot. (*compassion* = sympathy for the suffering of others which causes a desire to help them). Ask students to read or listen to the extract silently, noting down any words they do not know. It may help to write a few comprehension questions on the board, such as:

Why did Janet come round to the idea of a domestic robot?
How did her husband react?
What sort did they decide to have?

Exercise 4 Guess the meaning.

Students find the words in context and guess their meaning.

Exercise 5 Read and answer *True, False* or *Don't know*.

Students listen again or read the text in more detail to answer the questions. They may like to do this exercise in pairs.

Divide the class into groups of four. Each student should choose one of the four parts to read aloud (Janet, George, the doctor and the narrator). Each group then reads the story aloud, with students taking separate parts. Encourage more animated reading where necessary.

SUGGESTED LESSON BREAK

LISTENING

Exercise 6 Before you listen

Discuss the options with the whole class. Ask if students can use the four listed words in a sentence of their own.

Exercise 7

Play the tape a first time straight through for students to listen for the development of the story. Do not stop for any explanation at this point. Then play the tape again, this time pausing at each musical interlude for students to choose the best answer. Be prepared to stop and explain any difficult words and expressions as they arise.

TAPESCRIPT

/music/

NARRATOR: Four months later the housemaid robot, Hester, is now established in Janet's home as a friend as well as a maid.

JANET: Thank you, Hester. I suppose you must think me a poor, weak thing.

HESTER: Yes, I think all humans are weak. It's the way they are made. One must be sorry for them.

JANET: Compared with robots, we must seem so, I suppose. You are so strong. You never get tired. How I wish we were like that ...

HESTER: We were designed; you were just accidental. It is not your fault.

JANET: You'd rather be you than me?

HESTER: Certainly. We are stronger. We don't have to sleep. We don't grow old. If anything goes wrong with us or is broken, it doesn't hurt and is easily replaced. You have all kinds of pain and unhappiness. Human beings are so fragile. I feel very sorry for you. It disturbs my compassion-circuit.

JANET: Fragile. Yes, that's how I feel.

HESTER: If my arm or leg gets broken I can have a new one in a few minutes. People would be much more sensible to have a weak arm or leg replaced, but they don't seem to want to.

JANET: You mean they can be replaced? I didn't know that. I wish it were only arms and legs that were wrong with me. I don't think I'd hesitate... You heard the doctor this morning. He doesn't expect me to get any stronger. All he said was rest. What's the good of being alive if it's only rest, rest, rest! I'd rather anything than go on like this. I'd rather die.

HESTER: You've tired yourself out, Janet, dear. I'll take you upstairs. You'll be able to sleep a little before George gets back.

/music /

GEORGE: My wife. I rang you about an hour ago.

HOSPITAL ROBOT: Yes, Mr Shand. I'm afraid it has been a shock for you. But, as I told you, your house robot did quite the right thing to send her here to the hospital at once. She has been examined and the operation has been arranged for tomorrow, but of course we shall need your consent.

GEORGE: May I see the doctor in charge of her?

HOSPITAL ROBOT: He isn't in the hospital at the moment, I'm afraid.

GEORGE: Is it … er … the operation … absolutely necessary?

ROBOT: She must have been getting steadily weaker for some months now?

GEORGE: Yes, she has.

ROBOT: The only alternative is that she will get weaker still and have more pain.

GEORGE: I'd like to see her.

ROBOT: You may see her, but I must ask you not to disturb her. She's asleep now and it's better for her not to be woken.

/music/

ROBOT: Could I speak to Mr Shand, please?

GEORGE: Speaking.

ROBOT: It's the hospital here. It's about your wife. The operation appears to have been a complete success. The doctors are perfectly satisfied. There's nothing to worry about. Nothing at all.

GEORGE: Can I come and visit her?

ROBOT: No, it wouldn't be wise to allow any visitors for a few days yet.

/music/

GEORGE: Hello. It's Mr Shand here. I was just wondering if it was possible for me to visit my wife. It's been three days now ...

ROBOT: I'm sorry, Mr Shand. No visitors yet. We really don't recommend visitors.

/music/

GEORGE: Mr Shand here...

ROBOT: Yes, Mr Shand. Your wife has left the hospital. She's on her way home.

GEORGE: But it's only been five days! I thought it

was going to be weeks. O.K. Thanks. I'll go and get some roses to welcome her home.

/music/

GEORGE: Where is she?
HESTER: She's in bed. I thought it might be better if ...
GEORGE: Janet! Janet, I'm home!
JANET: Oh, George dear. Has she told you?
GEORGE: Has who told me what?
JANET: Hester. She said she would. Oh, George, I didn't mean it, at least I don't think I meant it. I wanted to be strong. I don't think I really understood.
GEORGE: Take it easy, darling. What on earth's all this about?
JANET: But George ...
GEORGE: I say, darling. Your hand's dreadfully cold. It's almost like ... GOD! NO!
JANET: But George. George darling.
GEORGE: No! NO! NO!
/music/

JIGSAW READING

Exercise 8 Follow the instructions.

Ask students how they think the story will end. Then ask them to complete the reading task to find the solution.

KEY

A(2): George turned and ran from the room.
B(3): In the darkness at the top of the stairs he missed the top step and fell down the whole flight of stairs.
A(1): Hester found him lying in the hall. She bent down and gently explored the damage. The extent of the damage disturbed Hester's compassion-circuit very greatly.
B(2): She did not try to move George, but went to the telephone and dialled. 'Emergency?' Hester asked, and gave the name and address.
A(4): 'I think his back is broken. There may not be a lot of time.'
B(1): 'Yes, you'd better send the consent form with the ambulance so that it can be signed at once.'
A(3): 'His wife will sign it.'

Exercise 9 Read and think.

Some students may still be puzzled by the ending, so get students who have understood what has happened to explain to the others.

SUGGESTED ANSWERS

1 He becomes a robot.
2 Because she has become a robot herself and has become converted.
3 Once you give machines a heart, they might eventually take over the human race.
4 *Nurse James; The perfect friend; The operation; A friend for Janet; A friend for life*

STUDY POINT

Before looking at the Study Point, ask students to look at some of the direct speech in the story and try and elicit from them some of the rules. Then read the information in the Study Point to reinforce them. Make comparisons with the students' own language if possible.

Exercise 10 PRACTICE

KEY

1 'How are you today?' the doctor asked politely.
2 'I'm very well,' he answered.
3 'Go away at once!' she shouted.
4 'If you want me to help,' she said with a smile, 'I'll do it with pleasure.'
5 'Don't look at me like that!' she said, 'I'm not lying.'
6 'How many times,' he said, 'do I have to tell you not to use my computer without asking?'

Exercise 11 WRITING

Start the summary with the students in class. Demonstrate that several options are possible and encourage them to use their own words as far as possible. Students can complete the summary for homework.

Exercise 12 Talk about it.

Round off the lesson with a quick appraisal of the story.

EXTRA ACTIVITIES

1 Your own radio story

Students rewrite the first part of the story, i.e. the text in the Students' book, as a radio play with parts and sound effects. If possible, record the best versions of this on tape.

2 Short story project

Students should find and read a short story, either in their own language or in English - preferably one with a 'sting in its tail', e.g: by O'Henry, Jeffrey Archer, Edgar Allan Poe, Muriel Spark, Dorothy Parker, Graham Greene. Students should write a short 50-100 word summary so that the whole class can decide on ten stories to put into an anthology called 'Ten of the Best'.

UNIT 30 Ten times more likely

Suggested lesson break: after Exercise 5

BACKGROUND NOTES

football pools: a competition where people risk small amounts of money every week on the results of certain football matches. Those who guess the results correctly can win large shares of the combined money.

Find out if students can explain the meaning of *odds* and use the word correctly in a sentence. Then ask them to read the dictionary entry. Point out that it is always used in the plural. You cannot say ~~The odd is....~~

Exercise 1 Talk about it.

Ask students to cover the text on the left while they do the quiz. This should be done rapidly, not allowing for second thoughts. Students compare their answers with their partner. Do not give them the correct answers yet.

Exercise 2 READING

Ask students to read the article to find out if they were right.

Exercise 3 Guess the meaning.

Discuss the words and check that students have guessed their meaning correctly. Spend a few minutes discussing the words and giving more examples of them in context before moving on.

Exercise 4 Read and think.

Discuss which statistics they found surprising and why. Find out if students think the statistics might differ in their own country, e.g: those to do with crime and punishment or car accidents. Take the opportunity to check how students are using comparative expressions and make a mental note of the areas to concentrate on later.

STUDY POINT

This is a common area of confusion for students and it is worth spending a few minutes helping them to distinguish between the differences in meaning and usage.

Read through the notes with them. Ask students to give you a few examples of sentences containing the words *chance* and *chances* so that you are sure they have grasped the difference in meaning.

Exercise 5 PRACTICE

KEY

1 chance of catching 2 chance to see 3 chance of getting 4 chances of seeing 5 chance to read

SUGGESTED LESSON BREAK

GRAMMAR REVIEW

KEY

How do you form the comparative and superlative?

a) add *-er, -est*, with spelling changes where necessary

b) use *more* or *most* in front of the adjective

c) same as in b)

Give the comparative and superlative forms of these irregular adjectives and adverbs.

good better best; well better best; bad worse worst; badly worse worst; fast faster fastest; hard harder hardest; a little less least; many more most; far farther//further farthest/furthest

Delete the incorrect words.

1 London is not as big as Tokyo.
2 New York is on the same latitude as Lisbon.
3 Oslo is one of the most expensive cities in the world.
4 São Paolo is much larger than Rio.

Ask students to make sentences comparing other towns and cities in their own and other countries.

Exercise 6 PRACTICE

Ask students to look at the map of Britain and to describe what it indicates and what is going to be compared. Point out the note that all times are door to door (which accounts for the length of the flight time). Work with the whole class to complete one or two examples and then ask students to work in pairs. Ask students to make similar statements about travel in their country.

Exercise 7 Talk about it.

Students work in pairs or groups to make statements under the headings. Encourage disagreement and discussion. Listen and check that the comparative forms are being used correctly.

GRAMMAR FOCUS

Note that *compared to/with* can be also used with the comparative form of the adjective, e.g. *Oslo is much more expensive compared to London.*

Elicit other sorts of adjectival phrases that can be used in this context, e.g: *able to, prepared to, inclined to.*

Ask students to find the sentences in the article on the first page of this unit.

Exercise 8 PRACTICE

Use the pictures to discuss with students where the two cities are and what they know about them. Go through the headings in the list, making sure that the students understand *pace of life, environment* and *cultural amenities*, and what adjectives might be used to talk about each category.

Tell students to copy the headings into their notebooks and write notes under each heading. When they have completed the activity, ask them to compare their notes with their partner.

Exercise 9

Bring the class together to discuss the two cities in relationship to the special requirements.

EXTRA ACTIVITIES

1 Alphabet comparisons

In groups, students sit in a circle. S1 starts by giving an adjective beginning with the letter *a*. S2 must give the comparative form and S3 the superlative form. S4 then gives an adjective beginning with the letter *b*. S5 gives the comparative form, S6 the superlative and so on. Any student who provides an incorrect form must drop out. The game is complete when there is no one left in the circle, or when the last letter of the alphabet has been reached. (It is best to exclude letters *k, x* and *z*.)

2 Points of comparison

Write a list of ten three-word groups on the board, e.g: *chair stool armchair*; *apple orange banana*; *slipper shoe boot*; *car bicycle motorbike*; *caravan tent youth hostel*; *house bungalow flat*; etc.

Students work in groups and compare the items in each group. They must try and find at least three different points of comparison for each group, e.g: *A chair is more solid than a stool*; *an armchair is more comfortable than a chair; a stool is more useful in a kitchen than a chair.*

CHECK 6 Units 26-30

(For adviced on handling this section, see the notes on Check 1 Units 1-5.)

KEY

Ex. 1

1 What will you have achieved by the year 2000?
2 In two years' time, my parents will have been married for twenty-five years.
3 Giles won't have finished medical training until he is twenty-six.
4 I'll have read it by then.
5 They won't have completed the motorway before 1996.
6 Unless we leave now, the film will have started when we get there.

Ex. 2 1 pick up 2 pick on 3 picking out 4 picked up 5 picked up

Ex. 3 1 instead of spending 2 without spilling 3 by talking 4 without ever stopping 5 instead of frying 6 by using

Ex. 4 1 juice extractor 2 acid rain 3 nuclear waste 4 endangered species 5 overpopulation 6 food processor 7 video recorder 8 natural resources 9 global warming 10 rain forest

Ex. 5 1c 2b 3c 4c 5a 6b

Ex. 6 1 will you be staying 2 'll be doing 3 will your parents be travelling 4 'll be earning 5 'll be holding 6 Will you be seeing 7 won't be using 8 will be watching

Ex. 7 1 on time 2 one at a time 3 for the time being 4 in time 5 all the time 6 at times 7 For a time

Ex. 8

1 'How long will you be?' she asked politely.
2 'I have no idea,' he said quietly, 'how we are ever going to repay you.'
3 'Get out and stay out!' he shouted, and slammed the door loudly.
4 'I didn't imagine the meeting would take so long,' she said as she paced impatiently around the room.
5 'That's not the right way to do it,' he said, snatching the paint brush from her hand. 'Let me show you how to do it properly.'

Ex. 9 1 chance to 2 chances of 3 chance 4 chance of 5 chance to 6 chance of 7 chance

Ex. 10 1 worse/worst 2 friendlier/friendliest 3 more quietly/most quietly 4 farther/farthest (further/furthest) 5 more/most 6 fewer/fewest 7 more fascinating/most fascinating 8 fitter/fittest

Ex. 11 1 less 2 much 3 with 4 as 5 as 6 much worse 7 than 8 from

UNIT 31 Faraway places

Suggested lesson break: after Exercise 5

BACKGROUND NOTES

(Note that a good world map or atlas would be useful for this unit.)

The photographs: top: office and apartment blocks in the centre of the city of Caracas in Venezuela. middle left: the beach of a seaside resort in the Algarve, Portugal .
bottom: houses in a suburb of Toronto in Canada. middle right: a village in the Italian Dolomites.

1 Talk about it.

Ask the questions to the whole class and find out if anyone has been to any places similar to the ones shown in the photographs. If so, find out what they liked or didn't like about the places. Ask students if they can categorise what each place is, e.g: *a mountain village*.

Exercise 2 VOCABULARY

Students work in pairs consulting the vocabulary in the chart and building up a detailed description of where they live. If some of the students finish early, ask them to describe features of their capital city, using the last section of the chart. Bring the class together to ask individual students to say exactly where they live.

Exercise 3 PRACTICE

Ask one or two students to describe where their relatives live. Make sure the vocabulary from the previous exercise is used as far as possible. The rest of the exercise could be done orally.

GRAMMAR FOCUS

Which is correct?

Work through the task with the whole class, first asking for the correct choice of answer and then asking individual students to say what and where the places are where appropriate. As you work, see if students can make their own rules about using the definite article.

KEY

1 the Bahamas 2 the Himalayas 3 Mount Etna 4 the Pacific Ocean 5 Rouen Cathedral 6 the Station Hotel 7 the National Gallery 8 the River Seine 9 the Gobi Desert 10 Lake Eyrie 11 the United States of America 12 Beijing University 13 Oxford Street 14 Tienanmen Square 15 the south of France 16 the Apollo Theatre 17 the Netherlands 18 Heathrow Airport

Exercise 4 PRACTICE

Students work individually. When you check the answers, ask individual students to say why an article is necessary or not.

KEY

the, –, the, –, the, the, –, –, the, the

Exercise 5

Students work in pairs, discussing the mistakes in the student's composition and correcting them.

KEY

insert definite article: should be *the Mediterranean Sea*
confused vocabulary: *stay* should be used instead of *rest*
confused vocabulary: *opportunities* should be used instead of *possibilities*
spelling: should be *quarter,* not ~~*quater*~~
confused vocabulary: *souvenirs* should be used instead of *curiosities*
use gerund after *enjoy*: should be *enjoy going shopping* not ~~*enjoy to go shopping*~~
spelling: should be *proximity,* not ~~*proxemity*~~

SUGGESTED LESSON BREAK

STUDY POINT

Read through the Study Point asking students to provide a sentence of their own for each word or phrase. Check the stress on words like *opportunity, possibility, possibilities, curiosity, novelty* and *souvenir.*

Exercise 6

Work through the exercise with the whole class and then ask students to make 6-8 new sentences for homework using the words and expressions.

KEY

1 Life 2 stay 3 cost of living 4 curiosity 5 possibilities 6 way of life 7 possibility 8 visit 9 souvenir 10 possible 11 novelty 12 opportunity

Exercise 7 READING

Ask students to close their books and form groups. Give them a few minutes to pool their knowledge about what they already know about the People's Republic of China, Beijing and the Great Wall of China.

Ask students to read the text on Beijing and note down information according to the headings. Allow plenty of time for each student to read the text and complete the information asked for.

Check the notes with the whole class and ask a few comprehension questions such as: *Where is Beijing? What forms part of China's border? What is unusual about many ancient Chinese cities? What is The Great Hall of the People used for? Who was Mao Tse Tung?*

Check that students understand the following words from the text: *spreads, border, stretches, compass, rallies, founder, outstanding.*

Practise saying the dates mentioned in the text. Ask what important dates students know from their own country's history.

Exercise 8 WRITING

Tell students either to write about the place where they live or about a city/town in their country. Remind them about the vocabulary in Exercise 2. Ask them to re-read the description of Beijing so that they can use it as a guide. Also revise general procedures for essay writing by referring to the Study Skills Review at the front of the Students' Book.

This writing activity can be linked to Extra Activity 2 below.

EXTRA ACTIVITIES

1 A geography quiz

Read out a list of place-names. Students must say what each place is and where it is located, e.g:

T: Bilbao.
S1: Bilbao is a port/coastal town in the north of Spain.

Either make your own list of places or choose from the following:

1 Bilbao 2 New Delhi 3 St Tropez 4 Oxford 5 Rouen 6 Recife 7 Zermatt 8 Beverley Hills 9 the Danube 10 the Prado 11 The Shetlands 12 Yosemite 13 the Sorbonne 14 the Taj Mahal 15 St Mark's 16 Portobello Road 17 La Scala 18 Bora Bora 19 Alice Springs 20 Wembley

2 Essay competition

Ask students to imagine that an international holiday company has invited all students of English to enter an essay competition. The competition rules are:

- The essay should be between 250 and 300 words long.
- It should give a personal view of a town or city.
- It should highlight any interesting or attractive features and say why the town or city could be attractive to ONE of the following categories of tourists:
  - a romantic young couple
  - a student on a budget
  - a family with young children

UNIT 32 Under threat

Suggested lesson break: after Exercise 4

BACKGROUND NOTES

River Mersey: the river that flows west from the Pennine Chain in the north of England into the Irish Sea. The city of Liverpool is situated on the River Mersey.

tonnes: a measurement of weight. 1 tonne = 1000 kg. Weights of cargo carried by ships are measured in tonnes.

Exercise 1 Before you start

Discuss the questions with the whole class. Prompt the students' memory, if necessary, of Chernobyl in Russia, the Exxon Valdez oil spill in Alaska and the destruction of Kuwait's oil fields during the Gulf War.

Ask students to explain in their own words what they understand by the terms *environmental disaster, an oil spill* and *damage.* Some of the vocabulary from the text and words in 'Guess the meaning' should occur during this discussion. Other words which might be useful are: *ecology/ ecological, environment/environmental, toxic waste* (n), *effluent* (n), *polluted/pollution, poison/ poisonous, extinct/extinction, threatened with (extinction).*

Exercise 2 Guess the meaning.

Ask students to read the text and work out the meaning of any words they still do not understand. Discuss each word separately.

READING

Exercise 3 Read and choose the correct answer.

Students now read the text and choose the best answer.

KEY

1b 2c 3a

GRAMMAR REVIEW

Go through the Grammar Review with the whole class, asking individual students to complete the tasks. Refer back to the newspaper report and work through it in detail, identifying each use of the passive and the tense used in each case. Finally, ask them to suggest why the passive is used in this sort of writing.

KEY

Which sentence is in the passive?
b)

How is a passive sentence formed?
By using the past participle with part of the verb *to be.*

What is the passive form of these modals?
a) She can be released.
b) He might be attacked.

Examples of the passive in the text.
It is feared; is being threatened; was washed; has been declared/ have been called in/ has been hampered; will not be known; cannot (easily) be broken down; to be fined; without being (unduly) affected

Exercise 4 PRACTICE

KEY

1 The birds are washed in detergent (by volunteers).
2 Food supplies are being prevented from reaching Somalia.
3 The oil was washed onto the beach by the tide.
4 In the programme we watched, elephants were being killed for their tusks.
5 A new president is going to be elected soon.
6 In future, a fine will be demanded if the law is broken.
7 The officials have been notified about it.
8 Chemicals had been released into the water.

SUGGESTED LESSON BREAK

Exercise 5

(Note: if available, some example headlines from recent English-speaking newspapers would be useful for this section.)

Ask individual students to read aloud the headlines. See if they can guess the meaning of *trap.* Then ask them to work in pairs expanding the headlines. Check these by asking individual students to read out their sentences for other students to correct if necessary.

KEY

1 A child star has been nominated as best actor in this year's Oscar awards.

2 Bangkok has been chosen to host an international pop festival. The profits will be donated to save the forests.
3 Flash cameras are being used by the police to trap high speed drivers.
4 The cosmonaut will be/is going to be rescued this week from the space station.
5 Rain is desperately needed in Southern Africa.
6 Dolphins in the Mediterranean sea are being destroyed by an unknown disease. Toxic wastes have been revealed as the cause.

GRAMMAR FOCUS

Read through the grammar notes with the whole class and ask individual students to make their own sentences using the structures described in the box. Direct students' attention to examples of the passive infinitive and gerund in the oil slick text.

Exercise 6 PRACTICE

Ask individual students round the class to provide the correct complete sentences and to identify which tense or form of the verb is being used.

KEY

1 to be told 2 Being spoilt 3 should have been told 4 being asked a question 5 can't be trusted 6 must have been used/mustn't be used 7 being paid for it 8 to be given/to have been given

LISTENING

Exercise 7 Before you listen

Ask individual students to explain the words and expressions, referring to a dictionary where necessary. Then ask them to look at the photographs and the captions of the people and suggest what the radio programme is going to be about.

Exercise 8

Ask students to copy the chart into their notebooks. Play the tape once for students to listen for gist and then a second time for them to complete the chart. Check these with the whole class.

After listening, ask students if they know of any people in their own country who are noted for their environmental concern and if anything unpleasant has happened to them.

TAPESCRIPT

NARRATOR: The title of today's programme is 'endangered species'. No, not owls or elephants but human beings who are fighting to save the environment and who are putting their lives at risk.

LINK: For most of us who are interested in protecting the environment, our support involves maybe paying money now and then and joining in on the occasional protest march. But for others it's much more serious and the cost much higher. Around the world, more and more environmentalists are being threatened and imprisoned, some even assassinated. Margaret Scott from Canada reports.

MARGARET: Colleen McCrory is fighting to save the forests in British Columbia. McCrory is a divorced mother who runs a small clothing store in New Denver to support her family. Twenty years ago she founded Canada's Future Forests Alliance, and demanded that 12% of all land should be set aside as wilderness. Since that time she has been constantly attacked in the newspapers by the 'Red Necks' who approve of 'logging'. This same pro-logging group organised a three-year boycott of her clothing store with the result that she has been forced to close it. She is now deep in debt. Not only that, but her children have been bullied at school and a friend of hers has been beaten.

LINK: It's a similar story in Malaysia. Jonathan Andrews reports from the rain forests Sarawak.

JONATHAN: Anderson Mutang, who has grown up in Sarawak's forests, has led many protests against the destruction of the forests. In the past six years, Mutang has directed six blockades of logging roads. He has spent four weeks in prison, including ten days in solitary confinement in a room without windows. During this time he was questioned by police sometimes for as much as seven to eight hours a day and threatened with torture.

LINK: These are only two of hundreds of courageous men and women all over the world who are trying to turn back the forces which are destroying the world's natural resources.

Exercise 9 ROLEPLAY

Ask a student to read the 'riots' headline aloud and then ask another to explain in their own words what the headline is about. Check that students all know what a nuclear missile site is.

Divide students into 'A' students and 'B' students who then refer to their respective rolecards. 'A' students must use their imagination to add to the details behind the news story. 'B' students prepare questions to ask about the incident. The questions should begin with *Who, What, Why, Where, How, When,* etc.

After five minutes 'A' students join with their opposite 'B' students to carry out the conversation. (If you wish, choose a recent incident which relates more to the students' own lives, such as a protest against building a new airport, motorway, or power station.)

Exercise 10 WRITING

Students can either base their writing on the headline provided or write about the incident they discussed in the Roleplay in Exercise 9.

EXTRA ACTIVITIES

1 Make your own crossword

Write the words below on the board and ask students to make a crossword which includes all of them. (Other words will have to be included as well). They should then write the clues for each word and give their crossword for someone else in the class to solve.
effluent, poison, waste, polluted, environment, extinct, ecology

2 Campaign

Students work in groups and choose an environmental issue they feel strongly about. They should work out plans for a campaign of protest. This could include making posters and leaflets, thinking of slogans, writing letters to newspapers and important people and thinking of ways to raise money for the campaign. The groups come together to compare their ideas.

UNIT 33 Speculation

Suggested lesson break: after Exercise 6

BACKGROUND NOTES
badger watching: Badgers are fairly large, dog-like nocturnal animals which can be found in secluded woods and country areas all over Britain. They have a distinctive blackish-brown and white striped markings on their head.
Similaun Glacier: a glacier (a mass of ice which moves slowly down a mountain) in the Austrian Alps in Europe.

Exercise 1 LISTENING DIALOGUE

Read the introduction to the dialogue and ask the students to look at the photograph and suggest why the woman is looking frightened. Check the meaning of the words *isolated, cottage* and *edge of some woods.*

Ask students to read the responses a) to h) below the dialogue and look at the same time at Exercise 2 'Guess the meaning'. Students may use a dictionary afterwards to check the meaning of *binoculars, badger* and *spade.* Ask students to try and place the responses in the right order in the dialogue.

Play the tape for students to check their answers. Then play it again for students to speak at the same time as the speakers.

Students then read the dialogue in pairs, reading the responses as fluently as they can.

TAPESCRIPT AND KEY

SUSAN: I think I'm going to give the police a ring.
BARRY: (1e) The police! Why?
SUSAN: I saw something strange in the woods just now.
BARRY: (2c) What do you mean 'strange'?
SUSAN: There was a man with a pair of binoculars.
BARRY: (3f) So? What's wrong with a pair of binoculars?
SUSAN: Well, why would he want them at this time of the evening?
BARRY: (4a) He might have been badger watching, you never know.
SUSAN: Badger watching? I doubt it. He had a spade with him.
BARRY: (5h) I can't see why a spade is so suspicious. He could have been digging for mushrooms.
SUSAN: (6b) With a spade? Don't be daft! Anyway, it's not the mushroom season.
BARRY: Did he see you?
SUSAN: Yes, he sort of gave a half smile and a wave.
BARRY: (7g) It must have been the farmer from up the road.
SUSAN: Well, I didn't recognise him.
BARRY: (8d) Listen, he can't have been doing anything very serious or someone would have contacted the police by now. I think you're being unnecessarily suspicious.
SUSAN: Do you think so? I'm not so sure.

Exercise 2 Guess the meaning.

KEY
1b 2c 3b

Exercise 3 Study the words.

KEY
1 What are you suggesting? 2 You don't know. (There could be all sorts of reasons why he was in woods.) 3 I don't think so. 4 Don't be silly/ That's rather a silly explanation.

Exercise 4 Answer the questions.

KEY
1 a) Because he had a spade with him.
  b) Because it isn't the mushroom season
  c) Because she didn't recognise him.
2 Students will probably use expressions like *He was probably..., Perhaps he was ..., Maybe he was ...* . Do not insist on past modals at this stage.

Exercise 5 LISTENING

Play the tape for students to listen and find out the solution to the story. Words which may cause difficulty are *cautionary tale, spotted, revealed, owl, fox, dazzled, headlights, bury* and *alerted.*

TAPESCRIPT AND KEY
And that's the end of our local news roundup. And finally, here's a cautionary tale for all you night-time bird watchers. A man who was being questioned by police last night after being spotted acting suspiciously in Seven Acre Woods has been released. The man, whose name has not been revealed, explained that he was a keen bird-watcher with a special interest in owls. On his way to the forest on Friday evening, he had unfortunately run over a fox which was dazzled by his

headlights and he decided to bury it in the woods. Police were alerted by a local woman who had spotted the man acting suspiciously. This is Neil Radford, Radio GFM.

Ask students to work in groups of three and retell the whole story from different points of view, i.e. 1 Barry's 2 Susan's 3 the man's.

Exercise 6 About you

Close the lesson by bringing the class together and asking students to recount any strange or frightening experiences of a similar nature they might have had.

SUGGESTED LESSON BREAK

COMMUNICATION FOCUS

Write the following sentences on the board:

a *The speaker is almost 100% certain that the event happened.*
b *The speaker is not sure.*
c *The speaker is almost 100% certain that the event didn't happen.*

Read the sentences aloud from the Focus box and ask the students to say which sentence (a, b or c) on the board best describes each of them.

KEY
The first and second sentence = b
The third and fourth sentence = a
The fifth and sixth sentence = c

Revise how the modal verbs are formed in the past simple and continuous forms.

Write the following two sentences on the board and ask the students to explain their difference in meaning:

1 He might have been looking for something.
2 He must have been looking for something.

Point out that the past continuous of a modal is used when we are speculating about a continuous activity in the past. For further practice, read out the sentences below and ask students to see if they can think of a comment using one of the structures exemplified in the Communication Focus box. You can prompt them with the first two words if necessary.

1 Your aunt didn't answer the door although I rang twice. (She might...)
2 His eyes were very red. (He must ...)
3 His flat smelt of onions. (He must ...)
4 He said he'd been waiting for ages but I didn't believe him. (He can't ...)
5 I tried phoning him several times but there was no answer. (You might ...)

Exercise 7 SPEECHWORK

Play the first example on the tape and get students to repeat the sentence. Stop the tape.

Now ask different students to read the listed sentences, encouraging them to say them with speed (otherwise the contractions are not natural).

Play the rest of the tape for the students to listen and repeat. The first four sentences are the same as those in the book, but they are followed by some other examples.

TAPESCRIPT
He must have been digging.
He must have been lying.
She can't have known.
They might have been looking.
He could have found out.
She must have been joking.
They might have gone to the police.

Exercise 8 PRACTICE

Students work individually to complete the exercise.

KEY
2 can't have lost 3 might/could have missed
4 can't have been 5 must have had

Exercise 9

Students work in pairs. Encourage them to think of more than one explanation for each situation. Collect as many different explanations as possible from the class.

Exercise 10 and 11 READING

Ask students to look at the 'Iceman' in the picture and scan the two headings. Ask: *How old is the body of the man? How old do you think he was when he died? Why do you think he still looks like that? Where was he found?* Ask students if they know the names of all the 'ages' (Ice Age, Stone Age, Bronze Age, Iron Age).

Ask students to read the text and try to guess the meaning of the words listed. They should make a note of any other words they do not understand. On their second reading, they should note down the information under the headings supplied.

Exercise 12 WRITING

Ask students to cover the text and note down what they think are the ten most important facts in the article. Collect these suggestions on the board and prune these down to about eight.

Ask students to try and link these into a caption for a museum exhibit.

SUGGESTED CAPTION
This exhibit shows the 4,000-year-old remains of a man found buried and mummified in a glacier in the Austrian Alps. He is the oldest human specimen from the Bronze Age. The cause of his death is not known but his weapons and clothes suggest he may have been hunting in the mountains at the time of his death. The body was discovered by some German climbers in 1991.

EXTRA ACTIVITIES

1 The time capsule

Imagine that scientists are planning to make a 'time capsule' of this decade which will include for posterity items of interest that best represent the age in which we live. Students work in groups to make a list of ten items which they would include in the time capsule.

2 Problem-solving

Read out the following problem situations and ask the students to think of as many solutions as possible.

1 You received some money from your aunt in a letter this morning. You think you left it on the kitchen table before you went out. You come back home in the afternoon and you can't find the letter or the money anywhere. What do you think has happened to it?

2 You notice at five o'clock in the morning your next door neighbour climbing through his living room window dressed in rubber boots and pyjamas. What do you think has happened?

3 A car is parked outside your house with all the windows open and the car radio on very loudly. What do you think has happened?

UNIT 34 The call of the wild

Suggested lesson break: after Exercise 5

BACKGROUND NOTES

golden eagles: a large golden-brown meat-eating bird of prey found in mountainous parts of the northern hemisphere.

the Soviet Union: The Soviet Union or USSR (The Union of Soviet Socialist Republics) was, until 1991, the largest country in the world and was made up of fifteen republics. It was formed after the Russian Revolution in 1917 as a communist state. After the break-up of the Soviet Union in 1991, eleven of the newly independent states grouped together to form CIS (the Commonwealth of Independent States), one of which was Kazakhstan.

communism: the system of government in which a single party controls the means of production with the aim of establishing a classless society. One of the features of communism is the restriction of free trading. Most British and American people associate communism especially with the Soviet Union and the People's Republic of China.

Exercise 1 Before you read

Ask the first question and list any new vocabulary on the board, e.g: *game* (wild animals or birds that are hunted), *wild boar, deer, elk, pheasant, partridge, wild duck, hare*.

Ask students to look at the main picture and ask them to identify the bird (a golden eagle). Now refer to the map and ask what part of the world it represents. Elicit what students know about the area, the climate, the type of landscape and the people who live there. Introduce words like *grassland* and *nomadic*. Draw an eagle on the board and get the students to label its beak, wing, tail, claws and feathers. Explain the term *wingspan* (the width of the wings when extended).

Ask students to write down some questions they would like to ask about hunting with eagles. Suggest areas like: training method, feeding, breeding, etc. Collect the questions and write them on the board.

Exercise 2 READING

Ask students to read the text. Draw the class together and ask which of their questions were answered and what they found was interesting or surprising in the text. Ask them to note down any words they are uncertain of as they go along but tell them not to use a dictionary at this stage.

Exercise 3 Read and answer.

Students reread the text, working with their partner to find the answers to the questions. The questions will need some interpretation. Then tell them to close their books and give you the answers in their own words as far as possible.

Exercise 4 Study the words.

After students have found the words, spend a few minutes discussing them and their general usage.

KEY

1 nomadic 2 incompatible 3 eliminated 4 prey 5 grooming

Exercise 5 Read and think.

SUGGESTED ANSWERS

1 Because the Soviet authorities didn't believe in individual trading for private gain.

2 Little bits of meat, mice, sheep's eyes, other organs, etc.

After discussing the two questions, ask if the students have ever seen, either in real life or on television, an animal being hunted for prey. Ask what their reactions were.

SUGGESTED LESSON BREAK

VOCABULARY

Exercise 6

At this point of the lesson, it would be useful to have some pictures or a reference book to demonstrate the different animal and bird species.

Students do the exercise in pairs.

KEY

1 cow 2 chicken 3 horse 4 sheep 5 duck

Exercise 7

KEY

a) birds of prey: eagle, hawk, owl
b) reptiles: snake, lizard, crocodile
c) big cats: tiger, lion, leopard
d) apes: gorilla, chimpanzee, monkey
e) dogs: wolf, fox, hyena
f) farm animals: cow, chicken, horse, sheep, duck

Exercise 8

Discuss and explain the animal expressions within the sentences. In order to avoid potential embarrassment, check beforehand if any of the animals, e.g. sheep, might cause insult to any members of the class.

Discuss if they have equivalent sayings in their own language and what other animals they use in expressions.

Exercise 9

Ask students to try and work out the answers from the context, and to say why the use of the animal word is effective.

KEY

1 wolf 2 hawk 3 leopard 4 lion 5 chicken
6 mouse

GRAMMAR FOCUS

Read through the notes with the students.

KEY

What's the difference in meaning?
Sentence 1 expresses a known fact but Sentence 2 expresses 'hearsay', a fact that has not been proven.

Students read through the note and the sentences and then provide some 'hearsay' statements about their own country, either historical facts or some topical controversy.

Exercise 10 PRACTICE

KEY

1 It is said that one elephant is killed every minute of the day.
2 It is commonly believed that the rhinoceros will be extinct in fifty years' time.
3 Bears are thought to be gentle animals but they can be quite aggressive.
4 Nepal is said to be a very beautiful country.
5 Fox-hunting nowadays is considered to be very cruel.

Exercise 11 Talk about it.

For the closing few minutes of the lesson, ask students to discuss the first question, naming any products which use birds of prey or other animals as their symbol and saying what they stand for.

The last question can be touched on briefly or treated in depth in the form of a debate.

EXTRA ACTIVITIES

1 Animal rights and wrongs

In groups, students discuss the rights and wrongs of the following issues concerning animals: dolphin shows, fox-hunting, performing animals in a circus, zoos, bull-fighting, cock-fighting, dog fighting.

3 Star gossip

For the next lesson, students find out a sensational piece of gossip, which is not necessarily proven, about a famous figure, either living or dead, e.g: *It is said that Marilyn Monroe had/Marilyn Monroe is said to have had affairs with two of the Kennedy brothers.*

UNIT 35 Roots

Suggested lesson break: after Exercise 8

BACKGROUND NOTES

The engraving: black slaves picking cotton on a plantation in one of the southern states of the USA in the early 19th century.
Alex Palmer Haley: (1921-92) a black American writer who shot to world fame after the publication and TV adaptation of his long, historically-detailed autobiographical novel, *Roots*.
The War of Independence: (The American Revolution) the uprising of the thirteen British North American colonies between 1775 and 1783 which resulted in the establishment of the United States of America.
The American Civil War: (1861-65) the conflict between the southern (Confederate) states of America and the northern (Union) states over the emancipation of slaves.
The First World War: (1914-18) sometimes called 'The Great War' or 'World War 1'.
Salvador Dali: (1904-1989) a Spanish surrealist painter notorious for his dramatic, distorted paintings and his outrageous behaviour.
Marilyn Monroe: (1926-63) one of the world's

most enduring sex symbols who made her most successful films in the 1950's and early 60's.
Gandhi: (1869-1948) an Indian political leader who led the long struggle for Indian independence from British rule by advocating non-violent resistance.
John Lennon: (1940-1980) an English singer and songwriter who was one of the four Beatles. He was shot outside his apartment in New York at the age of forty.
The photograph (page 104): this shows newcomers to the USA in 1900 waiting to complete immigration procedures at Ellis Island in New York Harbour.

Exercise 1 Before you start

Ask the questions of the whole class using the Background Notes above to help correct the students' answers.

Exercise 2

Ask students to complete the quiz in pairs and then discuss the correct answers.

KEY
1b 2c 3a 4b 5b

Exercise 3 LITERATURE

Read the introductory note about Alex Haley aloud to the students, explaining any new words as you come across them, e.g: *trace, maternal ancestors, ultimately, captured, shipped.*

Play the tape or ask students to read the text and think of answers to the questions: *Why do you think the other blacks avoided Kunta? What aspects of slavery does Kunta feel are most degrading?*

Discuss the answers with the whole class.

Exercise 4 Study the words.

Ask students to read the text once more in pairs and to find the equivalent words and expressions in the text. List these on the board and ask students to give you new sentences containing them.

KEY
1 shackled 2 went through the motions
3 melancholy 4 dingy 5 sinews 6 bred

Exercise 5 Answer *True* or *False*.

Work with the whole class, asking individual students to give a correct version of each of the false statements.

Exercise 6 Talk about it.

Students can talk about these issues in groups or as a whole class. They may like to consider where to draw the line between employment, exploitation and slavery. To help them think more widely about the issue, mention migrant agricultural workers and children employed in 'sweat shops', as beggars or as street vendors.

Exercise 7 READING

Ask students to explain what the word *obituary* means and where they would find examples of one. Ask them to read the text once through and ask some comprehension questions, e.g:

Where did Alex Haley die?
Where did his ancestors originally come from?
What largely inspired the book?
What job did Haley do before he became a full-time writer?
What special preparation did he make for 'Roots'?

Ask students to work in pairs reading the obituary to find out the theme of each paragraph. Finally discuss what the conditions must have been like on slave ships.

KEY
a) the second b) the last c) the first d) the fourth e) the third

Exercise 8 WRITING

Divide students into four groups and allot each group one of the famous people. The class then come together and pools their knowledge of the four people. Encourage students to use other sources of information, e.g: an encyclopedia or magazine articles.

Alternatively, suggest some personalities familiar to the students from their own country and ask them to discuss these in groups. Remind them to follow the structure of the obituary for the order of the paragraphs.

The writing can be started in class and continued for homework.

SUGGESTED LESSON BREAK

Exercise 9 PHRASAL VERB: *take*

Students use their dictionaries to find out what the phrasal verbs mean and then replace the words in italics in each of the sentences with the appropriate phrasal verb.

KEY
2 take to 3 take on 4 take in 5 takes after
6 take over 7 were taken in 8 taking off

Ask students if they know of any other meanings attached to these phrasal verbs, e.g: *take off* = to remove (of clothes) or to leave (of an aeroplane). Ask them to make sentences of their own with the phrasal verbs, either now or for homework.

STUDY POINT

Read through the Study Point, supplying more examples of sentences for students to transform either to formal or informal register. e.g: *The company for which she works has just been taken over./The family I stayed with are Polish.*

Exercise 10 PRACTICE

KEY

1 Last week I visited Seattle, the city in which Alex Haley died.
2 The woman to whom I was talking was a maths professor.
3 Virginia was one of the places to which slaves were taken.
4 The person for whom the party was being given was taken ill on the day.
5 *Roots* is the book from which I got most of my information.

Exercise 11 LISTENING

Ask students to skim-read the questions. Play the tape once through, asking students to listen to it with the questions in mind, but without writing anything. Afterwards they should try to answer as many questions as they can from memory.

Play the tape a second time for students to correct their answers. Discuss any problems and replay any parts that were difficult. Words which may cause difficulty are: *frustrating, drop out (of school), grade* and *steel mill.*

TAPESCRIPT

My grandparents came to the United States about 1912. They came from Russia, but they were actually German. They were children at the time so it's their parents who actually decided to make the move. Their ancestors were from Germany, but moved to Russia in probably the early 1800s. And so my ancestors lived there for several generations and were happy with things as they were until the beginning of the twentieth century when Russia was going through a period of wars, as was Europe, and that basically caused the family to realise they didn't really want to be part of this and so they left for the United States. So they came to the United States as 12, 13-year-olds and lived in a German area near Chicago.

When my grandparents came to the United States they both spoke German. They didn't … to my knowledge … they didn't know any Russian and their parents spoke German. They first started learning English when they went to public school. My grandfather found this very frustrating, he … people made fun of him and so he dropped out of school quite early, but my grandmother continued to about the eighth grade. When my grandfather left school, he started working where most of the men in the family worked which was at the local steel mill in the neighbourhood and my grandmother worked local farms and basically really didn't have any job until they met and were married which was in 1919. They were each about nineteen, twenty years old.

They had five children. The older ones went to work in the factory. My father was one of the younger children and he ended up going to college. My father was the first member of the family to go to college. He eventually came to California to take up a career as an engineer. A few years later my grandparents followed him out to California where they retired and they never went back to Russia. They never, as far as I knew, even had any contact with people from the old village. They came to the United States and just never looked back.

Exercise 12 About you

Ask students to work in groups. Each group should choose a 'secretary' to note down any interesting details about people's families which may arise during the discussion and collate these to report back to the whole class. Draw the class together to share the information.

EXTRA ACTIVITIES

1 Preposition chain

Write a list of people on one side of the board (e.g: *my doctor, my boss, my sister, the postman, Madonna*) and a list of prepositions on the other side (e.g: *to, with, for, by, from, in*).
S1 starts by calling out a person, e.g: *My doctor...*
S2 continues by choosing a preposition and making a relative clause, e.g: … *with whom I had lunch yesterday …*
S3 finishes the sentence, e.g: … *was arrested by the police this morning.*
S4 continues with another person from the board, and so on. This can also be done as a written game of consequences, where each element is folded over and hidden from the next person.

2 Video Club

There are many videos which can be shown in connection with this unit, e.g: (if available) some parts of the original major TV series of *Roots*; *Gone with the Wind*; Marilyn Monroe films like *Bus Stop, Some Like it Hot* or the *Seven Year Itch*; the long epic film, *Gandhi*; the Beatles' film *Let it Be*, etc.

3 One minute family history

Students prepare to talk for one minute about their own ancestors, as far back as they have knowledge of.

CHECK 7 Units 31-35

(For notes on handling this section, see Check 1 Units 1–5.)

KEY

Ex. 1 1 hilly 2 suburb 3 cathedral 4 river 5 rural 6 valley

Ex. 2 1 the 2 the 3 - 4 the 5 - 6 - 7 the 8 the

Ex. 3 1 spent 2 living 3 chance of earning 4 had spent 5 souvenirs 6 stay

Ex. 4 1 The house was used ... 2 Millions of fish are being poisoned … 3 … they were being followed. 4 A major earth tremor has been reported … 5 A lot of people in our town have been made redundant recently. 6 She had been given … 7 The winners of the competition will be announced … 8 The papers are usually marked … 9 When is the new ring road going to be finished? 10 … all the flights had been cancelled.

Ex. 5 1 ought to be thrown away 2 must have been put 3 might have been put 4 should have been given in 5 could have been taken 6 can't be traced

Ex. 6 1 She doesn't like being teased. 2 ... they are afraid of being caught. 3 Being told that you are no good ... 4 ... being asked stupid questions. 5 ... without being instructed. 6 ... at being kept waiting.

Ex. 7

1 London's Piccadilly Circus is going to be closed for a year.
2 Three top police officers have been charged with bribery and corruption
3 The $20 million Broadway musical of 'Anna Karenina' has been voted the flop of the year.
4 All cigarette advertising is going to be banned at sports events.
5 A famous sports star has been named in a new royal scandal.

Ex. 8

1 She can't have had much sleep.
2 You might have put them in your jacket pocket.
3 He must have been asleep at the wheel.
4 He might have gone to the other entrance.
5 He can't have been waiting long.
6 You must have been sitting in a funny way.

Ex. 9

1 chicken 2 owl 3 mouse 4 gorilla 5 snake 6 leopard 7 sheep

Ex. 10

1 It is said that there's going to be an election soon.
2 The Seychelles are said to be very unspoilt.
3 It is expected that an official announcement about the Prime Minister's health will be announced shortly.
4 The terrorists are supposed to have already left the country.
5 It has been reported that another earthquake has occurred in Northern California.
6 The dolphins' immune system is thought to have been damaged by pollution.

Ex. 11 1 begin 2 employ 3 understand 4 like 5 resemble 6 imitate 7 assume control of 8 be deceived

Ex. 12

1 This letter is from the Jones family with whom I stayed last summer.
2 He is giving a big party to which we are all invited.
3 We didn't recognise the hotel in which we had stayed the year before.
4 Last night we went to see an old film called *The French Lieutenant's Woman* in which Meryl Streep plays the leading role.
5 They bumped into the young couple to whom they had sold their house three years ago.
6 Mr and Mrs MacBride are the Irish couple from whom we rented the cottage.

UNIT 36 Irritating habits

Suggested lesson break: after Exercise 3

1 Talk about it.

Ask students to say what is happening in each of the pictures and discuss the questions with the whole class, introducing new vocabulary such as: *to empty (out), to read over someone's shoulder, cigarette ends/butts, deafening,* etc as you do so. Find out if students think the habits are irritating or not, and to name any other irritating habits. Make a note of these to refer back to in Extra Activity 1 below.

Ask questions to find out about the students' own country, e.g: *Can you be fined for dropping litter in the street or playing loud music in public places such as parks and streets? Are you allowed to use your car horn in built-up areas whenever you want?*

Exercises 2 and 3 LISTENING DIALOGUE

Ask students to cover the text of the dialogue while you play the tape. Ask the questions in Exercise 2, and replay the tape afterwards for students to check their answers.

Now ask students to look at the printed dialogue and find the matching expressions from Exercise 3 in the text.

KEY

1 for ages 2 That's not the point. 3 for instance 4 to bump into 5 will do 6 Honestly 7 to put up with 8 to give someone a hand

Ask individual students to make sentences using the expressions they have found. Point out the different terms used for an evening meal in the dialogue, e.g: Derek says, *for a meal* and Kate says *supper*. They could also have used *dinner* but this would have implied something more formal. Point out also the expression *anything much,* by which Kate means that she hasn't got any special food which she thinks would be suitable for her guests. At this point, students may like to speak at the same time as the speakers on the tape and then read the dialogue in pairs.

If time allows, use the following gapped sentences for extra practice. They can be copied onto the board or an OHT, or they can be read out with a finger snap signal or a slight pause to indicate the gap to be filled.

PRACTICE SENTENCES

1 I'm looking for a present for my sister. Do you think this new Whitney Houston CD ...? (*will do*)
2 You'll never guess who I ... yesterday. (*bumped into*)
3 I don't know how she ... her husband. He's so rude to her. (*puts up with*)
4 Some hobbies are quite expensive. Take photography, ... (*for example*)
5 I'm in the kitchen Derek. Could you come and ... with the washing-up? (*give me a hand*)
6 Oh, haven't you seen that Kevin Costner film? It's been out on video ... (*for ages*)
7 Quite ..., I don't think I've got a chance of passing my driving test next week. (*honestly*)
8 I know they're our best friends, but ... . You should have told me you had invited them for supper. (*that's not the point*)

If there is time, ask students to close their books and roleplay the dialogue situation in their own words from memory.

(Note that this might be an appropriate point to do Extra Activity 1 below.)

SUGGESTED LESSON BREAK

COMMUNICATION FOCUS

Ask students to read the introductory note and say whether it applies to their country. Ask about students' own attitudes to criticising people, and to being criticised themselves. Ask them also if they think that British behaviour is hypocritical.

Criticising habits

Read the sentences aloud and ask students to repeat them individually and chorally. Backchain any sentences which might cause difficulty.

Criticising past behaviour

Ask students to read the note about the intonation of sentences like *He might have phoned* and see if they can say them with two different patterns. The 'critical' version has a fall-rise intonation at the end.

Exercise 5 SPEECHWORK

Play the tape for students to say which tone is being used in each sentence.

TAPESCRIPT AND KEY

1 She's always leaving her dirty clothes in the bathroom. (critical)
2 You might have put it in the wastepaper basket. (neutral)
3 He could have caught an earlier train! (critical)

Write the following sentences on the board.

1 a) *It's an awful habit of hers.*
  b) *That's where we put our dirty laundry.*
2 a) *It was disgusting of you to throw the apple core on the floor.*
  b) *I can't find that letter from Jenny anywhere.*
3 a) *It's very rude of John to be late when you've got guests coming.*
  b) *John wasn't at the station when I got there.*

Play the three pairs of similar sentences on the tape, explaining that the sentences on the board give the correct context for each sentence they hear on the tape. Finally, play the tape again for students to listen and repeat the sentences.

Exercise 6 Practice

Ask individual students round the class to expand the notes in Exercise 6 into sentences using one of the structures in the Focus box.

KEY

2 You could have phoned to tell me!
3 I wish you wouldn't snap your fingers at the waiter.
4 You're always trying to impress other people.
5 I wish she would be more honest with me.
6 She might have introduced me to them!
7 I wish you wouldn't borrow my things without asking.

Make sure students say these sentences with the correct intonation pattern.

Exercise 7

Ask different students to describe what is happening in each picture and then complete the bubble as appropriate.

SUGGESTED ANSWERS

1 I wish he wouldn't smoke all the time/so much.
2 You're always losing your glasses!
3 He's always phoning to cancel at the last minute!
4 I wish he/she would turn the sound down.
5 Well, they might have cleared up after them!
6 You're always buying new clothes!

Exercise 8 PHRASAL VERBS AND IDIOMS: *do*

Ask students to study the exercise silently for a minute and then work through the exercise with the whole class asking individual students in turn to change the sentences. Then ask them to work in pairs to see if they can make sentences of their own using the expressions provided in the box. Finally, ask if they know of any other expressions or phrasal verbs with *do*. This might be a good time to revise expressions with *make* and *do*.

KEY

2 do without 3 has something to do with

4 do up 5 could do with 6 did away with 7 do my best 8 do you good 9 do me a favour

Exercise 9 ROLEPLAY

To set the context for the roleplay, find out how many of the students go to special classes for anything. What arrangements do they make? Divide the class into 'A' students and 'B' students and direct them to their appropriate role cards.

Allow sufficient time for them to think about their conversations. Point out that it is important that they really sound annoyed, and that they should try to include at least one of the ways of criticising from this unit. Monitor students as they converse and choose one or two pairs to perform in front of the whole class.

EXTRA ACTIVITIES

1 Discussion: what annoys me most

Write the following list of annoying habits on the board. Students work in pairs or groups and list them in order from the most to the least annoying. Reassemble the class to decide on the three most annoying habits.

- never washing up cups or mugs
- finishing other people's sentences for them
- never paying for a 'round' of coffee or drinks among a group of friends
- never putting the cap back on the toothpaste
- talking during a film in the cinema
- cutting toenails and leaving them on the floor
- always borrowing other people's things, especially clothes
- spoiling other people's jokes by saying the punchline
- sniffing instead of using a handkerchief
- leaving doors open and lights on

2 Mime the habit: A game

Students form groups. In turn, each student thinks of an irritating habit and mimes it for the others to guess by asking a maximum of ten *Yes/No* questions. To make it more challenging, they should avoid simple actions, such as cracking knuckles, twisting hair, etc.

UNIT 37 Happy families?

Suggested lesson break: after Exercise 2

BACKGROUND NOTES

nursery rhymes: simple poems for children with a strongly marked rhythm and rhyme, which have been handed down from generation to generation by oral tradition.

asthma: difficulty in breathing caused by spasms in the air passages in the lungs. Asthma attacks can be caused by allergies and infection as well as by stress and emotional upsets.

dropped out: discontinued either work or full-time education. The expression also implies that a person who 'drops out' takes up an unconventional life-style (see note below)

'hippie (hippy)' lifestyle: In the 1960s and 70s 'hippies' (also known as 'flower children' or 'drop outs') was the label given to a certain group of people who were against conventional standards and tastes, particularly in clothes, music and lifestyle.

Freud: Sigmund Freud (1856-1939) is the founder of the theory and practice of psychoanalysis. He pioneered the study of the subconscious mind.

Exercise 1 Before you read

Discuss the questions with the class as a whole, selecting different students to answer the first question. Introduce words such as *jealous, aggressive, feel left out, want attention, give/devote attention to* and any others that seem appropriate.

READING

Ask students to look at the cartoon picture of the children fighting and say how it relates to the title of the article. (We normally talk of a bond of love, not hate. The title of the article implies that brothers and sisters are often bonded by hate instead of love.)

Exercise 2 Read and answer.

Ask students to read the text and find the answers to the following questions (to be written on the board):

What did Mary do to her brother?
What did Bobby do to his sister?
Why did the teenage boy drop out?
What did Lisa do when her mother started to feed the baby?
How do the two teenage boys react if someone is unpleasant to one of them?

Check the answers, then ask students to work in pairs to answer the questions in their book. They may need to re-read parts of the text to do so. After checking the answers, ask if students have come across any experiences similar to those mentioned in the text.

SUGGESTED LESSON BREAK

Exercise 3 VOCABULARY

Do the exercise with the whole class or ask students to work in pairs.

KEY

1a 2d 3b 4c 5a 6d 7b 8c

Check the answers, and elicit from students the correct collocation, if appropriate, for the 'odd word out', i.e: 1 do some damage 2 make an excuse 3 pay a bill 4 miss a bus 5 lose a wallet 6 (no obvious collocation) take a holiday/end a holiday 7 (no obvious collocation) 8 pick a fight

Go round the class asking different students to make sentences for each of the possible collocations, e.g: *make money, make war, make trouble* (there are a possible total of twenty-four sentences).

If time is short, students can write the sentences for homework. Stress that they may need to check in a dictionary to see if any special prepositions are required by the collocation, e.g: *make trouble for somebody, break a record for doing something, draw a picture of something, miss an opportunity to do something,* etc.

GRAMMAR FOCUS

Ask students to find a sentence in the text starting with or including *not only* and *no sooner*. Ask why the structure of these sentences is different from a normal sentence.

Read through the first part of the notes with the students and give more examples of inversion with other tenses, e.g: *Not only does he ... / Not only did she ...* . Then write a couple of sentences on the board for them to combine with *not only*. Do the same with the other adverbs, presenting more examples with other tenses and giving some on-the-spot practice. Explain that another adverb that can be used in place of *no sooner* is *hardly: Hardly had he sat down than the telephone rang again.*

Finally point out the note at the end of the box.

Exercise 4 PRACTICE

KEY

1 No sooner had I sat down than the telephone rang.
2 Not only is he talented, he is also very modest.
3 Never has there been such high unemployment.
4 On no account must you speak to anyone.
5 Not only did she come top in maths, she also won the geography prize.
6 No sooner had he begun to speak than someone started to shout at him.
7 On no account should you touch that wire.

GRAMMAR REVIEW

Students will have met the reflexive pronoun in various forms during their course of study. This is an opportunity to bring all the uses together. Revise the different forms on the board, i.e: *myself, yourself, himself*, etc. Then ask students to do the task in the box.

KEY

How is the reflexive formed?
Singular: *My/your/him/her/it + self*
Plural: *Our/your/them + selves*

Note that the third person singular and plural use the object pronoun (*him, her, them*) not the possessive adjective (*his, her, their*) to form the reflexive pronoun.

The reflexive is used when the subject and the object of the sentence are the same person, e.g: *He looked at himself in the mirror*. In other words, the reflexive pronoun usually refers to the subject of the sentence.

Compare sentences 2a) and 2b).
In sentence 2a) *enjoy* is one of a group of verbs in English (e.g. *amuse, blame, cut, hurt, introduce)* which are frequently followed by a reflexive pronoun. These verbs cannot be followed by an object pronoun if the subject and object are the same, e.g: *He cut himself shaving.* not ~~*He cut him shaving*~~.

In sentence 2b) the reflexive pronoun is emphatic, i.e. it can be used with nouns to give the special meaning 'that person/thing in particular'. When reflexive pronouns are used emphatically they may refer to the subject or the object, e.g:
Subject: *We did the decorating ourselves.* or
We ourselves did the decorating.
Object: *We met the president himself.*

Exercise 5 PRACTICE

KEY

1 burn yourself 2 enjoyed ourselves 3 itself 4 hurt herself 5 look after myself 6 teach himself 7 themselves 8 help yourselves

LISTENING

Exercise 6 Before you listen

Start a general discussion about twins and draw out students' own experiences either of being a twin or of knowing twins.

Ask students to think of some questions they might like to ask someone who is a twin, and write these on the board.

Exercise 7

Discuss the words with the students and explain how they are used in a sentence. Ask students to look at the questions and explain *to tell them apart*. Play the tape once through without stopping. Elicit the answers and then play again for a more detailed study.

TAPESCRIPT

I am an identical twin and as children we looked exactly identical. So identical that we had to wear initials on our shirts so that teachers could tell us apart in school. And I think that's quite often the case with identical twins – that when they are young children they tend to be more identical physically than when they grow up and I think that twins tend to diverge more as they get into adolescence and then into adulthood.

And I think it reaches its climax when you're an adolescent because as an adolescent you are striving to be an individual but of course everybody looks upon you as one of a pair, so you have this real problem of identity.

My theory is that twins actually look alike physically but often they complement each other when it comes to their personalities and natures, if you like. And I think in our experience we complemented each other, we were the mirror image of each other. So my brother was more introvert ... was more academic, schoolish. I was, perhaps, or still am, you know, extrovert ... more extrovert than him and I think that's what we've carried through our childhood really.

As children going through primary school we got on very well. We were ... we always played together, we had common interests. Our parents actually encouraged that, so that when we were, you know, young children we had piano lessons and we did this and we did that together, and we were just like very, very close friends. And it was natural for us to play together rather than to play with other children.

When we got to adolescence, then that's where the truly competitive element came in and we found ourselves more likely to want not to be together. Not that we argued tremendously but that we just were searching for our own identities and therefore we would clash more.

Up until the age of eighteen we were always together, but when we left school I went to teach in France for a year, my brother went straight to university to read sciences - I was doing languages. So that when I came to go to university, he was a year ahead of me and by sheer chance we ended up in the same college in the same university, so the interesting factor was that we had deliberately aimed not to go to the same university ... to be separate ... but because I had this year off and he went straight in and through a quirk of the selection process, we ended up in the same college. This college, one of the Cambridge University colleges, seemed to specialise in twins because there were about half a dozen sets of twins in the college in that year and ... but what we discovered was that we were very unlike them because in virtually all cases those sets of twins in our college were reading the same subjects, lived in the same rooms, wore the same clothes, went to the same lectures and we actually felt quite different, because my brother was doing sciences, I was doing languages, we had different rooms, we had different friends in different years. So we realised that we were actually not anything like as close as other twins that we came into contact with.

WRITING

Exercise 8 Before you write

Ask students to read through the list. Check that they understand the words *discipline* and *protective*. Students work in small groups. Tell them that they have to decide on three points, even if it means a compromise. Draw the class together to see if the groups agree.

Exercise 9

Ask students to construct a paragraph around each of the points chosen in Exercise 8. They should introduce each point in turn and give examples where appropriate. They can also write a few lines about why they don't think certain actions are harmful.

Build up a framework for the paragraphs on the board with the students, e.g:
Paragraph 1: *In my opinion, one of the most harmful things a parent can do when bringing up a child is to ... . As far as I'm concerned this is far worse than ... . In fact, I think it's quite natural for parents to ...*

Paragraph 2: *I also think that (wanting ...) can be very harmful. I remember when I was ...*

Paragraph 3: *Another thing I disagree with is when parents ... . To give you an example, a friend of mine ...*

EXTRA ACTIVITIES

1 Scale of values

First dictate the statements listed below and ask students to mark them each on a scale of 0 to 5 with the following values: 0 = totally disagree, 5 = totally agree. Then students form groups and compare their opinions.

1 If a sibling hurts the new baby, she or he should be punished.
2 The needs of a new baby are more important than those of a four-year-old child.
3 Siblings shouldn't be allowed to say anything unkind about the new baby.
4 It is best to stop siblings fighting.
5 Sibling rivalry is something that all children grow out of eventually.

2 Negative adverbs: noughts and crosses

See Unit 20 Extra Activity 2 for instructions on how to play this game. In the boxes write the following adverbs: *no sooner, on no account, not only, never, hardly, rarely, little, seldom and only then.* (Students will need to consult the note on inversion after negative adverbs on page 132 of the Grammar Reference)

Students form two teams. One person from one team must make a grammatically correct sentence starting with one of the negative adverbs and inverting the subject and verb. If they get it right, the team earns a O or a X to be placed on that square. The game continues until one team gets a straight line of noughts or crosses.

UNIT 38 Missing

Suggested lesson break: after Exercise 7

(Note that a map of Asia would be useful to use with this unit.)

BACKGROUND NOTES
Himalayan: the Himalayas, the largest and highest mountain chain in the world, stretches for 2,410 kilometres through Pakistan, India, Tibet, Nepal, Sikkim and Bhutan. Mount Everest, the highest peak of the Himalayas and the highest mountain in the world, is in Nepal.
Brisbane: the capital city of the state of Queensland, Australia.
Nepal: a land-locked country bounded to the south and west by India and to the north by Tibet and China.
Kathmandu: (sometimes spelled *Katmandu*) is the capital of Nepal and a popular centre for trekkers.

Exercise 1 Before you read

Ask students to keep their books closed and use a map to find out if they can place Nepal, the Himalayas and Kathmandu. Ask if there are any hilly or mountainous areas similar to the one in the picture in the students' own country where people might go trekking. Then ask the 'Before you read' questions to the whole class and list their answers in note form on the board. Find out if there have been any incidents concerning lost mountaineers or mountain accidents in recent years.

Exercise 2 READING

Ask students to look at the pictures and the title of the article. Then set a time limit (e.g: thirty seconds) for them to skim the text. Ask one or two students to tell you what they think the story is about.

Exercise 3 Guess the meaning.

Tell students that they are going to read the text in sections and that they should guess the meaning of these words from their context.

Exercise 4 Read and complete.

Ask students to work in pairs. They should read the first paragraph down to *'not to be seen again for forty-two days'* and complete the appropriate diary dates. They should decide on a simple sentence each time to summarise the event.

KEY
(Paragraph 1)
Dec. 18th: James Scott and Tim Hooper set off trekking.
Dec. 19th: They met up with Mark Fulton, another Australian trekker.
Dec. 20th: Tim Hooper had strained his thigh and decided to turn back. He arranged to meet up with James in Kathmandu on December 25th. James and Mark continued.
Dec. 22nd: It began to snow. Mark wanted to continue but James turned back.

Students now read the next two paragraphs and work in the same way.

Finally, ask students to take turns in summarising the story in their own words without looking at the text. They needn't be too precise at this point about the dates.

Discuss what students feel about the way James' trekking party behaved and whether people who purposefully put themselves in situations involving danger deserve a lot of sympathy.

Exercise 5 Make questions for these answers.

Work with the whole class for the first few questions, then ask students to complete this and the following exercise for homework.

KEY
1 Why did Tim Hooper decide to turn back?
2 At what point did Tim send a fax to James' father saying James was missing?
3 What was James' sister, Joanne, doing when her father phoned with the news about James?
4 Why couldn't James' brother go to Nepal to look for James?
5 Had the French-Canadian walkers seen James?
6 When did Joanne leave Australia to go to Nepal?
7 What did the girl Joanne talked to at the airport suggest that she should do?
8 How did the Buddhist lama help Joanne?
9 Why did many people tell Joanne there was no point searching for James in the place the lama had indicated?
10 How long had James been sheltering on the ledge in subzero temperatures?

Exercise 6 Study the words.

KEY
1 to start talking to a stranger
2 to stop thinking about something for a while/to ignore something for the time being
3 without success
4 just about to agree
5 how she had almost admitted defeat and stopped her search for James

Exercise 7 Talk about it.

Students can discuss these questions as a whole class. This might include topics such as fortune tellers, palm readers, miracles, etc.

SUGGESTED LESSON BREAK

GRAMMAR FOCUS

Some of this will be revision for students, but encourage them to copy down the verbs in two separate lists in their notebooks. The phrases that usually cause problems are *It's no use ...ing; There's no use/point (in) ... ing, It's not worth ... ing.*

Divide the text up among the students and ask them to search for the verbs and expressions with *to* or the gerund.

Exercise 8 PRACTICE

SUGGESTED ANSWERS

1 staying in/watching TV/going to the cinema
2 to meet tomorrow night instead.
3 going to discos
4 to be a wild animal/to be tourists abroad.
5 to go trekking in winter on my own.
6 taking warm clothes.
7 to reach the harbour safely.
8 smoking
9 going out to eat
10 to be broken.
11 talking to him
12 hoping she will.

Students can write ten sentences for homework using a mixture of verbs.

Exercise 9 LISTENING

Ask students to read the questions and see if they can guess what the answers are going to be. Play the tape, pausing at intervals for students to respond.

TAPESCRIPT

WOMAN: Wow! This is weird. This Australian guy was missing in the Himalayas for forty two days and a lama helped his sister find him by locating him on a map.

MAN: You're kidding! I've just been reading about that.

WOMAN: How does he survive. Does it say?

MAN: Yeah, he survived for forty three days. How many weeks is that? That's six weeks with no food.

WOMAN: No food at all?

MAN: No, he had some chocolate bars at the beginning.

WOMAN: For how long? I mean how many chocolate bars did he have?

MAN: I think he had two or three chocolate bars, but basically the chocolate bars ran out.

WOMAN: When did they run out though?

MAN: Um, after about the first week.

WOMAN: Three chocolate bars in a week — that's amazing!

MAN: But then, the rest of the time, the rest of the forty three days, he had … he lived on snow, and because he was a medical student he knew that the only way he was going to survive, was not to be dehydrated. He had to keep liquids coming into him. So although the snow lowered his body temperature, he knew that he had to keep water and he survived on snow only. He used to suck these snowballs.

WOMAN: Didn't he think he was going to die?

MAN: He did think he was going to die. He thought he was going to die to the extent that he wrote lots of letters to his fiancée and his parents which were terribly sad.

WOMAN: Were they in there?

MAN: He says most … make me cry here … he says 'Please don't grieve too long, but go and live your lives to the fullest. Always remember me, I will watch down on you from heaven and take care of you. I hope that one day this letter is found and you get to read it. I love you with all my heart, all my mind for eternity.'
What really hit me was he wasn't frightened for himself at all. All he was frightened … all he was worried about was the fact that his family were going to suffer so much, and also the other thing he said was … that what a waste … everything they had done for him, what a waste, all his education, all his training, all the things, all the love that his parents had given him.

WOMAN: So he blamed himself a bit.

MAN: Yeah, completely.

WOMAN: Was he in a lot of pain?

MAN: No, not after a while. It was a terrible pain of hunger to start off with, and the pain of the frostbite that was in his feet, to start off with.

WOMAN: Because I would I think maybe you'd want to kill yourself or something if that happened.

MAN: It came to a point towards the end. He was determined to survive and then he thought he would try and get out. He'd been … he'd basically sheltered underneath a rock for all the time. And then he decided to try and get out and he set off and after only a few hours it became obvious that with his frostbitten feet and he was so weak by this time, he'd lost so much weight, he couldn't. At that point he kind of gave up hope and he came back.

WOMAN: What happened after they got him?

MAN: Well, from his point of view all that happened was that suddenly there was this helicopter three hundred feet away and people waving and shouting at him and then it went away.

WOMAN: Because it says they got him the next day, which … that time in between must have been crazy.

MAN: Well, he thought they had gone then, and then he was just lying there and he heard voices and he thought he was hallucinating, and then slowly suddenly these people came up and said …

WOMAN: … 'You're saved.'

MAN: 'We're here,' and he said that was the first time he cried … when they came to him … he just cried and cried and cried. Then they hoisted him up into a helicopter and took him back and he was in hospital in Kathmandu for weeks and weeks while he was recovering. Then finally he got taken back to Brisbane (I think it was Brisbane). He went back to his farm, to his parents where he slowly, slowly got better, with the obvious deep, deep love of his fiancée, who I presume by now he's married.

Exercise 10 WRITING

Encourage students to use their imagination but to base their writing on the facts they have learnt from the text and the listening exercise. Explain that the 'diary' would probably be an account written after the event and the writer would try to recreate his or her thoughts at the time.

EXTRA ACTIVITIES

1 Pack a backpack

In groups, students have five minutes to discuss what fifteen items (excluding passport and travel documents) they would pack for a week's trekking holiday in the Himalayas. After the time is up, bring the class together to discuss the final list. (N.B. Multiple items, such as three pairs of socks, count as one item.)

2 Write a dialogue

Choose one of the situations from the text and write the dialogue that you think might have taken place at that point (e.g: between James' father and Joanne when he announces the news; between Joanne and the girl at Kathmandu airport; between Joanne and Carl Harrison when she persuades him to make a final attempt in the helicopter to find her missing brother).

UNIT 39 Points of view

Suggested lesson break: after Exercise 6

BACKGROUND NOTES

Sumo-wrestling: a Japanese form of wrestling, involving special ceremonies as well as entertainment, in which two wrestlers try to force each other to the ground or out of a ring marked on the floor. Sumo wrestlers are known for their great size and strength.

Kung Fu: a Chinese style of fighting without weapons.

Introduce the topic of boxing and find out what students think of the sport. Ask them to name some famous boxers. Make a list of words to do with boxing, e.g: *box, boxer, boxing ring, boxing gloves, gumshield, the ropes, the referee, heavy/middle/light/featherweight title, countdown, knock out* (verb and noun), *punch, blow.*

Exercise 1 Before you listen

Ask students to read the newspaper report to find the answer to the questions. Ask if any students can explain the term *blood clot.*

Exercise 2

Students discuss their reaction in pairs. Ask for a show of hands for each statement.

Explain that you are going to play a dialogue in which two people take opposing views. Explain that as the people are giving strong opinions, they emphasise certain words. Students may like to see if they can complete the dialogue before listening.

Exercise 3 LISTENING DIALOGUE

Play the tape and ask students to complete the gaps in the dialogue.

TAPESCRIPT AND KEY

PENNY: Look at this! Granger is on a life-support machine.

DICK: Who?

PENNY: The boxer who got knocked out the other night in the World Heavyweight Championship.

DICK: Yes, *that was hard luck*. It was a good match, though.

PENNY: Well, I didn't think so. How *can it be* a good match when people get brain damage like that? I *really think it should be* banned as a sport.

DICK: Oh come on! It's not *that* dangerous. Boxers don't get hurt very often.

PENNY: But they *do get hurt*. And seriously too. Look what happened to Terry Granger. In fact *what amazes me is why* it doesn't happen to more boxers.

Play the tape again for students to check their answers. Comment on the use of *though* to show contrast. This is only used in conversation. Play it again asking students to 'shadow' the dialogue, speaking at the same time as the tape. They can then read the dialogue in pairs.

GRAMMAR FOCUS

Go through each section separately spending a little time on each to allow students to practise saying the sentences with emphatic stress where appropriate, and making similar sentences of their own. Give special attention to the second section where students have to add an auxiliary. Also, it is important that students get the phrasing and intonation right with cleft sentences. They should pause slightly before the verb *is* and end the sentence in a high fall, e.g:

What I CAN'T underSTAND

is how they managed to FIND that sort of money.

Exercise 4 SPEECHWORK

Ask students to look at the sentences and to write down the auxiliary verb on which the emphatic stress will fall. Then ask them to practise saying the sentences to themselves with spirit and enthusiasm. Finally, play the tape so that the context is provided and ask different students to provide the response.

TAPESCRIPT

1 Surely he's not going to charge us £100 for one lesson!
2 Mr Henley told me you weren't at the lecture.
3 I'd like to take this book back, but I'm not sure if Susan had read it yet.
4 The trouble is, you just don't care!
5 I thought Martha worked in a bank, but then Frank told me she was in advertising or something.
6 I imagine my contribution didn't make much difference, did it?

Exercise 5 PRACTICE

KEY

1 What seems strange is that is that so many people like watching it.
2 What appals me is how much money has been spent.
3 What amazes me is me how he can run so far.
4 What I can't understand is how people can call fox-hunting a sport.
5 What I can't see is why they don't ban it.
6 What worries me is that they don't teach anything about politics at school.

For extra practice, ask students to write down something that they think is a) surprising b) interesting c) frightening about some aspect of modern society, maybe to do with education, politics, environment, crime or people's habits and behaviour, etc.

Ask each student to convert their sentences into statements starting with: *What amazes/interests/ frightens me is ...*

Exercise 6 ROLEPLAY

Ask if students regularly watch videos and how often they buy new videos on which to record programmes from the TV. Ask if they ever ask other people to record programmes, and if not, why not.

Set the context for the roleplay and ask students to read their respective rolecards. Allow some time for them to prepare their roles. Ask what sport the *Grand Prix* refers to. Go round and monitor while students practise in pairs, making a note of any recurring errors. Choose a pair of students to perform before the class.

SUGGESTED LESSON BREAK

Exercise 7 LISTENING

Ask if students are familiar with the idea of 'phone-in' programmes. Explain that many phone-in programmes are to do with topical matters. The programme presenter selects topics of interest in the news and asks listeners to telephone the radio station to air their opinions.

Ask students to read the list of statements. If necessary, explain *morally wrong* and *naturally aggressive*. Play the tape without stopping and see how many of the statements students can respond to. Play the tape again for students to check their answers. Pause and replay the middle part (in brackets) where the woman uses emphatic stress and cleft sentences for emphasis.

TAPESCRIPT

PRESENTER: Hello. Mrs Williams from Bury St Edmunds. Are you there?

MRS W: Hello, Nick. Good morning.

PRESENTER: Good morning.

MRS W: Yes, it's about boxing.

PRESENTER: Yes?

MRS W: (I'd just like to say that I agree with your previous caller. I've got a son who did boxing at school but fortunately he's given it up now and all I can say is 'thank goodness'. Every weekend he used to come back with a swollen eye or a bleeding mouth. Once he was punched in the side of the head so badly he was concussed and had to go to hospital. What I can't understand is how they can call it sport. And I *don't* think it's right to make children do it at school. What you're actually saying to young children is 'It's O.K. to fight'. You're actually *teaching* them to fight and hurt people.)

PRESENTER: But wouldn't some people argue that at least they were being taught the right way to fight, the safe way, so to speak, and that boys, young men, get into fights anyway?

MRS W: Well, I don't agree that boys always get into fights. I think, on the contrary, boxing brought out an aggressive streak in my son that wasn't there before. And I blame it on the school. I really do.

PRESENTER: Right. Thank you, Mrs Williams. Let's have our next caller, Mr Hatton from Winchester. Good morning, Mr Hatton.

STUDY POINT

There are several different ways of balancing an argument. Some of these ways are listed in the Study Point box. Students may have heard of other ways, and it might be useful to 'brainstorm' any other expressions they know, e.g: *in point of fact, in effect, if the truth be known, but the fact is, but the fact of the matter is.* Ask different students to read through the examples. Point out that they are fairly formal and are often found in written English.

Exercise 8 PRACTICE

Make sure that students understand the following words: *brutal, tedious, wrestling, primitive, barbaric* and *ban*.

Tell students that there may be more than one appropriate way of combining the sentences but students should aim to choose what sounds best. Point out that statements of subjective opinion should be preceded by *as far as I'm concerned.*

SUGGESTED SENTENCES

1 At first sight boxing looks very brutal but in actual fact the sport requires a lot of skill.
2 Many people argue that motor-racing is very dangerous but on the whole there are very few serious accidents.
3 Many people think that tennis is exciting to watch but as far as I'm concerned it's extremely tedious.
4 It may be true that wrestling requires a lot of skill but as far as I'm concerned it's primitive and barbaric.
5 In theory you might be able to ban it but in practice it would still continue.

Exercise 9 Talk about it.

Ask what students know about martial arts, which countries they originate from and if they are popular in their country. Ask students to form groups to discuss what they feel about these and other similar 'sports'. Encourage them to use some of the new expressions from the Study Point. All students should take notes of the main points raised both for and against the sports discussed.

Exercise 10 WRITING

Students may write the letter about a sport or about any other topic which they feel strongly about. Stress that it is important for them to jot down a couple of points both for and against the topic in order to be able to write a balanced middle paragraph. Students should not feel obliged to introduce any of the expressions in the Study Point unless they seem to fit the argument. It is better that the letter should flow. Students can start the letter in class and complete it for homework.

EXTRA ACTIVITIES

1 Accusations!

Students sit in a circle and accuse each other of something trivial, e.g:

S1: You were late this morning.
S2: I WASN'T late this morning.

In other words, S1 'accuses' S2, and S2 has to react by contradicting S1, using emphatic stress on the auxiliary. S2 then chooses someone else to accuse, who has to retaliate, e.g:

S1: Maria, you didn't phone me last night!
S2: (Maria) I DID phone you! Bruno, you've lost my pen.
S3: (Bruno) I HAVEN'T lost your pen! George, you aren't concentrating.
S4: (George) I AM concentrating! etc.

2 What does the panel think?

Students choose a panel of five or six people to discuss the following statements. (The panel can be changed for each statement.) The rest of the class may give their opinions from the 'floor' after each panel member has had her/his say.

1 The minimum age for a driving licence should be raised.
2 Smoking should be banned in all work places.
3 All zoos should be closed.
4 Censorship of films on television is a waste of time.

UNIT 40 Educating Rita

Suggested lesson break: after Exercise 8

BACKGROUND NOTES

Julie Walters: an English TV and film actress well-known for her comedy acting.
Michael Caine: (now Sir Michael Caine), an English film actor, well-known internationally and noted for his Cockney accent.
bleedin': a euphemism for the swear word 'bloody' which itself derives from the expression 'By our Lady!' and has nothing to do with blood at all.
The Open University: a 'self-study' university education scheme in which mature adult students without formal qualifications can gain a university degree by following television and radio lectures at home. They also correspond with individual personal tutors and take part in residential summer courses.
William Blake: (1757-1827) an English poet and philosopher

LITERATURE

Exercise 1 Before you read

Find out if any students have seen the film, *Educating Rita*, on video or TV. If so, they might be able to give a brief summary of the plot. If students have not heard of the film, see if they can suggest what sort of film it might be from the title, and from looking at the picture. Ask questions like: *Do you think it is going to be a serious or a funny film, or both? Do you think there will be any romance in it? How old do you think the two characters are?*

Explain that Rita is a 'mature student', i.e. someone who returns to education later in life and ask: *What are the advantages or disadvantages of starting an academic course of study when you're in your late twenties or thirties?*

Exercise 2

Ask students to read the background piece on Willy Russell. Students who know nothing about the play will benefit from reading the introduction (in the pink box at the top of the page) alongside the background notes on Willy Russell.

The parts that may have influenced his writing of the play are: his northern background and his job as a hairdresser as well as a teacher.

Exercise 3

Pre-teach the words *outspoken, struggle, disillusioned* and *seek refuge in*. Ask students to read the questions and skim-read the introduction. Students can now reconsider their answers to Exercise 1.

Exercises 4 and 5

Go through the text with the students line by line either with or without the tape. Explain that as Rita comes from the north, she speaks with a northern accent. Also, that she uses a lot of slang and colloquial expressions. This is reflected in the way some of the words are written. Point to a couple of words to illustrate this, e.g: *bloody borin'* for 'extremely boring' in the first line, *Y' said* for 'You said' and *feller* for 'fellow' (man).

Read the stage directions in between the speech. Explain *flounce* and *dump* and refer to the glossary to help students understand the authors' names and works.

As you work through the text, get students to explain the words and expressions from Exercise 5. Once you have worked through the whole piece, select a part of it (e.g: the first half of the first page) and ask students to practise reading it in the way in which they think it will be spoken by the actors. Ask a pair to 'perform' their reading.

Play the tape of the scene for students to compare their version. Finally, ask students to choose the best answers in Exercise 4.

KEY (Exercise 4)
1b 2c 3b

KEY (Exercise 5)
1 really irritates me 2 refer to/ mention other authors 3 Don't keep criticising me! 4 Isn't that marvellous! (spoken sarcastically) 5 read hungrily and in large quantities 6 marvellous/ very good/excellent book 7 man 8 more refined/ of better quality 9 you apparently believe/think 10 making good judgements

Exercise 6 Read and think.

Discuss the questions with the class as a whole.

Exercise 7 STYLE

Ask students to look through the text again to find instances of words and expressions to support their answers. Ask them to give a more formal equivalent in Rita's case and a less formal equivalent in Frank's case.

SUGGESTED ANSWERS

1 He writes sentences like *That's justice for y'* and *just cos I'm more well read*. Other examples are *an'* for 'and' and the use of slang expressions like *dead fantastic book* and *posher*.
2 He uses longer words and more formal expressions, e.g: *in your favour, selective, under the impression that* and sentences like: *It's merely a question of being discerning in your choice of reading material*.

Exercise 8 Talk about it.

Ask students to discuss the question of 'pulp fiction' versus 'literature' in groups. Ask them to note down any features of pulp fiction which they think distinguishes it from literature, or vice versa. Ask them also to discuss whether Frank's attitude to 'pulp fiction' is helpful for Rita.

SUGGESTED LESSON BREAK

VOCABULARY

KEY (Exercise 9)
1 sarcastic 2 exasperated 3 decisive 4 indignant

KEY (Exercise 10)

SUGGESTED ANSWERS

indignant
Oh that's prime, isn't it! That's justice for y'.

decisive
Right, that's it. I'll never read a Harold Robbins novel again.

exasperated
I've had enough of this. It's borin', that's what it is, bloody borin'.
But surely you can see the difference between Harold Robbins and the other two.

sarcastic
It's a bleedin' piece of paper, isn't it?
I don't think the examiner, God bless him, will have read 'A Stone for Danny Fisher'.

LISTENING

Exercise 11 Before you listen

Ask students to find *subjective* and *objective* in the dictionary and to give examples of what the words mean. Explain that Rita has come a long way since the beginning of the play and has made lots of friends on the course. One of them is called 'Trish' (short for Patricia).

Exercise 12

Ask students to read the sentences and, as they listen, to try and decide which of the possibilities best sums up Frank's reaction (c). They should explain why the other three options do not apply.

TAPESCRIPT

FRANK: I want to talk to you about this. Rita, what's this?
RITA: Is there something wrong with it?
FRANK: Look, the poem is a simple, uncomplicated piece about a blossom, as if seen from a child's point of view.
RITA: Yeh, that's what you say, Frank, but Trish and me and some others were talkin' the other night about Blake, and we came to the conclusion that the poem works on other levels as well.
FRANK: So? You think it gains from being interpreted this way?
RITA: Is me essay wrong then, Frank?
FRANK: It's not ... not wrong. But I don't like it.
RITA: You're being subjective.
FRANK: Yes, yes. I suppose I am.
RITA: If it was in an exam, what sort of mark would I get?
FRANK: A good one.
RITA: Well, what the hell are you sayin' then?
FRANK: What I'm saying is that it's up to the minute, quite trendy stuff about Blake; but there's nothing of your views in there.
RITA: Or maybe Frank, there's nothing of <u>your</u> views in there.
FRANK: Maybe that is what I mean.
RITA: But when I first came to you, Frank, you didn't give me any views. You let me find my own.
FRANK: And your views I still value. But, Rita, these aren't your views.
RITA: But you told me not to have a view. You told me to be objective, to read other books. Well that's what I've done. And I've now come up with these conclusions.
FRANK: Yes. All right.
RITA: Look, Frank, I can have a mind of my own, can't I?
FRANK: I sincerely hope so, my dear.
RITA: And what's that supposed to mean?
FRANK: It means - It means be careful.
RITA: What d'y' mean, be careful? I can look after myself. Just cos I'm learnin', just cos I can do it now and read what I wanna read an' understand without havin' to come runnin' to you every five minutes y' start telling me to be careful.
FRANK: Because - because I care for you- I want you to care for yourself.
RITA: Tch. I- I care for you, Frank... But you've got to leave me alone a bit. I'm not an idiot now, Frank. I don't need you to hold me hand as much...I can - I can do things on me own more now ... and I am careful. I know what I'm doing - just don't - don't keep treatin' me as though I'm the same as when I first walked in here. I understand now, Frank; I know the difference between - between - Somerset Maugham an' Harold Robbins. You understand, don't you Frank?
FRANK: Entirely, my dear.

Exercise 13 Study the words.

KEY

1 as a child might describe it 2 has other possible interpretations 3 modern 4 quite fashionable stuff 5 being able to think for myself 6 I am very fond of you 7 I don't need your advice and guidance

Exercise 14 Think about it.

Discuss the questions as a class.

SUGGESTED ANSWERS

1 Through her own reading, she has discovered that she can think for herself and can make her own value judgements. She has discovered that education has given her self-confidence and the possibility to make choices in life.
2 He is disappointed because a) she no longer echoes his views b) she is adopting trendy views and forgetting her own and c) she doesn't need him any longer.
3 (Open answer)

Exercise 15 IDIOMS: *life*

Discuss the idioms to do with 'life' and ask if students can paraphrase them in their own words. Give examples of occasions on which they might be used. If they know of others in their own language to do with 'life', ask them to try and translate them into English.

KEY

1 for dear life 2 the life and soul of the party
3 the light of his life 4 a new lease of life
5 walk of life 6 risked life and limb 7 had the time of his life

EXTRA ACTIVITIES

1 Lucky Numbers: a communication game

Divide the class into two equal teams. Write the numbers 1 - 30 on the board. These numbers correspond to the list of communicative functions below. In turn, a member of each team chooses a number at random. The teacher reads out the function which corresponds to the number. The student must immediately give a sentence that interprets the function. The teacher awards a mark on a scale of 1-3 according to the accuracy, appropriacy and fluency of the student's interpretation. The winning team is the one that scores the most marks.

COMMUNICATIVE FUNCTIONS

1 State a preference about TV programmes.
2 Express dislike about a certain type of food.
3 Give a balanced opinion about horse racing.
4 Make an accusation and deny it emphatically.
5 Criticise someone's bad habits in the sitting room.
6 Criticise a friend's behaviour at a party last night.
7 Make a request to a friend about clothes.
8 Make a request to a stranger in the street.
9 Ask permission to do something in the classroom.
10 Ask to do something in someone's home and refuse permission politely.
11 Ask politely for some factual information at an airport.
12 Ask a friend to do you a favour and say what it is.
13 Invite a friend to the cinema
14 Find out if someone is free one day next week.
15 Give and refuse a formal invitation.
16 Agree on a time for a class meeting.
17 Ask for a suggestion about where to buy some fresh bread in the area.
18 Make and respond to a suggestion about a class party.
20 Ask for a suggestion about what birthday present to buy for a friend.
21 Give an opinion about a current film.
22 Offer someone a reward of £10 for singing 'Happy Birthday to You' loudly outside the school entrance.
23 Comment critically on the result of a past sports event.
24 Express approval or disapproval about a recent school event
25 Express regret about some aspect of your past education.
26 Find out about someone's plans for the summer.
27 Draw a definite conclusion about someone who was absent from class last week.
28 Ask someone to speculate about their future activities.
29 Report what someone has told you or asked you to do today.
30 Give someone a warning about having a barbecue.

2 Amateur dramatics

Students make groups of four to plan, prepare and act a 3-5 minute playlet based on the following ideas or on their own ideas:

1 The Uninvited Guest
2 Strangers on a Train
3 Noises in the Night
4 Family at War
5 Confrontation
6 Love Story

Check 8 Units 36-40

For notes on handling this section, see Check 1 Units 1–5.

KEY

Ex. 1
1 I wish she wouldn't use the phone without asking.
2 He's always folding back the pages of a book!
3 I wish he wouldn't leave all the lights on.
4 She's always leaving her clothes lying around!
5 I wish he would wash up occasionally.
6 She's always playing Dire Straits!

Ex. 2 1 made 2 lend 3 do 4 break 5 lose 6 make 7 do

Ex. 3
1 No sooner had we started eating than the telephone rang.
2 Not only was he a brilliant journalist, he was a competent poet too.
3 Never have I been so insulted!
4 On no account should you pay this bill.
5 Not only does she enjoy swimming, she loves an early morning run as well.

Ex. 4 1 yourself 2 myself 3 ourselves 4 herself 5 himself 6 themselves 7 yourself 8 yourselves

Ex. 5 1 to be 2 watching 3 going 4 not to marry 5 complaining 6 to make 7 phoning 8 not having 9 thinking 10 to say

Ex. 6 1 does like 2 do (survive) 3 does (rain) 4 did live 5 have seen 6 did hear

Ex. 7
1 What I'd really prefer is a glass of milk and a sandwich.
2 What I like being able to do is to lie in bed on Sunday morning.
3 What I hate is having to tell lies.
4 What I can't understand is why people choose to go on holiday in Britain.
5 What I think is strange is that he wants to sleep on the floor.

Ex. 8 1 At first sight, in actual fact 2 In theory, in practice 3 believe 4 As far as I'm concerned 5 On the whole

Ex. 9 1 lease 2 walk 3 dear 4 soul 5 time 6 limb

Ex. 10 1 sent 2 was having 3 runs 4 is sitting 5 had already left 6 had been raining 7 see 8 will be lying 9 have lost 10 have been working 11 will be/will have been used up 12 have just made 13 had she started 14 wouldn't play 15 had worked 16 would have fallen 17 paid 18 knew 19 be prevented 20 have been told

FLUENCY PROJECTS

The four fluency projects can be used at any point during the course to help students consolidate what they have learnt and to provide an opportunity to practise a range of language in different contexts. Some teachers may like to use them for an informal test of students' oral proficiency.

Although the projects appear in a group after Unit 40, it is suggested that one Fluency Project is used after every ten units. Projects 1 and 2 are better suited to the first half of the course, and 3 and 4 to the second half. Fluency Project 4, which is based on a radio programme, could take longer to cover and is possibly best left until the end, where it can serve as a round-up project for the whole course.

FLUENCY PROJECT 1
A new product

Allow a double lesson or two separate lessons to cover the work.

Suggested lesson break: after Exercise 1

Exercise 1

Some teachers may like to bring into the class a selection of yoghurts and drinks to provide a background context for the project. Ask if students have noticed any new icecreams or drinks on the market and what is different about them. Read the introductory text with the students and ask them to explain what *to launch a product* means.

Go through the agenda making sure students understand the headings for each section. Ask a student to explain the difference between *to package* and *to pack*.

Before students break into groups, revise the names of different types of fruit. Write the following headings on the board: *citrus fruits, tropical fruits, soft and berry fruits, orchard fruits,* and ask students to name as many as they can under each heading.

Citrus fruits (e.g. oranges, lemons, limes, grapefruit)
Tropical fruits (e.g. bananas, melon, pineapple, mango, kiwi, guava)
Soft and berry fruits (e.g. peaches, nectarine, apricots, cherries, redcurrants, blackcurrants, raspberries, strawberries, blackberries, bilberries)
Orchard fruits (e.g. apples, pears, plums)

Revise also the names of different containers: *can, jar, tub, carton, bottle*.

Divide the class into groups. Students who are elected to 'chair' the meetings in each group should be told to ask everybody's opinion in the group before taking a decision.

Teachers with access to a tape recorder and microphone may like to record parts of the discussion, moving from group to group. This will be useful for assessment and for giving students' feedback at the end of the lesson or in a subsequent lesson.

Set a time limit for the discussion (e.g. thirty minutes) and allow time for each group to report back the decisions.

SUGGESTED LESSON BREAK

Exercise 2

In the same groups, students work out the script for a commercial for their product. It can be for radio or TV and should be no longer than sixty seconds.

If you are based in Britain or the US and have a video recorder in class, you could try to collect a few typical commercials to play to students beforehand to stimulate their ideas. They can then analyse what makes something sell, how much repetition of the brand name there is, if the price is mentioned and so on.

Students in each group pool their ideas and select one or two to act out the commercial.

Exercise 3

Students write the results of their decisions in the form of a report which they would give to the company. The report can be divided between the members of the group and can be written up after completing the work on the radio commercial. The report can be either formal or informal in style. It may be helpful to write the initial framework of the report on the board for students to copy. e.g.

<u>Report of meeting on (date)</u>
The meeting was to discuss and make certain decisions concerning the launch of a new brand of (yoghurt). The following decisions were made:

<u>Flavour</u>
We decided/It was decided to launch three flavours only to start with: blackcurrant, strawberry and raspberry.

<u>Comparison with other products</u>
The yoghurt has larger pieces of real fruit in it and it is less sweet. It will be low-fat and it will cost less.
etc.

Each group then reads out their report followed by a performance of their commercial.

FLUENCY PROJECT 2: Questionnaires

Suggested lesson break: after Exercise 2

Exercise 1

Before starting work, ask students to copy the framework of the questionnaire in their notebooks, e.g:

Name : *Nationality:* *Age:*
1
2
3
4 a
b etc.

They can use one colour pen for their own answers and another colour pen for their partner's answers. Allow some time for students to discuss with their partner their choice of rating for the subsections a) - f) in Question 4 of the questionnaire. This could also be the basis of a whole-class discussion if the ratings differ considerably.

Exercise 2

Students can ignore the 'Age' section if they are studying in school and their ages are all the same. Ask one student to write the headings from the questionnaire on the board leaving plenty of space between them. He or she then asks all the pairs in turn to give their results for each question. As they do so, the student at the board should put a stroke (/) for each person who has marked that category.

For Question 4, a number rather than a stroke should be given. After asking three pairs, the results may look like this:

Age

15-20	21-30	31-40	over 40
////	//		

Qu 1

YES	NO
////	//

Qu 2

holiday	business	study English	other
//		/	/ (visit relatives)

Qu 3

The USA	Australia	New Zealand	Canada
//	/	/	
Britain	other		
/	/ (Malta)		

Qu 4
a) 3 4 4 4 5 5
b) 5 5 5 5 5 5
c) 3 3 3 4 4 5
d) 1 1 2 2 3 3
e) 4 4 4 5 5 5
f) 5 5 5 5 5 5

When all the results have been tabulated in this way, ask students to make a 'pie chart' showing percentages for Question 1, 2 and 3, and a bar chart for the ages and for Question 4. For Question 4, the total number for each section a) - f) should be added up and the bar chart should show the relative importance of the six categories. If you have a large class, allot a different section for each group to work out. A representative for each group should then pin up on the class noticeboard the statistical pie or bar chart for their section.

SUGGESTED LESSON BREAK

Exercise 3

Divide the class into groups. Ask each group to choose one of the suggested topics listed in their books and to construct a questionnaire around it. The questions should only require the interviewee to do the following operations:

- answer yes or no
- tick a box
- circle a letter
- circle a number or word
- give a one-word answer

Explain that questionnaires may use a combination of these types of question.

Ask students if they can see why 'open questions' are to be avoided e.g: *What do you like doing in your spare time?*

Students now think of some questions to ask in their questionnaires and how to frame the answers. Go round each group and help them with any difficulties. Each group should produce a short questionnaire which can be circulated round other groups for discussion and correction if necessary. The final version of the questionnaire should then be written out neatly (or typed) and photocopied so that each member of the original group has a copy.

Exercise 4

Each student should question six different people before the next lesson. The results are then collated by the original groups and reported to the rest of the class. Discuss any interesting experiences that may have occurred while the surveys were being carried out.

FLUENCY PROJECT 3:
Life decisions

Suggested lesson break: after Exercise 2.

BACKGROUND NOTES
'A' (Advanced) Level: the higher standard of examination in the British education system necessary for entry into university. It is usually taken at the age of eighteen. Most students take between two and four subjects, often in related subject groups, e.g: sciences, arts, modern languages. Universities specify which grades they require for entry onto specific courses.
Harvard Business School: The Harvard Business School in the USA has a reputation for being one of the world's leading schools of business.
Boston: the state capital of Massachusetts on the north-east coast of the USA.
medical school: Students can either go to university to read medicine for two years followed by a three-year clinical training course at a teaching hospital or they may go straight to a teaching hospital where they spend five years before they qualify. Medical students may be forced to leave medical school if they fail any major exams.
General Practitioner: (usually called a GP) a doctor who is trained in general medicine and whose work (General Practice) is to treat people in a certain local area.
Harley Street: an area of London where important doctors, especially specialists, have their clinics. It is a famous and expensive place to get medical treatment.

Exercise 1

Open a general discussion on what qualifications and qualities are necessary to become a doctor and what sacrifices have to be made. Ask the students to read Sam's dilemma and then cover the text while you ask the following comprehension questions:

How do we know that Sam is intelligent?
What sort of personality has Sam got?
What does his father want him to do and why?
Why is Boston an attractive option for Sam?
What is Sam thinking of doing?
Why is he not sure about it?

Crisis Point 1

Students briefly discuss in pairs which of the options Sam should choose, and what they would do if they were in Sam's position. They can also argue the case for each option, in a form of a roleplay. Student A takes the part of either Sam's father or Sam's uncle and Student B takes the part of Sam.

Ask students to look at the photos and say what it reveals about his decision, and at what point in Sam's life the photos are taken. They should then say what problems Sam's decision might cause.

Exercise 2

Write the following headings on the board to help students listen. (The key is in brackets). It may be necessary to pre-teach *pharmacist.*

Sam's girlfriend:
Name: (Penny)
Occupation: (pharmacist)
Age: (three years older than Sam)
Her living arrangements: (shares a rented flat in South London with a nurse)
Sam's living arrangements: (shares a house with seven other medical students in north London)

His problems:
1 (lives a long way from medical school, and from Penny)
2 (pays a lot in rent but spends very little time there)
3 (pressure of exams- has already failed one)

Play the tape once for students to make a mental note of the information they need to extract. Play again for students to note down the details, pausing if necessary. Check the answers and, as you do so, ask additional questions to draw out some more background information for the roleplay, e.g: *What do you think Sam's house is like? What does Penny think of it? Why isn't he working hard?* etc.

Ask a student to explain the word *ultimatum* (a final statement of conditions that must be met between two parties), then discuss with the students Sam and Penny's dilemma and what Penny's ultimatum is.

TAPESCRIPT
In the end, Sam decides to go to medical school and gets a place at King's College in London to study medicine. During his third year, he meets and falls in love with Penny, a pharmacist at a London teaching hospital. Penny, who is three years older, shares a rented flat in south London with a nurse.
Sam is now in his fourth year. He lives in a large, unmodernised house in north London with seven other medical students and it takes him nearly an hour to get to college every day. He pays £65 a week in rent and uses his room only as a place to sleep, as he spends most of his spare time with Penny. The pressure of exams is beginning to increase for Sam. He has already failed an important exam and has had to take it again. In the last few months, he and Penny decided not to spend so much time together but this has just caused more tension between them when they do meet. One Saturday evening after a meal, Penny gives Sam an ultimatum: either they get married or they go their separate ways. /bleep/

Crisis Point 2

Students now read Crisis Point 2 and decide which part they are going to play. Students perform in pairs while you go round and listen. Select a couple to perform their roleplay.

SUGGESTED LESSON BREAK

Exercise 3

Play the tape and ask students to follow the instructions in their books. Pause the tape after 'final exams' and elicit the answer to the first part of the task.

Now play the tape as far as 'aid is desperately needed' and ask: *What happened after Sam qualified? What is their problem three years later? What do they both want eventually? What does Sam need to do? What do they really want to do with their medical skills?*

Tell students that you are now going to play the rest of the tape and that they should note down the three options which Sam and Penny have to choose from. Before playing the tape, write on the board: *Harley Street, GP, Swindon, World Health Organisation.* Ask students if they know what the names stand for and where the places are. Use the background notes to help with your explanations. Play the tape and check the three options.

TAPESCRIPT

Sam and Penny agree to separate and not to see each other until he has qualified as a doctor. He concentrates on his studies and does well in his final exams.

After qualifying, Sam realises that he does want to spend the rest of his life with Penny and they decide to get married.
Three years later, Sam is now 27 and Penny is 30. They are happy in their jobs but are not quite sure what direction their lives are going in. They both want to start a family before their mid-thirties and would like to move out of London. Penny's job is not very well-paid and Sam needs a job that will keep them financially secure. However, at the back of their minds, he and Penny feel that they would like to put their medical skills to some real use in countries where medical aid is desperately needed.

By chance, three different options present themselves. An old school friend, Mark, says there is a vacancy for Sam as a GP (General Practitioner) in their recently modernised medical practice in Swindon, a large town in the west of England. The hours are long but it is a good, steady position and it would be an ideal place to bring up children.
A friend of Penny's, who works for the World Health Organisation, is trying to persuade Sam and Penny to join her medical aid team on a two-year project in Ethiopia. She says their medical skills are needed urgently. They would get their travel, board and lodging and would receive a small daily allowance. Meanwhile, a rich businessman, whom Penny once treated successfully, tells her about a position which has just become available in a private clinic in Harley Street, a famous area of private medical clinics in a well-to-do part of London. He assures Penny that the work would be extremely well-paid and that Penny could choose her hours of work.

Crisis Point 3

Students then form groups to discuss the advantages and disadvantages of each option and decide which they think Sam and Penny should choose. Point out that they might like to combine some of the options.

Exercise 4

Students write the letter for homework, based on their decision. To help students focus their letter, suggest that Sam writes to one of the friends he shared a house with, or that Penny writes to the nurse she used to share a flat with. They should try to make the letter friendly and informal, and they should assume that the 'friend' is aware of what the options are and what Sam and Penny have been doing.

Exercise 5

Finish the lesson by drawing the whole class together to discuss the questions in the book. Some useful expressions that you may need to introduce during the course of discussion are: *a six/seven-year course, a junior doctor, a houseman, a surgeon, consultant, clinic, general/private practice, salary, the national health service, private health scheme, responsible, cynical, dedicated.*

With the last question, remind students of any current cases in the news where doctors have made the headlines.

FLUENCY PROJECT 4: A radio programme

Suggested Lesson Break: after Exercise 2

Make sure you have allowed enough time for the preparation, rehearsal and performance of the radio programme and for feedback, i.e. at least two double periods.

Open the lesson by asking students how often and when they listen to the radio, what sort of programmes they like and what are the qualities of a good radio programme.

Ask them to read the advertisement 'Over to You' and ask if they can explain the concept of a Community Broadcasting Company (people helping to make their own programmes based on the interest of specific groups within the community).

Exercise 1

Read the introductory paragraph aloud and ask students to skim-read the 'Ideas for Items' and to mark the sections which interest them most. Students then consider the other items listed in Exercise 1. Your role at this point is to help the students make decisions at each stage without trying to influence them too much. If students decide to include musical links, someone will have to be chosen to select and coordinate the music.

For the last item, use your knowledge of the students' capabilities to influence the choice of producer. Note that the person chosen to be producer will have an ongoing task of checking the progress of each group so that he/she can start planning the outline of the complete programme from an early stage.

Exercise 2

At this point, act as a facilitator helping students to find the research material they may need, e.g: newspapers, magazines. Suggest that each group starts by discussing possible styles of presentation for the feature they have chosen. The preparation and writing stage may take a whole lesson and this may be the most appropriate place to break the lesson. Any students who haven't finished their writing can do so at home. Others can polish what they have written.

SUGGESTED LESSON BREAK

Exercise 3

When students next meet, the groups write a short description of their programme. This will be similar (and in some cases identical) to the 'Ideas for Items' description, but should specify programme topics in more detail with the name of the presenter. It would be helpful for the 'producer' if the group also attached some programme notes about timing, type of music required and the names of the presenters. At this stage the producer should write the order of items on the board.

Exercise 4

While students are rehearsing their features, the producer should walk round listening and offering suggestions.

Exercise 5

Draw the class together to record the items in the desired sequence, (or to perform them as a class), pausing to change items and to include the link music or link voice if necessary. If the programme has been recorded, it can be played back for comment and criticism of the content, production quality and language.

Grammar Index

(R) = *item appearing in a Grammar Review section*

Workbook tapescript

Unit 2

Exercise 3

Make comments. Look at your book and listen to the examples.

T: lovely day
S: *It's a lovely day, isn't it?*
T: fantastic party
S: *It's a fantastic party, isn't it?*

Now you speak. Substitute the different phrases in your book each time.

1 lovely day [bleep]
It's a lovely day, isn't it?
2 fantastic party [bleep]
It's a fantastic party, isn't it?
3 exciting match [bleep]
It's an exciting match, isn't it?
4 fascinating documentary [bleep]
It's a fascinating documentary, isn't it?
5 incredible story [bleep]
It's an incredible story, isn't it?
6 interesting article [bleep]
It's an interesting article, isn't it?
7 depressing sight [bleep]
It's a depressing sight, isn't it?
8 wonderful view [bleep]
It's a wonderful view, isn't it?

Exercise 4

Ask questions with certainty. Look at your book and listen to the example.

T: I think I've seen you somewhere before.
S: *Haven't I seen you somewhere before?*

Now you speak.

1 I think I've seen you somewhere before. [bleep]
Haven't I seen you somewhere before?
2 I think we've seen this film before.
Haven't we seen this film before?
3 I think I met you at Tim's house last week. [bleep]
Didn't I meet you at Tim's house last week?
4 I think that's Jan's new boyfriend. [bleep]
Isn't that Jan's new boyfriend?
5 I think she was working in Peru at the time. [bleep]
Wasn't she working in Peru at the time?
6 I think they got married recently. [bleep]
Didn't they get married recently?
7 I think you've forgotten something. [bleep]
Haven't you forgotten something?

Exercise 5

Ask questions with uncertainty or surprise. Look at your books and listen to the example.

T: You're surprised that John has made a mistake.
S: *John hasn't made a mistake, has he?*

Now you speak.

1 You are surprised that John has made a mistake. [bleep]
John hasn't made a mistake, has he?
2 You are not sure if you and your friend are lost. [bleep]
We aren't lost, are we?
3 You're not sure if the glasses are your friend's. [bleep]
These aren't your glasses, are they?
4 You are not sure if your father has phoned yet. [bleep]
My father hasn't phoned yet, has he?
5 You don't think your friend left the door open by mistake. [bleep]
He didn't leave the door open by mistake, did he?
6 You are surprised that some friends are getting married. [bleep].
They aren't getting married, are they?
7 You are surprised that Sue is leaving. [bleep]
Sue isn't leaving, is she?

Unit 3

Exercise 4

Listen to the extract from a radio show and decide which partner - Number 1, 2 or 3 - Gerry chose for his evening out.

COMPERE: Now, Gerry, can you tell us a bit about yourself before you ask the questions?

GERRY: Sure, Jim. I'm an outdoor person and lead a very active life. I spend a lot of time working out and playing sports. I suppose I'm not really an intellectual at all. As for night life, I prefer going to a pub with a group of friends to going to expensive restaurants. My type of date? Well, nobody too serious. Someone with a good sense of humour - who likes sport!

COMPERE: O.K, Gerry. I have the three young ladies at the end of the phone. Let's have the three questions.

GERRY: Right. Well here's my first question. What would be your idea of a good evening out? Number 1.

NO 1: A film and then a meal in a restaurant. Nothing too smart but it has to be good food.

GERRY: Number 2?

NO 2: Going to a disco with some friends is my idea of fun.

GERRY: Number 3.

NO 3: Well, I'm very fond of classical music, so my idea of a good evening out would be a concert and a meal afterwards.

GERRY: O.K. How do you prefer to spend your Saturday afternoons? No 1.

NO 1: Well, I'm a bit lazy so I'd prefer to stay in bed, but I might go out shopping, I suppose.

GERRY: Number 2?

NO 2: You'll find me at the health club on Saturday afternoon. I usually go for a swim and work out every Saturday afternoon.

GERRY: Number 3.

NO 3: I never have a special routine. Sometimes I see friends. Sometimes I read a book. It depends on my mood.

GERRY: Right. And my last question. What would you do if we were going out for a drive in my car, it broke down in the middle of a snowstorm and I asked you to get out and push. Number 1?

NO 1: I'd be extrememly annoyed but I'd do it.

GERRY: Number 2?

NO 2: I would tell you to push and I would get into the driving seat and steer.

GERRY: Nice one. Number 3?

NO. 3: I think I'd walk off and leave you.

GERRY: Right! Thanks very much!

COMPERE: Well, Gerry, which one is it to be? Number 1,2 or 3?

GERRY: It's difficult but I think I would have to go for number [bleep]

Unit 7

Exercise 2

Listen to an interview with a man who has just been to New York and tick the ideas in your book which he agrees with.

PRESENTER: Today Selina Kahn is in the arrival area at Gatwick Airport checking out today's topic - national stereotypes. Selina …

SELINA: Thanks, John. I have with me Eric, who's just flown in with Virgin Atlantic from the USA.

ERIC: That's right. I've just come back from New York.

SELINA: Is it as dangerous there as they say?

ERIC: No, New York isn't dangerous, no more than any other big city, especially if you're careful and don't advertise the fact that you're a tourist.

SELINA: And is it true what they say about New Yorkers, that they're rude, and that they only care about themselves?

ERIC: Well, I found the people were very friendly. However, they do have a reputation for not caring about other people. I think the reason for this is that life in New York is incredibly stressful. People just don't have the time to think about anybody else. It isn't that they don't care.

SELINA: Is there anything else you noticed about New Yorkers?

ERIC: Two things I had heard about before I went to New York did seem to be true, though. First is that they are always talking about money and how much things cost. Secondly, it's that people eat all the time as they go about their daily lives, you know they 'graze on the hoof' as they walk about the streets.

SELINA: Thanks Eric, and now I have with me, Sue, who's been to the south of France.

Unit 8

Exercise 4

Make polite requests on a train journey. Look at your books and listen to the examples.

T1: You want to buy a newspaper and you ask another passenger to look after your bag.

S: *Would you mind looking after my bag?*

T2: I'm sorry?

S: *Could you possibly look after my bag?*

T2: Oh yes, of course. No problem.

Now you speak.

1 You want to buy a newspaper and you ask another passenger to look after your bag. [bleep]
Would you mind looking after my bag?
I'm sorry? [bleep]
Could you possibly look after my bag?
Oh yes, of course. No problem.

2 You ask the assistant at the newspaper kiosk to give you a 50p piece in the change. [bleep]
Would you mind giving me a 50p piece in the change?
I'm sorry? [bleep]
Could you possibly give me a 50p piece in the change?
Oh yes, of course. No problem.

3 On the train, you want to do the crossword in your newspaper. You wonder if your neighbour could lend you a pencil. [bleep]
Would you mind lending me a pencil?
I'm sorry? [bleep]
Could you possibly lend me a pencil?
Oh yes, of course. No problem.

4 You feel a little chilly. You would like the person next to the window to close it a little. [bleep]
Would you mind closing the window a little?
I'm sorry? [bleep]
Could you possibly close the window a little?
Oh yes, of course. No problem.

5 Your suitcase is on the rack and you would like the person opposite to lift it down. [bleep]
Would you mind lifting my suitcase down?
I'm sorry? [bleep]
I said could you possibly lift my suitcase down?
Oh yes, of course. No problem.

6 A woman in the corner has got her walkman on very loud. You would like her to turn it down a little.

[bleep]
Would you mind turning your walkman down a little?
I'm sorry? [bleep]
I said Could you possibly turn your walkman down a little?
I'm sorry. I can't hear you!

Exercise 5

Ask for permission in different situations. Look at your book and listen to the examples.

T: You are in a café. You want to borrow the salt and pepper from another table.
S: *Excuse me. Do you mind if I borrow your salt and pepper?*

Now you speak.

1 You are in a café. You want to borrow the salt and pepper from another table. [bleep]
Excuse me. Do you mind if I borrow your salt and pepper?
2 You are in a hospital waiting room where there is a TV. You would like to change the channel. [bleep]
Excuse me. Do you mind if I change the channel?
3 You are in the reception area of a hotel. You would like to use the phone. [bleep]
Excuse me. Do you mind if I use the phone?
4 You are on an aeroplane. You would prefer to sit in the aisle seat. [bleep]
Excuse me. Do you mind if I sit in the aisle seat?
5 You are in a dentist's waiting room. You would like to turn the radio on. [bleep]
Excuse me. Do you mind if I turn the radio on?

Unit 10

Exercise 5

Listen to four people talking about the British police and put a tick next to the people who hold the opinions listed in your book.

Pauline Davis
From what I have seen since arriving in Britain, the police here are very friendly. And you see more policemen patrolling the streets than in Canada and when you ask them for directions they are very helpful.

Brian Dobson
A lot of policemen come across as heavy-handed. They seem to take the attitude that everyone is a criminal until proved different. I know they have a stressful job but I am not sure they are doing enough to identify with young people in the community.

Terry Smith
I had my mountain bike stolen last week. I reported it at the local police station and they were extremely friendly and helpful even though they didn't think I'd get it back.

Yvonne Tate
I think the police should do a lot more to get rid of their racist reputation especially now that we live in a multi-cultural society. Lots of my friends who are black have been picked up several times by the police for no real reason.

Unit 11

Exercise 5

Listen to two people talking about an event that occured in the middle of the night and number the events listed in your book in the correct order.

STEVE: Hi, Sue.
SUE: Steve! Nice to see you. You look a bit tired.
STEVE: Well, I didn't get a very good night's sleep last night.
SUE: Oh?
STEVE: Mm. You won't believe it but at about three o'clock in the morning there was a knock at the door and there was my neighbour, Roger, standing there in his pyjamas asking if he could come in.
SUE: What on earth was he doing ...?
STEVE: Well, what he said was that he had woken up in the middle of the night and heard his dog barking. So he thought it might have been someone prowling round his garden so he got up and went outside to have a quick look. Well, what he didn't realise was while he'd been asleep a strong gale had blown up and so the front door slammed shut behind him. So suddenly there he was, in his pyjamas, outside in a howling gale and unable to get back in.
SUE: But why didn't he ring the doorbell of his own house? Surely there was someone else in the house.
STEVE: No, no, that's it, you see. His wife had gone away to visit her parents for a couple of days so he was alone in the house. Anyway he couldn't face spending the rest of the night outside, so he came and knocked on my door.
SUE: And you were of course delighted to see him at that hour.
STEVE: Well, I didn't mind, actually. I gave him a mug of hot tea and a sofa for the night but in fact we stayed up all night chatting. So yes, I'm a little tired this morning.

Unit 13

Exercise 2

Inquire about days and times. Look at your book and listen to the example.

T: You want to know if your friend is free on Wednesday night.
S: *You're not free on Wednesday night by any chance, are you?*

Now you speak.
1 You want to know if your friend is free on Wednesday night. [bleep]
You're not free on Wednesday night by any chance, are you?
2 You want to know if your friend is free on Thursday morning. [bleep]
You're not free on Thursday morning by any chance are you?
3 You want to know if your friend is free on Thursday evening. [bleep]
You're not free on Thursday evening by any chance, are you?
4 You want to know if your friend is free on Friday at four. [bleep]
You're not free on Friday at four by any chance, are you?
5 You want to know if your friend is free at the weekend. [bleep]
You're not free at the weekend by any chance, are you?
6 You want to know if your friend is free for Sunday lunch. [bleep]
You're not free for Sunday lunch by any chance, are you?

Exercise 4
Agree days and times. Look at your book and listen to the example.
T: Is Friday O.K?
S: *Yes, Friday suits me fine.*

Now you speak.
1 Is Friday O.K? [bleep]
Yes, Friday suits me fine.
2 Shall we say two o'clock? [bleep]
Yes, two o'clock suits me fine.
3 What about Thursday morning? [bleep]
Yes, Thursday morning suits me fine.
4 Would three o'clock be all right? [bleep]
Yes, three o'clock suits me fine.
5 How about Saturday afternoon? [bleep]
Yes, Saturday afternoon suits me fine.
6 Shall we fix it for Monday morning, then? [bleep]
Yes, Monday morning suits me fine.

Exercise 3
Invite people informally and formally. Look at your book and listen to the examples.
T: Ask a friend to join you for a meal this evening.
S: *Do you fancy joining me for a meal this evening?*
T: Invite someone you have met for the first time to come out for a meal.
S: *Would you like to come out for a meal?*

Now you speak. Invite people informally or formally.
1 Ask a friend to join you for a meal this evening. [bleep]
Do you fancy joining me for a meal this evening?
2 Invite someone you have met for the first time to come out for a meal. [bleep]
Would you like to come out for a meal?
3 Ask a friend if she wants to see Robocop 3 with you. [bleep]
Do you fancy seeing 'Robocop 3' with me?
4 Invite some friends of your parents to stay for tea. [bleep]
Would you like to stay for tea?
5 Invite a business colleague to look round your company. [bleep]
Would you like to look round our company?
6 Ask a friend if she wants to go to the jazz concert in the park. [bleep]
Do you fancy going to the jazz concert in the park?
7 Invite your landlady to look at your family photos. [bleep]
Would you like to look at my family photos?
8 Ask a friend to come swimming with you. [bleep]
Do you fancy coming swimming with me?

Unit 15

Exercise 1
Listen to Julie talking about her great-aunt, and answer the questions in your book.

ALAN: Who's that, Julie?
JULIE: That's a picture of my great-aunt. She isn't alive any more but I have very strong memories of her. I used to go and stay with her in the holidays when I was little. She was so kind to me. She used to spoil me, I suppose. I was only about eight at the time, but she'd let me stay up late in the evenings and have supper with her in front of the television, and then she'd bring me a glass of milk and a biscuit in bed before I went to sleep. I remember once there was a very bad thunderstorm. I was really frightened, and I remember her pulling me into bed with her and we both lay there with our sheets over our head. She was so funny and full of life. I really miss her sometimes.

Unit 16

Exercise 4
Listen to the instructions for making a simple supper dish and number the illustrations in your book in the order in which they occur in the recipe.

PRESENTER: And now over to Anton who has our recipe for today.
ANTON: We all lead very busy lives so it's useful to have a number of recipes for quick and tasty supper dishes. Today I have chosen one of my favourites based on a typical dish called Rosti from my country. This is what you need:
- half a kilo of firm potatoes
- two medium sized onions
- some olive oil for frying

- some salt and pepper and, if you want, some mature Cheddar cheese. This is what you do.

First you peel and finely chop the onions and set these aside on a plate.

Now peel the potatoes and make sure you put them in a bowl of cold water so they don't turn brown.

Grate each potato in turn. You will need to do this quickly or the potatoes will go brown.

Now take a large heavy-bottomed pan and fry the chopped onions in two tablespoons of olive oil until they are golden.

In the meantime, dry the grated potato with kitchen paper. It's best to do this in small handfuls.

Add the potatoes to the onions in the frying pan and fry gently until the potato and onion mixture forms a type of pancake and has a nice brown crispy layer at the bottom.

Add salt and pepper according to taste. If you like, add some grated cheese to it and put it under the grill for a few moments.

I like to serve this with a simple green salad but you might like to serve it with grilled bacon, ham or even fried eggs.
Have a nice supper!

Unit 18

Exercise 3

Make and repeat suggestions. Look at your book and listen to the example. A friend of yours wants suggestions for entertaining his aunt and uncle for the afternoon. The trouble is, he's isn't listening properly when you answer, so you have to repeat your suggestions.

T: What shall I do with my aunt and uncle?
S: *Why don't you take them for a walk in the park?*
T: I'm sorry. I wasn't listening.
S: *I said, couldn't you take them for a walk in the park?*

Now you speak.

1 What shall I do with my aunt and uncle? [bleep]
Why don't you take them for a walk in the park?
I'm sorry. I wasn't listening. [bleep]
I said, couldn't you take them for a walk in the park?
2 No, I'm not keen on a walk in the park. It's too cold. [bleep]
Why don't you go to a concert with them?
I'm sorry. I wasn't listening. [bleep]
I said, couldn't you go to a concert with them?
3 No, I don't want to go to a concert. [bleep]
Why don't you treat them to tea at the Crown Hotel?
I'm sorry. I wasn't listening. [bleep]
I said, couldn't you treat them to tea at the Crown Hotel?
4 No, I don't think they'd be that impressed by tea at the Crown Hotel. [bleep]
Why don't you show them the new Dockland building?
I'm sorry. I wasn't listening. [bleep]
I said, couldn't you show them the new Dockland building?
5 The Dockland building's a bit boring. [bleep]
Why don't you take them to the Botanical Gardens?
I'm sorry. I wasn't listening. [bleep]
I said, couldn't you take them to the Botanical Gardens?
6 No, flowers bore me. [bleep]
Why don't you let them have a rest for a change?
I'm sorry. I wasn't listening. [bleep]
I said, couldn't you let them have a rest for a chnage?
Now that's the best idea you've had all day!

Exercise 4

Make suggestions. Look at your book and the pictures and listen to the example. A friend of yours is on her own for a Saturday evening and doesn't know what to do with herself.

T: What am I going to do with myself this evening?
S: *You could always read the paper.*

Now you speak. Look at each picture and make suggestions in the same way. Speak when you hear the 'bleep'.

1 [bleep] *You could always read the paper.*
2 [bleep] *You could always wash your hair.*
3 [bleep] *You could always make a cake.*
4 [bleep] *You could always read a book.*
5 [bleep] *You could always phone your mother.*
6 [bleep] *You could always go to bed.*

Exercise 5

Disagree with suggestions. Look at your book and listen to the example.

T: Let's go to the theatre.
S: *Won't that be rather expensive?*

Now you speak.

1 Let's go to the theatre. [bleep]
Won't that be rather expensive?
2 Shall we go to the football match? [bleep]
Won't that be rather crowded?
3 What about sitting on the patio? [bleep]
Won't that be rather hot?
4 We could always go on an open-top bus. [bleep]
Won't that be rather cold?
5 Why don't we go up on deck? [bleep]
Won't that be rather windy?
6 Couldn't we go and see the new Finnish film? [bleep]
Won't that be rather depressing?

Unit 20

Exercise D

Listen and name the animal and the sound it is making.
1 [cow mooing] 2 [horse neighing]
3 [dog barking] 4 [lion roaring] 5 [owl hooting]
6 [wolf howling] 7 [cat miaowing]
8 [hen clucking]

Unit 22

Exercise 4

Listen to the conversation in the shop and answer the questions in your book.

GIRL: Excuse me. I want to buy some earphones for my boyfriend's walkman. Are there several different sorts?

MAN: Well, earphones do come in different prices, yes, depending on how sensitive you want them to be.

GIRL: Mm. The trouble is, my boyfriend is so particular about everything. They've got to be good.

MAN: Well, you can't go wrong with this pair. And there's a special offer on them. Only £18.99. Reduced from £21.50.

GIRL: Mm. But what if they're not exactly what my boyfriend wants?

MAN: Don't worry. You can bring them back provided you have the receipt.

GIRL: Really?

MAN: Yes, as long as you bring them back within seven days, that is.

GIRL: I see. And I would be able to exchange it for a different pair, would I?

MAN: Yes, as long as you haven't damaged them of course. You know, if they're damaged, we wouldn't be able to take them back.

GIRL: No, all right then. I'll take them.

MAN: Thank you. Now how would you like to pay?

Unit 23

Exercise 1

Express approval and disapproval (1). Look at your book and listen to the examples.

T: What did you think of the film?
S: *I didn't think much of it, actually. In fact, it's one of the worst films I've seen this year.*
T: What did you think of the restaurant?
S: *I was quite impressed by it, actually. In fact it's one of the best restaurants I've ever been to.*

Now you speak.

1 What did you think of the film? [bleep]
I didn't think much of it, actually. In fact, it's one of the worst films I've seen this year.
2 What did you think of the restaurant? [bleep]
I was quite impressed by it, actually. In fact, it's one of the best restaurants I've ever been to.
3 What did you think of the book? [bleep]
I was quite impressed by it, actually. In fact, it's one of the best books I've ever read.
4 What did you think of the documentary? [bleep]
I didn't think much of it, actually. In fact, it's one of the worst documentaries I've seen this year.
5 What did you think of the hotel? [bleep]
I was quite impressed by it, actually. In fact, it's one of the best hotels I've ever stayed in.
6 What did you think of the concert? [bleep]
I was quite impressed by it, actually. In fact, it's one of the best concerts I've been to this year.
7 What did you think of the meal? [bleep]
I didn't think much of it, actually. In fact, it's one of the worst meals I've ever had.

Exercise 2

Express approval and disapproval (2). Look at your book and listen to the example.

T: Did you enjoy the meal?
S: *I thought the first course was excellent but I didn't think the main course was very interesting.*

Now you speak.

1 Did you enjoy the meal? [bleep]
I thought the first course was excellent but I didn't think the main course was very interesting.
2 Did you enjoy the film? [bleep]
I thought the story was O.K. but I didn't think the acting was very impressive.
3 Did you like the hotel? [bleep]
I thought the rooms were comfortable but I didn't think the service was very efficient.
4 What did you think of the concert? [bleep]
I thought the first half was excellent but I didn't think the second half was very exciting.
5 How did you like the car? [bleep]
I thought the design was very elegant but I didn't think the performance was very impressive.

Unit 24

Exercise 4

Listen to someone recounting a travel incident and complete the sentences in your book using a third conditional.

Did you hear what happened to me last week? It's typical of me, I suppose. I was going to Tunisia on business with a colleague of mine. We were going to use my car to go to the airport and leave it in the long term car park. I had allowed plenty of time, which was fortunate, because when we got to the airport and I took the bags out of the car I realised that I had forgotten my passport! I couldn't think what to do at first. Then I thought, well, maybe my wife, Sue, could bring my passport to the airport. So I found a phone and telephoned home in the hope that she hadn't yet left for work. The phone rang six or seven times and I thought 'That's it. She's already left. There's no way I'm going to get my passport now.' I was just about to put the phone down when my colleague persuaded me to hang on for a few moments more. He said Sue might be in the bathroom or something. So I did, and then a second or two later Sue answered the phone. She had, in fact, already left the house but by mistake she'd left a window open so she could hear the phone ringing from the street and rushed back in. Luckily, we live quite near the airport so she was able to jump in a taxi and bring me my passport. She got to the airport just in time and we caught the flight by the skin of our teeth!

Unit 28

Exercise 2

Listen to the news extract and answer the questions in your book.

NEWSREADER: And now for some news. Thousands of football fans have arrived in Munich in Germany today for the final of the World Cup between England and Denmark. Many fans will be queuing all night in the hope of getting a ticket for tomorrow's match. The organisers are concerned that it will be a peaceful event. According to one German official:

OFFICIAL: We will be putting the English fans at one end of the stadium and the Danish fans at the other. Police will be controlling the crowds all the time so we don't expect there to be any trouble.

NEWSREADER: And the question on every English fan's lips is 'Will Paul Gascoigne be playing tomorrow?' The controversial football star suffered a knee injury in his last match and it is uncertain whether he will be fit to play tomorrow. And that's all from our news room today.

Exercise 4

Make conversational responses. Look at your book and listen to the examples.

T: Will you be working late tonight?
S: *I'm afraid so.*
T: We're not going to be late, are we?
S: *I don't think so.*
T: Is your cold any better today?
S: *I'm afraid not.*

Now you speak.

1 Will you be working late tonight? [bleep]
I'm afraid so.
2 We're not going to be late, are we? [bleep]
I don't think so.
3 Is your cold any better today? [bleep]
I'm afraid not.
4 I wonder if the weather will clear up by tomorrow. [bleep]
I hope so.
5 Have you finished with that book yet? [bleep]
I'm afraid not.
6 Will Simon be bringing that dreadful friend of his? [bleep]
I hope not.
7 Does the film start at nine? [bleep]
I expect so.
8 Is it February 15th today? [bleep]
I think so.

Unit 29

Exercise 1

Listen to the following sentences and match them with the adverbs and adverbial phrases from the box.

1 Can you hurry up please? I haven't got all day.
2 I can't believe you could do such a thing!
3 You don't have to go if you don't want to.
4 Get me to the hospital as fast as you can!
5 It's good of you to come. Please take a seat.
6 Can we open it now, Mum?
7 Oh dear. I..I..I hope I haven't broken it.

Unit 30

Exercise 2

Listen to Brian's conversation with another journalist and note down the advantages of working as a foreign correspondent compared with being on the news desk in London.

JACK: Brian, hi! Have you just got back?

BRIAN: Yes, just this minute. I haven't even had a chance to unpack yet.

JACK: How are you enjoying life as a foreign correspondent, then?

BRIAN: Well, I'm certainly finding it a lot more exciting than working in the newsroom here.

JACK: Yes, I can imagine.

BRIAN: I mean, you have to work incredibly fast, so it's a lot more demanding.

JACK: Mmm. Sounds like hard work to me.

BRIAN: Sure but you're much more involved in events than you are when you're writing about them back in England. And it's a much more active life. You're running around all the time. It suits me better than being stuck behind a desk.

JACK: Mm. I'm not convinced. I mean there are advantages to working here in Britain, you know.

BRIAN: Such as?

JACK: Such as: it's a lot less stressful, the hours aren't so long and you're far less likely to get shot while you're on the job!

Unit 31

Exercise 3

Listen to the conversation and write the couple's route in your book.

FRANK: Well, this is us at Heathrow Airport before we set off. First stop United States. That's the Empire State Building and that's Times Square.

JUDITH: Did you get a chance to see the Museum of Modern Art?

MARVA: Well, no. There wasn't time, really.

FRANK: Now this is Day Two. Both of us on the beach in the Bahamas taking it easy.

JUDITH: And this is Day Three, is it?

MARVA: Yes, this is in South America, sailing down the Amazon.

JUDITH: Oh, those must be the Andes!

FRANK: No, that's Mount Fuji in Japan, actually. It's Day Four, you see.

JUDITH: Oh, I see. That's you recovering from the climb, is it?

MARVA: Well no. We didn't actually have time to climb it.

FRANK: Ah! Day Five.

MARVA: Yes, that's the two of us, sunbathing in the south of Thailand.

FRANK: Day Six. That's me in front of the Taj Mahal in India.

JUDITH: It looks more like the Vatican in Rome to me.

FRANK: Oh, perhaps it's Day Seven, then. That's right. We did the Vatican after the Taj Mahal.

JUDITH: And who are those two people?

FRANK: Ah, that's Day Eight. That's Marva and myself asleep at Heathrow Airport!

Unit 32

Exercise 3

Listen to some news items and note down the details of each item under the headings in your book.

And now here is the eight o'clock news.

Florida was hit yesterday afternoon by a hurricane of up to a hundred miles an hour. Twenty people are believed to be dead and over a hundred injured. Relief workers are being sent in to help clear the damage. Emergency aid of three million dollars was promised last night by the US government.

A bank in Manchester was robbed at gunpoint yesterday as five men burst in at lunchtime wearing masks and carrying shotguns. The robbers escaped with over 10,000 pounds. Three customers who were in the bank at the time were held hostage until the robbers made their escape. No one was injured but one of the bank clerks is still being detained in hospital for shock.

And finally, Ben, the world's oldest dog, died on Tuesday in Toronto, Canada, at the ripe old age of thirty. 'It's a very sad day for me,' said his owner, Sam Harris. 'Ben was the best friend a man could ever wish for.' Ben is now assured of a place in the Guinness Book of Records.
And that ends the news for today.

Unit 33

Exercise 4

Draw possible conclusions. Look at your book and listen to the example.

T: He was found wandering around the house at three in the morning.

S: *He might have been sleepwalking.*

Now you speak

1 He was found wandering around the house at three in the morning. [bleep]
He might have been sleepwalking.

2 I don't know who she was talking to for so long. [bleep]
She might have been phoning her boyfriend.

2 Why did you tell me to turn down the music? [bleep]
The neighbours might have been trying to sleep.

3 There was a strange sound outside the sitting room window last night. [bleep]
Someone might have been trying to break in.

4 I phoned her but her number was engaged. [bleep]
She might have been trying to phone you!

5 You weren't in when I called yesterday. [bleep]
I might have been sitting in the garden.

Exercise 5

Draw definite conclusions. Look at your book and listen to the two examples.

T: I couldn't see the little boy anywhere.

S: *He must have been hiding.*

T: She suddenly forgot what she was saying.

S: *She can't have been concentrating.*

Now you speak.

1 I couldn't see the little boy anywhere. [bleep]
He must have been hiding.

2 She suddenly forgot what she was saying. [bleep]
She can't have been concentrating.

3 Sally wasn't home when I called. [bleep]
She must have been fetching the children.

4 He came last in the race. [bleep]
He can't have been trying.

5 The man was stopped in his car by the police. [bleep]
He must have been drinking and driving.

6 I didn't hear the announcement at all. [bleep]
You must have been dozing.

7 Don't you remember I said we'd be late? [bleep]
I can't have been listening.

8 Her eyes were red and puffy. [bleep]
She must have been crying.

9 She got burnt on the first day on the beach! [bleep]
She can't have been wearing any suntan lotion.

Unit 36

Exercise 2

Criticise habits. Look at your book and listen to the example. Mr Smith has returned from work and is asking his wife about her day with the children.

T: Anna broke a cup this morning
S: *She's always breaking cups!*

Now you speak. You are Mr Smith.

1 Anna broke a cup this morning. [bleep]
She's always breaking cups!
2 Then she cut herself with the bread knife. [bleep]
She's always cutting herself with the bread knife!
3. Then Tim lost his schoolbag. [bleep]
He's always losing his school bag!
4. And he missed his train. [bleep]
He's always missing his train!
5 And Harry got into trouble with his teacher. [bleep]
He's always getting into trouble with his teacher!
6 And then I watched Neighbours on TV. [bleep]
You're always watching 'Neighbours'! It sounds like a very familiar day to me!

Exercise 3

Express irritation. Look at your book and listen to the example.

T: Mr Sanderson said could you type this letter?
S: *I wish he'd write more legibly.*

Now you speak.

1 Mr Sanderson said could you type this letter? [bleep]
I wish he'd write more legibly.
2 John says it'll be another half an hour before he's ready. [bleep]
I wish he'd hurry up.
3 Sarah's going out with Tom again this evening. [bleep]
I wish she wouldn't spend so much time with him.
4 We got this letter from the council this morning. [bleep]
I wish they'd express themselves more clearly.
5 Dave's coming to stay for three weeks. [bleep]
I wish you wouldn't tell me things at the last minute.
6 Penny isn't sure if she's going to come on Saturday. [bleep]
I wish she'd make her mind up.

Exercise 4

Criticise past actions. Look at your book and listen to the example.

T: Why didn't you tell me?
S: *You might have told me!*

Now you speak.

1 Why didn't you tell me? [bleep]
You might have told me!
2 Why didn't she write? [bleep]
She might have written!
3 Why didn't he pay the bill? [bleep]
He might have paid the bill!
4 I was a bit upset that they didn't lend a hand. [bleep]
They might have lent a hand!
5 I can't understand why he didn't offer us a lift. [bleep]
He might have offered us a lift!
6 Why didn't you ask me first? [bleep]
You might have asked me first!

Unit 38

Exercise 2

Listen to the conversation at an airport check-in counter, and choose the best answer for the questions in your book.

MAN: That's good. We've managed to get here with plenty of time to spare. I'll just go and check in.
WOMAN: There's our check-in desk over there.
GIRL: I'm awfully sorry, sir. There's been a slight problem. I'm afraid the 11.30 flight is fully booked.
MAN: It can't be. We're not late. It's only 10.30. There's at least an hour before the flight is due to leave.
GIRL: I realise that, sir, but there's been a problem with the computer and the flight's been overbooked. I really do apologise.
MAN: But this is outrageous!
GIRL: I'm sorry, sir.
MAN: So what do you intend to do about it?
WOMAN: Frank, do calm down. It's no use getting aggressive.
GIRL: I realise that it is the airline's fault, sir, and we are doing our best to sort it out.
MAN: Huh! We've arranged to meet some people in Manchester for lunch. There's no point in going if we can't get there in time. We really need to be on this flight.
GIRL: I'm sorry, sir, but it's just not possible but I'll try to get you on the next available flight.
MAN: And when will that be?
GIRL: 13.30.
MAN: You mean 1.30, in over two hours' time! That's ridiculous!
GIRL: Frank, it's no use shouting at her. It's not her fault. Can you promise to put us on that flight?
GIRL: Yes, madam. I'll do that right away.
WOMAN: Thank you. Come on, Frank. Let's go and have a coffee and find a telephone.
MAN: Hmph! I don't feel like waiting two hours in this place. And what about lunch? What are we supposed to …

Unit 40

Exercise 2

JANE: A lot of what I feel about the play is through having worked on it as an actress, through Rita's point of view.

INTERVIEWER: Is it a play with a message?

JANE: I think the play says an awful lot about education and emphasises the importance of it, especially the importance it was for Rita at that time in her life. I think it says it really can feed and nourish a person spiritually. But it also says that education doesn't have to be boring. Another interesting point, I think, is that education can be a threat like it is to Rita's husband, Denny.

INTERVIEWER: What do you think the play's really about?

JANE: I think one of the things that sticks in my mind which Rita mentions early on in the play and very much so in that last scene, is the word 'choice'. And that, I think, is the key word. Choice through education, not choice between which brand of washing powder to use, but on a higher level. So it doesn't necessarily mean you're a better person because you've got that education but it gives you the choice and, as Frank says and what Rita recognises, - well, Frank says it gives you a different song to sing. Rita feels it's giving her a better song to sing but at the end she's appreciated Frank's point of view as well.

INTERVIEWER: Now, the play has been a huge success. Why do you think that is?

JANE: I think it's because so many different people can relate to it in different ways and on different levels. I mean, on one level it's just a simple, touching love story, but there's also a lot of depth to it. It's also very funny and well written and the characters — even the ones that we don't see in the play — are totally believable.

AREAS OF DIFFICULTY IN SPEECHWORK

Section A Weak forms

1 Questions

Listen and repeat the questions.

When do they start?
When shall I come?
What can she say?
Who could he ask?
Why was he there?
Why should I pay?

Exercise 2 Modal verbs in the past

Listen and repeat the sentences.

They might have caught a different train.
He must have found it by now.
She can't have finished the book yet.
I could have sworn he was there.

Exercise 3 Grammar words

Listen and repeat the sentences.

I have to leave.
It's not the time of day to do it.
I drove from home to work in twenty minutes.
I said that it was mine.
I bought some bread and milk at the shop.
It's cheaper than in London but not as cheap as I thought.

Section B Contractions

Listen and repeat the sentences.

I've already paid the bill.
She's coming on the ten o'clock train.
They weren't at home when I called.
You couldn't give me a hand, could you?
I think you've broken your arm.

Section C Word linking

Exercise 1 Sound liaison

Listen and repeat the phrases and sentences.

a waste of time What a nice idea! How are you?
now and then high and low way out
here and there far and wide

Exercise 2 Sound deletion

Listen and repeat the phrases.

must pay the fact that next day stand still
good point won't be ten points one bed in case
one card this shirt secretary policeman library

Section D Pronunciation of individual sounds

1 /ɪ/ hit /iː/ heat

Listen and practise the difference.
his/he's live/leave sit/seat hit/heat fit/feet

Listen and underline the word you hear in each sentence.

1 I'm going to live on my own.
2 Can you feel this?
3 I saw the ship when I climbed the hill.
4 The boy beat the dog.
5 The note says 'We'll come tomorrow'.

Listen and repeat the sentences.

Please keep the streets clean. What's this in Japanese?
Peter lives at sixty-three Pitt Street.

2 /æ/ fat /ʌ/ sun
Listen and practise the difference.
hat/hut mad/mud run/ran drunk/drank much/match

Listen and underline the word you hear in each sentence.
1 She's worried about her uncle.
2 He bought a garden hat.
3 She's run all the way.
4 I crashed the car against the wall.
5 She used a rag to clear up the stain on the carpet.

Listen and repeat the phrases and sentences.
an African rug a mad uncle
a ham sandwich and a currant bun
She rang her mother on Monday, not Saturday.

3 /eɪ/ take /e/ said
Listen and practise the difference.
wait/wet main/men gate/get taste/test late/let

Listen and underline the word you hear in each sentence.
1 It's a big debt for him.
2 I'd like to sit in the shade.
3 I'm afraid it's already let.
4 Could you give me the paper, please?
5 The pain is in my hand.

Listen and repeat the sentences.
He's waiting to test it. It was a grey, wet day.
I'll fetch a pen straight away.

4 /əʊ/road /ɔː/ door
Listen and practise the difference.
note/nought coat/caught low/law bone/born cold/called

Listen and underline the word you hear in each sentence.
1 He was in the hole, crying.
2 She was given a yellow ball for her birthday.
3 It was a very big lawn.
4 He took the coal in the kitchen.
5 Please don't snore any more!

Listen and repeat the phrases.
no more snow It won't be boring.
a phone call for Joe The water is cold.

5 /t/ ten /θ/ think /ð/ then /d/ den
Listen and practise the difference.
tin/thin part/path tank/thank tree/three then/den there/dare breathe/breed than/Dan

Listen and underline the word you hear in each sentence.
1 I put it in a tin can.
2 He drew a large three on the piece of paper.
3 She made a cup of tea then left.
4 He threw the ball in the air.
5 He took the wrong part.
6 The animals can hardly breathe in here.

Listen and repeat the phrases and sentences.
Danny's mother and father
This is the third time I've thanked her.
Take a deep breath and count to thirty.

6 /p/ pat /b/ bat /t/ too /d/ do /k/ curl /g/ girl
Listen and practise the difference.
pat/bat ton/done cot/got pet/bet tore/door card/guard

Listen and underline the word you hear in each sentence.
1 I'm going to back the car.
2 Can you give me the time?
3 The peach was wonderful.
4 She's dyed her hair.
5 The bracelet was gold.
6 The class is too big.

Listen and repeat the phrases.
a cup of tea and a glass of milk
a piece of cake and a biscuit
a Burmese cat and a Pekinese dog
ninety pence for two peaches and a bunch of grapes

7 /b/ berry /v/ very
Listen and practise the difference.
berry/very bain/vain ban/van best/vest bet/vet bow/vow bat/vat beer/veer boat/vote

Listen and repeat the phrases and sentences.
a rubber ball five friends of Bob a very lively boy
He visited Bilbao. Have a biscuit.

8 /v/ vary /w/ wary
Listen and practise the difference.
veal/wheel vest/west via/wire vet/wet vary/wary

Listen and underline the word you hear in each sentence.
1 This area of France is famous for its wine.
2 She pointed to the west.
3 He didn't like the vet.
4 Do you call this worse?

Listen and repeat the phrases and sentences.
a very wet winter a week's work seven sandwiches
We won't invite her.
William went to Vienna on Wednesday.

9 /r/ red /l/ light
Listen and practise the difference.
red/led right/light row/low read/lead wrong/long

Listen and underline the word you hear in each sentence.
1 Could I borrow your red pencil?
2 Don't take the long road, will you?
3 Do you think the room is right?
4 The grass is almost green.
5 The insects glow in the dark.

Listen and repeat the phrases.
a red letter day green grass
the long road to London
the bright lights of Richmond

10 /s/ send /z/ zoo

Listen and practise the difference.

ice/eyes lace/laze Sue/zoo rice/rise once/ones price/prize

Listen and underline the word you hear in each sentence.

1 The first sentence begins with zed.
2 She let the horse loose.
3 I think you need a big sip.
4 I've only got two pens left.
5 I don't like zoos.

Listen and repeat the phrases and sentences.

She's won first prize. It's freezing outside.
It's used for sailing. These are easy sentences.
I need a razor. He wants a rise in salary.

11 /s/ saw /ʃ/ sure /ʒ/ pleasure

Listen and practise the sounds.

see she sell shell sock shock press pressure pleasure cushion action vision leisure measure usually beige

Listen and repeat the phrases and sentences.

six sheets She sells cushions.
I'm sure she sent it. She's at the leisure centre.
I usually read Shakespeare for pleasure.

12 The silent *r* /hɑːd/ hard

Listen and repeat the words and sentences.

hard word girl port better father sure wear cure fire iron earth
It's hard work. My father's sure to hear.
Where's the iron?
The farmhouse is on fire.
You'd better wear my jacket.

13 Consonant clusters beginning with /s/ student

Listen and practise the sounds.

school stop student Spanish Scottish slipped street stranger

Listen and repeat the sentences.

I started school at the age of six.
We spoke to some Spanish students.
She slipped in the street and strained her wrist.

14 /tr/ train /dr/ drain /str/ stretch

Listen and practise the sounds.

try/dry train/drain trip/drip trill/drill tread/dread trout/drought stress strain stretch straw stripe stroll strange

Listen and repeat the phrases and sentences.

a trip to Truro by train
He wore dreadful stripey trousers and a straw hat.
strangers strolling down the street
I tried to find something to drink.

Workbook key

Unit 1

1 Type of word: *adj(ective)* Definition: *brave, showing courage* (etc) Example sentence: *It was a courageous action by a courageous person.* (etc)

2 2 at 3 have 4 to 5 hear 6 for 7 trees 8 and 9 idea 10 full 11 ears 12 were 13 breath 14 as 15 for 16 to 17 shut 18 no 19 longer 20 like 21 surfboard 22 an 23 never

3 spoke spoken; flew flown; drove driven; threw thrown; rode ridden; spent spent; put put; gave given; taught taught; forgot forgotten; knew known

4 2 have just had 3 have swum 4 have won 5 has seen 6 Have you ever tried 7 felt 8 has been 9 saw 10 met 11 Has she had 12 have already died

5 2 anxious 3 brave 4 risky 5 nervous 6 safe 7 terrified 8 afraid/frightened

6 I promised to write; settling; I've been here for a week; I have already written; we all had to write; nervous; the first time I have written; language

Unit 2

1 2 would they? 3 doesn't she? 4 will you? 5 didn't he? 6 do I? 7 have they? 8 aren't I?

2
2 Aren't you enjoying the video?
3 Hasn't the post arrived yet?
4 Doesn't the train have/Hasn't the train got a restaurant car?
5 Aren't we/I going to have an English test today?
6 Isn't the weather cold for the time of year?

Unit 3

1
2 She doesn't mind ironing but he doesn't like/dislikes it.
3 She hates/detests/can't stand travelling by undergound but he doesn't mind it.
4 She quite likes/enjoys watching sport on TV but he dislikes/doesn't like it.
5 She loves/adores decorating the house but he can't stand/hates/detests it.
6 She detests/hates/can't stand not having a car but he doesn't mind it.

2 careful; unemotional; harmless; unkind; unoriginal; unsafe; unselfish; tactful

3
2 Jack would rather listen to his walkman than read a book.
3 Marilyn prefers going to the theatre to going to the cinema.
4 Jonathan would rather go out with his girlfriend than go out with a group of friends.
5 Sam prefers walking to taking a bus.
6 Gillian would rather study than babysit.

4 Number 2; Reasons: both like going out with friends, both like sport, both have a good sense of humour

5 **Across**: 1 couple 4 go 5 of 7 prefer to 9 separate 11 NY 12 tastes 14 ill 17 whereas
Down: 1 common 2 of 3 perfect 4 get 6 he 8 one 10 rather 13 live 15 she 16 mad

Unit 4

1 2 a 3 the 4 the 5 - 6 - 7 - 8 a 9 the 10 an 11 the 12 the 13 a 14 the 15 a 16 the 17 an 18 the 19 - 20 the

2

energy	energetic	energetically
music	musical	musically
emotion	emotional	emotionally
intellect	intellectual	intellectually
nature	natural	naturally
crisis	critical	critically
fortune	fortunate	fortunately
physique	physical	physically

3 2 critical 3 energy 4 physically 5 fortunately 6 crisis 7 physical 8 accidentally

Unit 5

1 2d so (that) I could 3a so (that) people won't 4f in order to catch 5g so (that) he wouldn't 6b in order to lose 7h so (that) you won't 8c so (that) we can have

2 2 am learning 3 am working 4 am writing 5 am enjoying 6 visit 7 am studying 8 buy 9 am currently working 10 need

3 Type 1: work out (a problem); clear up (a room), wake up, turn off, ring up
Type 2: get on with (someone), look after
Type 3: clear up (weather), wake up, go on

4 2 getting on 3 get into 4 get across 5 get away 6 got over

5
3 art. just finished secondary school
4 t I have been learning
5 sp Unfortunately
6 ʌ can't afford to pay
7 w.o. all my costs
8 t I won't be able
9 ʌ go to England
10 gr I like studying

11 t are asking for
12 gr improve my English (in order) to get a job
13 exp hearing from you

Progress Test Units 1-5

The progress tests are designed to give practice in some of the types of questions that the students will meet when they take the First Certificate examination. The three types of exercise, which are repeated in each test, are: 1) transformation 2) word formation 3) multiple choice vocabulary exercise. The first two are directly related to the language covered in the previous five units. The third exercise, however, may include words in a lexical set which have not necessarily occurred in the preceding five units, but which often cause confusion.
Total marks = 32
Suggested marking scheme:
Exercise 1: 2 marks per sentence = 16
Exercise 2: 1 mark per word = 8
Exercise 3: 1 mark per correct choice = 8

1 1 Aren't you a friend of John's?
2 I prefer listening to music to watching TV.
3 I haven't had such a good night's sleep for weeks.
4 I can't stand listening to country and western music.
5 It's the first time I've (ever) been to the opera.
6 This is the worst film I've ever seen.
7 It was the first time she had travelled by plane.
8 I'd like to interview him so (that) I can get a better impression of him.

2 1 courageous 2 daring 3 naturally 4 critical 5 explanation 6 application 7 costly 8 hopelessly

3 1B 2D 3C 4B 5D 6B 7B 8B

Unit 6

1 2 ear 3 jaw 4 neck 5 chin 6 forehead 7 eyebrow 8 cheek 9 moustache 10 throat

2 2 sun-tanned skin 3 long-haired dog 4 red-haired man 5 well-dressed 6 long-sleeved blouse 7 shoulder-length hair

3 2 with 3 in 4 by 5 in 6 with 7 in

5 Bestepapa: 1,7,9 Bestemama: 5 Eddoes: 3,4,11
The man from Harlem: 2,6,8,10

Unit 7

1 2 Joe came to stay last December and he's been living with us ever since.
Joe has been living with us since last December.
3 Barry went to Boston a year ago and he's been working there ever since.
Barry has been working in Boston for a year.
4 Sandra met Paul six months ago and she's been going out with him ever since.
Sandra has been going out with Paul for six months.
5 Peter got a job at the college in 1992 and he's been teaching there ever since.
Peter has been teaching at the college since 1992.
6 Bob lost his job when they closed down his factory and he's been looking for another job ever since.
Bob has been looking for another job since they closed down his factory.

2 Ticks against 4 and 5

3 2 have you been waiting 3 've been waiting 4 've only been 5 haven't made 6 've just dropped in 7 's been giving 8 Have you been 9 've ever been 10 've been coming 11 Have you just come in 12 've lost 13 Have you filled in 14 've already given

4 3 Look it up 4 Look for it 5 Look at it 6 Look in it 7 Look down it 8 Look after it 9 Look round it 10 Look through it

Unit 8

1 2 Do you know when he left?
3 Do you know when it starts?
4 Do you know how far he had gone?
5 Do you know if the bus has gone?
6 Do you know where she was sitting?
7 Do you know if they left a message?

2 2 Do you think you could lend me your camera for the weekend?
3 Do you think you could change a £5 note for me?
4 Do you think you could forward my post when I leave?
5 Do you think you could answer the phone while I'm out?

3 2 Do you mind if I turn the volume up?
3 Would you mind taking any messages for me while I'm out?
4 Do you mind if I turn the heating on?
5 Do you mind if I make myself a cup of tea?
6 Would you mind sending me another bill?

6 Suggested conversation

YOU: Do you mind if I sit here?
WOMAN: Not at all.
YOU: Do you think you could lend me/I could borrow your magazine?
WOMAN: I'm sorry? (I didn't realise you were talking to me!)
YOU: Would you mind lending me your magazine?
WOMAN: No, of course not.
YOU: Excuse me, but do you mind if we play our radio? We won't play it very loud.
WOMAN: Not at all.

Unit 9

1 1: good-looking, well-dressed, bald-headed, overweight 2: bad-tempered, big-headed, fun-loving, open-minded, quick-thinking, cold-hearted, good-hunoured, hard-working, narrow-minded, self-confident, warm-hearted 3: left-handed, Spanish-speaking, well-qualified

2 2 narrow-minded 3 well-dressed 4 cold-hearted 5 good-humoured 6 self-confident 7 Spanish-speaking

3 2A 3B 4A 5C 6A

4 2 happened 3 ago 4 in 5 which 6 filled 7 for 8 later 9 still 10 despite 11 days 12 Since/Despite/After 13 on 14 heard 15 sending 16 so 17 hearing 18 Yours

Unit 10

1 2B 3B 4C 5C 6A 7A

2 2 have to show 3 do young people still have to do 4 had to meet 5 don't have to watch 6 will have to pay for 7 Did you have to do 8 didn't have to wait/ haven't had to wait 9 doesn't have to work

3 disloyal; unenthusiastic; inexperienced; irreplaceable; dishonest; irresponsible; disorganised; unreliable; insensitive; inefficient

4

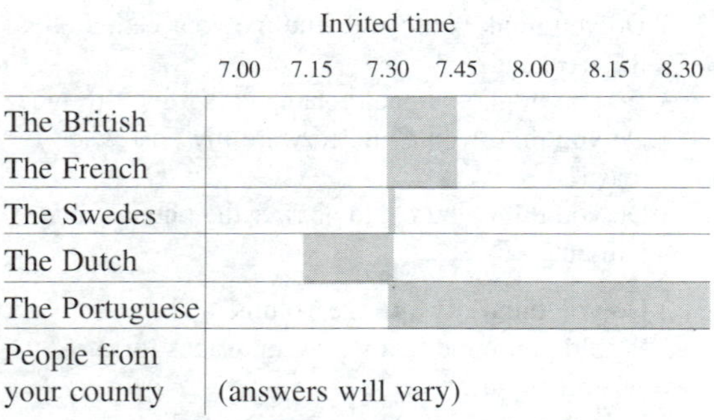

5 Pauline: 2, 4 Brian: 1, 5 Terry: 4 Yvonne: 3

Progress Test Units 6-10

1 1 Six months ago she started wearing contact lenses.
2 Even though she felt ill she went on the excursion.
3 I've been going to art classes for two years.
4 Would you mind picking me up at the station?
5 I wonder where the information desk is.
6 Despite its age the radio still works.
7 You ought to/should see a doctor.
8 You didn't need to bring a present/needn't have brought a present.

2 1 unemployed 2 strong 3 appearance 4 uncomfortable 5 energetically 6 inconvenience 7 response 8 reasonable

3 1A 2B 3D 4D 5C 6C 7B 8D

Unit 11

1 1A 2C 3C 4B

2 2 noticed 3 was pouring 4 realised 5 had stabbed 6 ran 7 was/were singing 8 treated 9 told 10 had had

3 2 didn't feel 3 had run 4 had just finished 5 got up 6 had known 7 had seen 8 saw

4 2 had been waiting 3 had been snowing 4 had been playing 5 had been overworking 6 had been smoking 7 had been trying 8 had been using 9 had been wearing

5 1c 2h 3e 4b 5d 6g 7a 8f

Unit 12

1 2 talking 3 moving 4 slam 5 leaving 6 saying 7 shout

2 **Across** 4 slap 6 shout 7 slam 9 shake 11 attack 12 cry
Down 1 push 2 knock 3 pat 4 scream 5 punch 7 steal 8 kick 10 hurt

Unit 13

1 2e 3a 4d 5b 6c

5 2 'm not doing 3 'll give 4 are you meeting 5 'm going to give her a ring 6 'll let you know 7 'll be 8 'm going to watch 9 'll call

6 1g 2c 3b 4d 5a 6h 7f 8e

Unit 14

1 1 - 2 - 3 - 4 the 5 a 6 The 7 the 8 a 9 the 10 the 11 a 12 a 13 - 14 the 15 - 16 the 17 A 18 a

2 2B 3A 4B 5B 6C

3 2 all of a sudden 3 In fact 4 In the end 5 The next day 6 However 7 all along 8 in future

Unit 15

1 1 No 2 She used to stay with her in her holidays. 3 She was allowed to stay up late and her aunt used to bring her a glass of milk and a biscuit in bed before she went to sleep. 4 There was a bad thunderstorm. 5 Pulling her into bed with her and covering their heads with a sheet.

2 2 grab 3 slap 4 jump 5 sniff

3 2 I remember walking to the bus stop.
3 I remember some boys coming up behind me.
4 I remember them pushing past me.
5 I remember dropping my briefcase.
6 I remember one of the boys running away.

4 2 My grandmother would break an egg into a glass and drink it.

3 My grandfather would talk to his flowers every night/at night.
4 My uncle would put on a jacket and bow-tie every evening for dinner.
5 My mother would read a book while feeding the baby.

5 1 letters, mints, lipstick, Coty powder 2 the woman's husband/the writer's father 3 They were softened and worn at the edges. 4 leather and powder 5 He may have been killed in the war.

Progress Test Units 11-15

1 1 After running/I had run two miles I felt tired.
2 As soon as I saw her I knew she'd been crying.
3 While I was watching television downstairs, a burglar broke in upstairs.
4 Do you fancy joining me for a meal?
5 I'll do the washing up (if you like).
6 When I got home, I realised (that) I had dropped my wallet somewhere.
7 The smell of newly-baked bread makes me think of/reminds me of my mother.
8 I remember taking the dog for a walk every day when I was little.

2 1 arrangements 2 suitable 3 dishonest
4 unbelievable 5 thoughtful
6 unnecessary/needless 7 speech 8 memory

3 1B 2C 3C 4A 5B 6D 7D 8C

Unit 16

1 2 I must leave now or I'll never catch my train.
3 They'd better come soon or they'll miss the start of the show.
4 Stop shouting or you'll wake the whole house up.
5 I must fill in this form or I won't get a refund.
6 She'd better turn up on time or she won't create a very good impression.

2 3 Always turn the car lights off, otherwise your battery will go flat.
4 Never drink coffee late at night or you won't/might not be able to sleep.
5 Make sure you get to the winter sales early otherwise all the bargains will be gone.
6 Make sure you don't arrive late for the performance or they won't/might not let you in.
7 Be careful not to leave the gate open or the cows will/might get out.
8 Make sure you have an injection, otherwise you might catch cholera.

3 2 milk 3 egg 4 steak 5 cheese 6 salt 7 flour
8 biscuits 9 tomato 10 milk

4 1E 2A 3I 4C 5D 6B 7H 8G 9F

Unit 17

1 2 She told her parents (that) she was leaving in ten minutes' time.
3 He said (that) they didn't have enough money to go abroad this/that year.
4 She wanted to know who was going to help her.
5 He asked if the station was far away.
6 She reminded him that they had met at the sports club last Friday/the previous Friday.
7 They wanted to know when lunch would be ready.
8 She told me not to wake her before eight o'clock.
9 He said (that) I/we had to catch the ten o'clock bus.
10 The girl said (that) she had to phone her parents before she went to bed.
11 He admitted that he hadn't been here/there for weeks.

2 2 She apologised for being late …
3 She agreed to lend her brother …
4 The hotel receptionist warned me not to leave …
5 I suggested he went/should go …
6 The doctor recommended taking …
7 He promised to take …
8 Although I offered to pay ..., she insisted on paying …

3 1 Hello. Is Eric there, please?
2 Well, I'd like to but I'm in a bit of a hurry, actually. 3 Can you give him a message instead?
4 I've booked a tennis court for tomorrow at eight. Could he pick me up at seven thirty? 5 Andy. He'll know who I am. 6 Could you also tell him I'm sorry I didn't phone yesterday. 7 Goodbye!

4 1 'We don't receive enough respect from our male superiors.'
2 'It's difficult to work for a woman manager.'
3 'I decided not to have children because of my career.'
4 'I've had children but my career has suffered.'
5 'The idea of a 'traditional management career' has to change. Both male and female managers should be allowed to work more flexible hours, and at home if necessary. I feel that this will/would enable them to combine work and outside responsibilities.'

Unit 18

1 2 along 3 in 4 through 5 to 6 of 7 round 8 at

2 A: Where do you think I should go to buy a good leather jacket?
B: Why don't you try 'Leather World' on the High Street?
A: Isn't that rather expensive?
B: Yes, perhaps it is. You could always try the second-hand market.
A: That's not a bad idea.

3 A: When do you think the best time would be to talk to Mrs Potts about our exam?
B: Why don't you talk to her after class?
A: Isn't she always in a hurry then?
B: Yes, perhaps she is. You could always phone her at home in the evening.
A: I'm not sure about that.

6 2 It's about time you gave up smoking.
3 It's about time you bought a new suit.
4 It's about time you saw a dentist.
5 It's about time you went to the launderette.
6 It's about time you went to bed.

Unit 19

1 (Suggested answers) 1 western, police drama 2 animated film, adventure film 3 horror film 4 adventure film, science fiction film 5 science fiction film 6 psychological thriller 7 police drama, adventure film, comedy 8 comedy
2 historical; romance; psychology; humour; confusing; animated; surprise; critical; fictional/fictitious
3 1C 2B 3C 4A

Unit 20

1 2 Rochester asked what the matter was.
3 She said (that) she would carry it in.
4 He ordered Jane to answer him and speak again.
5 He said to Jane that he couldn't see her but (that) he had to touch her.
6 She said (that) she had spilt half of what was in the glass.
2 2 It's a horse. It's neighing.
3 It's a dog. It's barking.
4 It's a lion. It's roaring.
5 It's an owl. It's hooting.
6 It's a wolf. It's howling.
7 It's a cat. It's miaowing.
8 It's a hen. It's clucking.
3 2 clapped their hands 3 pokes...in the ribs 4 close her eyes 5 shrugged his shoulders 6 pricks up its 7 snapped his fingers 8 curl up

Progress Test Units 16-20

1 1 She said that she couldn't come tomorrow/the next day.
2 He apologised for being rude.
3 They suggested going to the police.
4 She accused John of cheating.
5 You should/ought to see the new musical.
6 Give me back my money or I'll call the manager.
7 Make sure you don't put cash in your back pocket.
8 If you pour some oil in the pan, the mixture won't stick.
2 1 careless 2 recommendation 3 frightening 4 performance 5 lively 6 action 7 decision 8 refusal
3 1D 2A 3C 4B 5A 6B 7B 8A

Unit 21

1 2 live on 3 paid back 4 run out of 5 save up 6 pay for
2 2 loyalty 3 imagination 4 obsession, tidiness 5 extravagance 6 envy 7 meanness 8 intelligence
3 2 of 3 for 4 in 5 with 6 to 7 about 8 in

Unit 22

1 2 didn't give him 3 won't mind 4 Would you 5 'll definitely have 6 didn't finish 7 wouldn't be able to 8 will you
2 2 unless 3 provided that 4 even if 5 provided that 6 as long as
3 2 enjoyed 3 could 4 had 5 was/were 6 was able to 7 paid
4 1 ear phones for a walkman
2 £18.99
3 a) Provided that she has the receipt.
b) Provided that she returns them within seven days.
c) Provided that she doesn't damage them.
5 1b 2b 3c

Unit 23

3 2 should have rung 3 ought to have caught 4 shouldn't have overslept 5 oughtn't to have made 6 should have bought 7 ought to have told
4 2 He should have been studying for his exams.
3 They should have been wearing ties.
4 They shouldn't have been climbing in those conditions.
5 He shouldn't have been cycling on the pavement.
6 They shouldn't have been smoking.
5 2 nevertheless 3 In fact 4 as a result 5 but on the whole

Unit 24

1 2 If only we had enough money to redecorate the house.
3 I wish I didn't have to spend so long commuting to work every day.
4 If only I hadn't forgotten to lock the door.
5 I wish I could remember the number of the house.
6 I wish she'd told me she hated classical music.
7 If only I hadn't dropped out of college.
2 2 If I hadn't been in the shower, I'd have answered it.
3 If you hadn't reminded me, I'd have forgotten about it.
4 If I'd had the time, I'd have visited you.
5 If you had been standing/had stood further away, the photo would have been all right/much better.
6 If the salary had been higher, I'd have taken the job.
3 2 claim 3 trace 4 heat 5 spark 6 fire 7 burn

8 crash 9 fired 10 burnt
4 2 hadn't persuaded/told 3 hadn't left 4 wouldn't have heard 5 wouldn't have got

Unit 25

1 2 That their daughter had disappeared. 3 That she had been kidnapped. 4 £1,000 5 To the Grand Hotel in Brighton. 6 Beside a sofa in reception. 7 6 p.m. 8 His daughter arrived home. 9 The briefcase containing the £1,000. 10 It was a practical joke.
2 received informed inquired replied attempt withdrew entered placed approached returned refrain from transpired succeeded appreciate
3 2 She looks as if she's going to have tea with the Queen.
3 She looks awful.
4 She looks as if she's swallowed something nasty.
5 She looks very uncomfortable.
6 She looks like an actress.

Progress Test Units 21-25

1 1 There has been a considerable increase in the number of people over the age of eighty.
2 There have been complaints about the canteen food.
3 Unless I get paid I won't come.
4 I didn't think much of the breakfasts.
5 He shouldn't have left without a map.
6 Because of his broken leg he couldn't come trekking with us.
7 If there hadn't been a lifeguard on the beach, she might have drowned.
8 I wish I'd listened to my mother's advice.
2 1 behaviour 2 remarkable 3 unsuccessful 4 inquiry 5 disorganised 6 obsession 7 occasionally 8 excited
3 1C 2C 3A 4C 5A 6B 7C 8D

Unit 26

1 2 Will Sue have had the baby by then?
3 I don't expect we'll have finished eating by then.
4 We'll have run out of money by next week.
5 I'm afraid I won't have typed it by lunchtime.
6 He won't have arrived by then, I'm afraid.
7 Will you have read it by Monday?
2 2 antisocial 3 underweight 4 underestimate 5 anticlockwise 6 overcharge 7 antifreeze 8 underline 9 overlook

Unit 27

1 2 Instead of spending 3 by changing 4 without having to pay 5 Before making 6 after talking
2 1 portable television 2 electric toothbrush 3 sound system 4 video recorder 5 food processor 6 exercise bike 7 personal stereo 8 coffee machine 9 juice extractor 10 tin opener
3 examiner, examination; generator, generation; developer, development; trainer, training; recorder, recording; extractor, extraction

Unit 28

1 2 I hope I'll be acting in a West End musical but I expect I'll be working in a hotel in Brighton.
3 I hope I'll be playing in international tournaments but I expect I'll be coaching children at school.
4 I hope I'll be working as a foreign correspondent but I expect I'll be answering problem letters in a women's magazine.
2 1 The final of the World Cup. 2 In Munich, Germany. 3 Queueing for tickets. 4 They will be putting the English fans at one end and the Danish fans at the other end. 5 They will be controlling the crowds. 6 If Paul Gascoigne will be playing tomorrow. 7 He has got a knee injury.
3 2 I'm afraid not. 3 I expect so. 4 I don't think so. 5 Of course not. 6 I don't expect so.
5 Dear Mr Tsuji, (*insert date*)
Thank you for your letter. I *am writing* to tell you my travel arrangements for my trip to Tokyo on *Monday July 1st.*
I will arrive *at* Narita Airport at 1425 on flight number JAL325. I hope the flight will be *on time.* I'm 1.85 tall. When I arrive, I *will be wearing* a beige raincoat and (*I will be*) *carrying* a black briefcase. My friends tell me that the weather is fine in Tokyo at this time of year. I hope *so.*
I look forward to *meeting* you.
Yours *sincerely,*
Jean-Claude Trudeau

Unit 29

1 2 in a shocked voice 3 gently 4 urgently 5 politely 6 excitedly 7 nervously
2 'Have you got it?' Fred whispered.
'What do you mean?' replied Sam angrily. 'Of course I've got it!'
'But you don't seem to be carrying anything,' Fred protested, 'so I thought ...'
'Well, you thought wrong, didn't you?' Sam snapped. 'I've got it in my pocket.'
He pulled out a small package about the size of a matchbox.
'Now,' Sam whispered, 'give this to Bobo with this message from the boss. The boss says ...' He hesitated as he tried to recall the exact words.
'Happy birthday!'
3 **Across** 1 circuit 4 beg 6 me 7 lose 9 few 11 erase 12 again 13 visit 14 on 16 sad 17 noon 18 robot 19 pen 20 new
Down 1 complexion 2 compassion 3 ill 4 beef 5 grow 8 operation 10 estimate 15 now 16 son 18 re

Unit 30

1 2 The Finlux is not as expensive to buy as the Ferguson.
3 The screen on the Sony is a bit larger than the screen on the Philips.
4 The screen on the Ferguson is much larger than the screen on the Philips.
5 The Finlux is a bit more sophisticated than the Sony.
6 The Ferguson is not as sophisticated as the Finlux.
7 The Philips is a bit cheaper to rent than the Sony.
8 The Finlux is not as cheap to rent as the Sony.

2 1 More exciting 2 More demanding 3 More involving 4 More active life 1 Less stressful 2 Hours not so long 3 Less likely to get shot

3 2 Compared with her brother, Wen-Ling is much less confident/much more full of self-doubt/much more like to worry over things.
Chien-Kuo is much more confident than his sister.
3 Compared with her brother, Wen-Ling is not as interested in politics and economics.
Chien-Kuo is much more interested in politics and economics than his sister.
4 Compared with her brother, Wen-Ling is much more interested in people.
Chien-Kuo is much less interested in people than his sister.
5 Compared with her brother, Wen-Ling is not as patient.
Chien-Kuo is more patient than his sister.

4 2 They are less interested in buying single records.
3 They are more worried about getting a job.
4 They are less likely to suffer from ill health.
5 They are more able to express their feelings.
6 They are more interested in travelling abroad.

Progress Test Units 26-30

1 1 My sound system is better than his.
2 Is this the largest sweater you have/you've got?
3 Simon is not as good at playing the piano as Jill/is not as good a pianist as Jill.
4 Prices in the USA are much cheaper than in Britain at the moment.
5 Norway is less likely to win the Cup than Sweden.
6 By cutting down on salt, you'll reduce the risk of heart disease.
7 Instead of arguing with her, you should try to talk things over.
8 I'm afraid we won't be going abroad for our holiday this year.

2 1 useless 2 economical 3 reduction 4 incurable 5 discovery 6 unpronounceable 7 enjoyable 8 likelihood

3 1A 2B 3C 4C 5D 6B 7A 8C

Unit 31

1 2 mountainous 3 agricultural 4 coastal 5 commercial 6 industrial 7 historical 8 cultural

2 2 Birmingham is an industrial city in England.
3 Washington DC is the capital of the USA.
4 Uppsala is a university town in Sweden.
5 Newmarket is an agricultural town in England.
6 Rimini is a seaside town in Italy.
7 Wengen is a mountain village in Switzerland.
8 Fuzeta is a fishing village in Portugal.

3 Day 1 USA (New York); Day 2 The Bahamas; Day 3 South America (Amazon); Day 4 Japan (Mount Fuji); Day 5 Thailand; Day 6 India (Taj Mahal); Day 7 Rome (The Vatican); Day 8 Heathrow Airport

4 2 possible 3 possibilities 4 life 5 souvenirs 6 novelty 7 chance 8 curiosity 9 living

5 2 the 3 - 4 The 5 the 6 - 7 - 8 the 9 the 10 the 11 the 12 - 13 the 14 the 15 the 16 - 17 the 18 -

Unit 32

1 2 The rooms are cleaned thoroughly by the hotel staff every day.
3 The match has been postponed until next Saturday.
4 During the evening money was being raised for charity.
5 The video is being repaired at this very moment.
6 The parcel should have been posted on Thursday.
7 The college is going to be redecorated during the holidays.
8 Some Roman treasure was discovered in the middle of a cornfield in Sussex last week.

2 2 to be erected 3 being constructed 4 can be obtained 5 has to be bought/will have to be bought 6 to be abandoned 7 may be achieved 8 being completely fenced 9 being killed

3 Incident 1 WHAT: hurricane WHERE: Florida WHEN: yesterday afternoon DETAILS: Up to 100 miles an hour, twenty believed to be dead, over a hundred injured, 3m dollars aid promised by US government.
Incident 2 WHAT: bank robbery WHERE: Manchester WHEN: yesterday lunchtime DETAILS: five robbers escaped with £10,000, three customers held hostage, no one injured.
Incident 3 WHAT: Ben, world's oldest dog, died WHERE: Toronto, Canada WHEN: on Tuesday DETAILS: Ben was thirty, owner is Sam Harris, Ben will get a place in the Guinness Book of Records.

5 2 devastate 3 hamper 4 contaminate 5 migrate 6 imprison 7 assassinate 8 boycott 9 torture 10 bully

Unit 33

1 Number 1: 2, 5 Number 2: 3, 7, 9
Number 3: 1, 4, 6, 8

2 2 He can't have done the journey in three hours.
3 Jo might have decided to have an early night.
4 The train must have left early.
5 That can't have been an elephant.
6 You must have dropped the envelope as you were running for the bus.
7 One of our employees might have double-booked your ticket.
8 They must have decided to take the train after all.
9 They might have missed the turning.

3 2 might have been working late 3 might have already gone to bed 4 must have been shopping 5 might have been having 6 can't have been

6 **Across** 2 badgers 5 major 6 wrap 8 am 10 ate 11 rare 13 wear 15 do 17 dye 19 ham 21 axe 22 glacier 25 yes 26 studied
Down 1 tattoo 2 bow 3 arrow 4 roar 7 pray 9 me 12 area 14 Ed 15 dig 16 faces 18 heard 19 hay 20 mist 24 red

Unit 34

1 3 Columbus persuaded people that the earth was not flat./Most educated people already knew that.
4 He was a great and noble explorer./He was a ruthless imperialist responsible for the slavery and destruction of America's native tribes.
5 He was left to die in poverty./He died in obscurity.

2 3 Columbus is believed to have landed first in the Bahamas.
4 It is thought by some people that Columbus was an imperialist.
5 Columbus' real name is said to have been Cristobal Colon.
6 It is thought by a lot of people that Columbus died in poverty.

Unit 35

1 1E 2C 3A 4F 5B 6D

2 1 T 2 T 3 T 4 F 5 T 6 F 7 F 8 F 9 T

4 2 Mozart, about whom many books have been written, was a brilliant composer.
3 The woman from whom I heard the story is my neighbour.
4 The environmental issue about which I spoke yesterday is becoming more important.
5 The article in which your name was mentioned was written by a friend of mine.

5 2 The road you drove along this evening has now been closed.
3 The person I normally play badminton with has broken her wrist.
4 The house I was born in has now been demolished.
5 The apartment she moved from was quite dark and dingy.
6 The time we were supposed to arrive at was six o'clock.
7 Caroline is someone I have nothing in common with.
8 My assistant is someone I have the greatest confidence in.

Progress Test Units 31-35

1 1 All the crops have been destroyed by rain.
2 The woman is believed to have been murdered.
3 His parents should be told as soon as possible.
4 Being caught drinking and driving is a serious offence.
5 He might have dropped his wallet in the street.
6 She must have caught the early ferry.
7 They can't have left the restaurant without paying.
8 The man to whom I was talking was my Italian singing teacher.

2 1 deceptive 2 pollution 3 notify 4 threat 5 unreliable 6 agricultural 7 unduly 8 Environmental

3 1B 2A 3D 4A 5B 6D 7C 8A

Unit 36

1 2 You're always borrowing money from me.
3 You're always watching horror videos.
4 You're always using my hair gel.
6 I wish you wouldn't play your guitar at two in the morning.
7 I wish you would listen to what I say.
8 I wish you wouldn't hang around the flat when my friends come round to visit.

5 1c 2b 3b 4c 5a

Unit 37

1 2 No sooner had we finished our meal than the waiter presented us with the bill.
3 No sooner had Nick dropped off to sleep than the alarm clock rang.
4 No sooner had Jan got home than she realised she'd forgotten her dentist's appointment.
5 No sooner had she handed in her notice than she was offered a pay rise.
6 No sooner had I put the baby to bed than she started to cry.

3 2 Not only is the job very boring, it's also very badly paid.
3 Not only is Bob very bright, he's also got a great sense of humour.
4 Not only did she have to take them out for a meal, she also had to find them a hotel.
5 Not only do we have to pack our bags the night before, we also have to get up at half past four the

next morning to catch the train!
6 Not only did John Barnes score three goals in the Cup Final, he was also voted top player of the year.

3 2 ourselves 3 herself 4 themselves 5 ourselves 6 himself

Unit 38

1 1 eating 2 to give up, watching television, to give up 3 to eat, leaving, wasting 4 persuading, to be, inviting 5 living, feeling, getting, flying
2 1b 2c 3a 4a 5b
3 1 walk, rescue, pass 2 walk, path 3 bag 4 stick, trip, party 5 party
4 1 James explained that he had come to Nepal to work in a local hospital as part of his medical studies.
2 Mark suggested attempting a more exciting route
3 James promised to meet Mark in Kathmandu on December 25th.
4 Joanne offered to go out to Kathmandu and search for James.
5 The president of the Himalayan Research Association recommended that Carl Harrison should be hired/recommended hiring Carl Harrison/recommended Carl Harrison as the best man to hire.
6 A girl at the airport suggested that Joanne consult/should consult a Buddhist lama.
7 Joanne refused to give up hope.
8 The lama assured Joanne that she would meet her brother again.
9 Colonel Pun announced that they had spotted a person who was alive.

Unit 39

1 2 ... he did say he'd be a bit late. 3 ... they are going out ... 4 ... we did get ... 5 ... I do love ... 6 ... I did know that she was married.
2 2 What I have forgotten is the cheese!
3 What I don't understand is why you lied to me.
4 What he didn't tell me was that he'd burnt the kitchen table.
5 What I don't know is your last name!
6 What I can't stand is people who do it behind my back.
3 I'm not that rich! 3 They're not that tight! 4 It's not that bad! 5 I'm not that ill!
4 2 I really think ... 3 It was really stupid ... 4 I was really exhausted ... 5 ... he drives really well.
5 2 At first sight learning to play the piano looks easy, but in actual fact it requires a lot of practice.
3 At first sight modelling looks like a glamorous career, but in actual fact it is very stressful.
5 In theory it's possible to see the sights of London in a couple of days, but in practice you need at least a week.
6 In theory anybody can become the President of the USA, but in practice a candidate has to be fairly rich.
8 It may be true that the number of fast food restaurants is on the increase, but on the whole people are now more health-conscious.
9 It may be true that some young people are lazy, but on the whole most want to get a job.

Unit 40

1 1e 2i 3g 4c 5a 6h 7j 8f 9b 10d
2 1a, c, d 2a, b, d, f
3 2 a new lease of life. 3 had the time of his life. 4 the light of his life. 5 the life and soul of the party.

Progress Test Units 36-40

1 1 I wish she wouldn't use my perfume without asking.
2 He might have let us know in advance.
3 He's always using the phone when I want to use it.
4 On no account must you lean out of the train window.
5 Not only is Bill aggressive, he's also sarcastic.
6 No sooner had I got into the shower than the doorbell rang.
7 What amazes me is that people are so unconcerned about the famine in Africa.
8 There's no point in worrying about him. It's pointless.
2 1 dangerously 2 interpretation 3 Unfortunately 4 novelist 5 honestly 6 politically 7 furious 8 miraculously
3 1D 2A 3D 4C 5D 6A 7A 8C